Contemporary
German Stories

The German Library: Volume 100

Volkmar Sander, General Editor

CONTEMPORARY
GERMAN STORIES

Edited by A. Leslie Willson

CONTINUUM · NEW YORK

1998
The Continuum Publishing Company
370 Lexington Avenue
New York, NY 10017

The German Library is published in cooperation
with Deutsches Haus, New York University.
This volume has been supported by Inter Nationes, and a grant from the funds
of Stifterverband für die Deutsche Wissenschaft.

Printed in the United States of America

Library of Congress Cataloging-in-Publication Data

Contemporary German stories / edited by A. Leslie Willson
    p.   cm. — (The German library ; v. 100)
    ISBN 0-8264-0968-7. — ISBN 0-8264-0969-5 (pbk.)
    1. Short stories, German—Translations into English. 2. German
fiction—20th cetnury—Translations into English. I. Willson, A. Leslie
(Amos Leslie), 1923– . II. Series.
    PT1327.C67   1998
    833'.01080914—dc21   98-19078
                                                                CIP

Acknowledgments will be found on page 281,
which constitutes an extension of the copyright page.

· Contents

Introduction: A. Leslie Willson   ix

ALFRED ANDERSCH
Jesuskingdutschke   2
Translated by A. Leslie Willson

STEFAN ANDRES
El Greco Paints the Grand Inquisitor   15
Translated by Jeanne R. Willson

JÜRGEN BECKER
From the Story of a Separation   44
Translated by A. Leslie Willson

ULLA BERKÉWICZ
Hi, Wendy!   51
Translated by A. Leslie Willson

ELISABETH BORCHERS
Murder; or, This Story Is No Proof   67
Translated by James A. Hayes

GISELA ELSNER
The Engagement   72
Translated by Minetta Altgelt Goyne

HUBERT FICHTE
The Garden 87
Translated by A. Leslie Willson

GÜNTER BRUNO FUCHS
Confessions of an Elderly Cane Maker 92
Translated by A. Leslie Willson

MAX VON DER GRÜN
Shorthand Text 99
Translated by John Derrenberger

PETER HANDKE
The Goalie's Anxiety at the Penalty Kick 105
Translated by Michael Roloff

HERBERT HECKMANN
UBUville—The City of the Grand Egg 177
Translated by Thomas I. Bacon

HELMUT HEIßENBÜTTEL
Texts 194
Translated by Michael Hamburger

MICHAEL KRÜGER
The Pet 201
Translated by A. Leslie Willson

ULRIKE LÄNGLE
The Devil Is the Friend of Man 210
Translated by Scott G. Williams
(with Ulrike Längle, Grit Liebscher, Hiram Maxim, Ann Reitz)

FRIEDERIKE MAYRÖCKER
In a Rundown Neighborhood 214
Translated by Michael P. Elzay

HANS ERICH NOSSACK
The Pocketknife 217
Translated by Marc Tangner

Contents · vii

HELGA NOVAK
Journey of a Woman Nihilist to Verona in Late Autumn   225
Translated by Peter Spycher

LUTZ RATHENOW
Struggle   236
Translated by George F. Peters

JOSEF REDING
Disturbances All the Way to Baton Rouge   240
Translated by Ralph R. Read III

UWE TIMM
The Dinner Party   250
Translated by Rebecca Penn

WOLFGANG WEYRAUCH
Something's Happening   261
Translated by Earl N. Lewis

WOLF WONDRATSCHEK
German Lesson   269
Translated by A. Leslie Willson

Biographies   273

Introduction

The thematic content of contemporary German writing after 1945 is as infinite as a magical form-changer, ranging from simple shapes to experimental probings of the structure of language, from presumptuous and impertinent rebellion to a dreamlike reconfiguration of reality, from parable to layers of subjectivity, from formal dance and procession to riotous and reckless abandon.

The stories in this collection, which complements other volumes in The German Library (87, devoted to GDR stories, and 99, *Contemporary German Fiction*), reflect the times: the destructive threat to personal and artistic freedom by Nazi edict, the roiling waves of wartime emotional and intellectual dislocation, the insidious invasion of private liberty by an invasive East German regime, the evocation of stability and perception of instability through dream, the dangers of the ascendancy of subjectivity, a rollicking humor at one's own expense, the eruption of a youthful rebellion against a stagnant establishment, and monstrous fables of change.

The masterful story "El Greco Paints the Grand Inquisitor" by Stefan Andres is a thinly veiled but relentless attack on Nazi ideology, a parable of the confrontation between good and evil, between the freedom of artistic expression and the dictatorial suppression of the individual. The genius of El Greco unmasks the iniquitous soul of the master of the Inquisition. Published in Germany in 1936, the story unleashed a Nazi persecution of the author that resulted in his flight to Italy, where he spent most of the rest of his life and where he died.

A glimpse of wartime Germany is Hubert Fichte's "The Garden," which presents a boy who lives in Hamburg on the edge of a storm of fire and who, in the fascinating person of a visiting sailor, glimpses the future that lies waiting for him.

The restless spirit of a generation denied truth and exposed to the vagaries of conflict, the so-called sixty-eighters, is depicted in stories by Alfred Andersch and Wolf Wondratschek, themselves a generation apart. In his "Jesuskingdutschke" Andersch gives readers a snapshot of Berlin in the political debates and air of rebellion that resulted in the death by gunshot of student leader Rudi Dutschke in a melee between police and students. Wondratschek's story "German Lesson" expands the snapshot to a panoramic view of all of Germany through the eyes of a disaffected youth.

Lutz Rathenow was himself a target of unannounced and furtive investigations by the East German state police and in his "Battle" offers readers a parable about the threat that East Germans felt themselves impotent to combat, here with the intrusion of a portentous moth into a household. The idea of there being something "over there," outside a normal window in a parallel world, permeates Hans Erich Nossack's futuristic "The Pocketknife," where a malleable, translucent wall that separates two realities seems about to be pierced. A more palpable and present menace is "The Pet" in Michael Krüger's parable of a publishing empire.

With his "Something's Happening," a stroll down a single street populated by a bootblack, a taxi driver, and sundry others who stand for a whole city, Wolfgang Weyrauch captures the aura of threat of "when the big blast blows," without ever mentioning an impending nuclear wasteland that many people feared, concluding with an even more fearsome laser weapon.

In her story "Journey of a Woman Nihilist to Verona in Late Autumn" Helga Novak probes the mind and manner of a fugitive nihilist, one of a breed of destroyers who have been abroad since Euripedes, seen through the eyes of a girl who has been engaged to care for the nihilist's children. Nothing has changed.

The critical social atmosphere of the times encourages a closer examination of the norms of society and the sometimes risible, sometimes perilous situation which that portends for groups and individuals, here in the example of Henry in Elisabeths Borchers' "Murder; or, This Story Is No Proof." Max von der Grün's "Shorthand Text" chillingly reports on the increasing absence of society's concern for fellow human beings, the growing isolation and self-absorption of individuals and small groups. In "The Devil Is the Friend of Man" Ulrike Längle depicts a contemporary social problem (the smoking of cigarettes) in a clever parody of a "heavenly discourse" in a dialogue with the Devil, in whose domain Lucky Styx is the most popular brand. The petty purposes and spurious exaltations of a society are pinned down in miniature in the choreo-graphed muddle of an engagement party in Gisela Elsner's graphic "The Engagement," where petty disaster lurks on every side.

Authors often depict Germany's love-hate relationship with America with a setting in New York, here with the ubiquitous threat to all Manhattan in Jürgen Becker's inspired "From the Story of a Separation," where a cockroach lurks in every corner. The tendency to mix fact and fiction by some contemporary writers is evident here, too, in that Becker's characters are sometimes real people and sometimes literary inventions, a kind of neoromantic irony. The cockroach also plays a leading role in Uwe Timm's "The Dinner Party," where the host cooks up a lively dish for his guests, again in a New York apartment.

The ambiguous German opinion about American culture is re-flected most incisively in "Disturbances All the Way to Baton Rouge," where a visiting German joins in a freedom march and meets the American heartland, only to realize that Germany had its own "Blacks," who back home are called "Turks." But America also offers unexpected pleasures, as Ulla Berkéwicz demonstrates with "Hi Wendy," in which an American co-ed is seduced by a visiting scholar from Germany.

Günter Bruno Fuchs uses the occasion of his "Confessions of an Elderly Cane Maker" to complain that the walking cane, though a progressive invention, has for hundreds of years been misused and misappreciated, since it has often been lifted in a defensive gesture that is far beyond what might have been necessary—and he gives several examples of what he means. Progress is susceptible to regressive tendencies. In his experimental "Texts" Helmut Heißenbüttel offers linguistic variations on several themes: tradi-tion, politics, a final solution of his own, a catalogue of the incorri-gible, and the complexities of a short story. Also a writer with an original style and point of view, Friederike Mayröcker examines life and death and promises of serenity to come in her collage "In a Rundown Neighborhood," which centers on the French Quarter of New Orleans with its jazz and a red rose blooming in December in Texas.

The boundaries of reality, and how language defines existence, are touched and probed by Peter Handke in his novella *The Goalie's Anxiety at the Penalty Kick*, where effects do not always match causes, the expected may not happen, and a murderer's descent into madness is traced in exquisite detail. The work is a prime example of subjectivity at its literary best, where language's relationship to object can melt away.

The German scene in all its vagaries and routines, its customs and stereotypes is turned topsy-turvy by a visitor from UBUville in Herbert Heckmann's entertaining and ruthless "UBUville—The City of the Grand Egg." Here Germans have an opportunity to step back and take a look at their foibles and be amused at themselves, if they have an iota of humor.

Again, I acknowledge with gratitude the contribution of the translators, without whom this volume would not have been possible. They are equal to all challenges, and the reader should applaud them albeit silently.

All in all, this collection is to read and cherish and reread, to pass along and talk about: a cross section of German life and liveliness over the past half century.

A. L. W.

Alfred Andersch

Jesuskingdutschke

For Walter Heist

"That's only a laceration," said Carla while examining the top of Marcel's skull. "Just superficial."

She parted his black hair and traced the course of the wound as well as she could in the shine of the streetlight. Marcel stood leaning against the light pole. Blood was trickling down his face in two streams. He wiped it away carefully when it got in his eyes.

"It must be bandaged," Carla said to Leo. "Best by me in the clinic. Can we get a taxi here someplace?"

Carla was a medical student. She was just completing her period of practical training in the Moabit Hospital.

"First you ought to go home and change clothes," said Leo. "You must be soaked to your skin."

She shook her head. "Not necessary," she said, "my coat kept most of it off of me. I have things to change into at the clinic."

Her hair, which was just as black as Marcel's, clung to her head. She was wearing a bright raincoat that was closed with a belt.

While Leo forced himself to observe how the blood was trickling into Marcel's beard, he heard behind him the steps of the demonstrators who were withdrawing on Kochstraße. They were no longer running, because the police had engaged them only until the corner of Charlottenstraße. The water cannon were still in action, although the street was already empty. Leo, turning away from Marcel and Carla, saw the stream of water illuminated by the searchlights from beyond the Wall. Suddenly it was turned off. For seconds nothing but silence and the dark gleam of the wet roadway prevailed. Only then were the police in the background of the street visible. They were teeming, nothing but helmets and coats around the Press House, behind the windows of which all the lights were on. About a hundred meters in front of the water cannon, almost at the corner to Checkpoint Charlie, a man lay face down on the sidewalk. A civilian, apparently a doctor, let through by the police who had circled the Sector checkpoint with several chains, approached the prone man.

Possible that in spite of the tumult a few taxis are standing at the Kochstraße subway station, thought Leo, but going in that direction meant running directly into the claws of the police.

"Come!" he said. "There are taxis at Askani Square."

They were among the last who left the scene. As they were walking past Anhalter Straße, the night was any April night in Berlin, cool and empty. Every time they happened into a circle of light, Leo noticed that Carla was watching Marcel attentively; obviously she was afraid that the blood would begin suddenly to flow out, bright and in streams.

At the Green Tower of Askani Square a single taxi was standing. The driver had propped one arm on the steering wheel and put his head in his hand. He seemed to be asleep, but when Leo had his hand on the door handle, he said, without changing his position: "Keep your paws off! I'm not driving any students."

"We have a wounded man with us," said Carla. "He must be treated as soon as possible."

The man didn't answer but rolled up the window. They saw him grab the microphone of his radio unit.

"Let's go to Halle Gate," Leo suggested. "By subway to Wedding and then change for Pulitzstraße."

"And there we have to change again in the subway," said Carla. "If we go on foot through the Tiergarten, we'll get there sooner."

Leo had to admit she was right. But just now he would prefer to go by subway from Halle Gate to Wedding. On that stretch the trains traveled under Friedrichstraße along through East Berlin without stopping. The light in the mostly empty cars would be weaker, you sat in an achromatic twilight in which the stations emerged, yellow-tiled clouds. City Center, Französische Straße, Oranienburg Gate. Two People's policemen were always standing next to one another on the platforms, their rifles slung over their shoulders.

They arrived at the Landwehr Canal, turned to the right. Leo read, *Reichspietschufer*. The night ought really to smell of murder, he thought, of Köbis and Reichspietsch, of Liebknecht and Luxemburg, by right it ought to be a night screaming for help, but it was only badly lit and Aprillike. The water of the canal lay thick and meaningless between the bright stone embankments. Sometimes a car drove through the weakly moving circles of light that lay on the pavement of Uferstraße.

To the right now stood the Wall, sometimes only as a short hyphen between the walls of warehouses, then again in longer frontages. They followed it by bending in to the long, abandoned street northward, Linksstraße. Behind the Wall a diffuse glow of light; that made the side on which they walked even darker.

On Linksstraße Marcel opened his mouth again for the first time.

"Lukács's critique of Bucharin is still wrong," he said. "Bucharin saw a few things at the time that Lukács didn't see."

"Say," asked Leo, "did you by any chance find a Bucharin?"

"Yes," said Marcel, "in the antiquarian bookstore on Flensburger Straße. I couldn't believe my eyes. The German edition of 1922."

"Man!" said Leo. "When can I get it?"

"Not for the time being. We're going to hold a seminar about it first."

Marcel studied sociology. After the Institute had fallen apart, the students sometimes determined the seminar topics.

"Bucharin is the only one who sees the role of technology," declared Marcel. "He says: 'Every given system of social technology also determines the system of labor relationships between people.' And for that very reason Lukács attacks him. He asserts that Bucharin identifies technology with forces of production. . . ."

"Which wouldn't even be so wrong," Leo interrupted him. "For us in architecture both are identical, I'd like to insist."

"Well, OK," said Marcel, "but Bucharin doesn't even go that far. He just says that the development of society depends upon the development of technology. And Lukács calls that a 'false naturalism.'"

They suddenly stopped talking because a police Jeep stopped next to them. The policeman sitting next to the driver jumped out and approached them.

"May I ask for your ID!" he said.

"Why?" asked Leo. "Aren't we allowed to walk here?"

"If you want to cause trouble, you can just climb in!" said the officer.

Leo took out his Berlin ID and handed it to the man. As students they were used to being checked without cause; so they always carried their IDs with them.

The policeman looked at Marcel. "What's wrong with you?" he asked.

"He fell down and hit his head," said Carla.

"So," said the policeman. "Just fell down."

"No" said Carla, "didn't just fell down, fell down. That happens. I work in the Moabit Hospital, and we're taking him there."

She gave him her West German ID. He took out a notebook and began to write down their names.

"You don't have the right to take down our names," said Leo.

"You'd be surprised, if you knew what all I have the right to do," he replied, quite calmly.

Leo felt Carla put her hand on his shoulder.

"Don't worry," he said loudly. "I'm not going to do anything to him."

The policeman looked at him. "You're said to have threatened a taxi driver before," he said.

"That's not true," said Carla. "He refused to drive us, and we didn't say a word and left. Not a word! Although he said that he didn't drive students." She almost screamed it.

Not even the policeman could fail to hear that someone here wanted to assert his rights. He left Leo alone.

"Now your ID!" he said to Marcel, while he gave Carla and Leo their papers back.

When he saw Marcel's Swiss passport, he became concerned.

"We'll take you to the nearest emergency ward, if you wish," he said.

"I want," said Marcel, "you to write my name down in your book, too."

"That's not necessary," he replied.

Marcel grabbed his passport from the policeman's fingers, turned around, and walked on.

To leave the guy just standing there was not only a good way out, thought Leo, as he and Carla followed Marcel, but also the best tactic. Who knows what all might have happened, if I had stood in front of that polyp for very long. Oh hell, he thought immediately, that's showing off. I'm a braggart. Nothing at all would have happened. And maybe Marcel knows it. If a little while ago, before he received his blow, it was still capable of observing what was going on around him, then he had to know it. Then maybe he was so quick to leave because it was embarrassing for him to listen to me be so insolent. Insolence and nothing else.

But Marcel seemed to be thinking of something else completely. While they still heard the Jeep behind them turn around and drive away—the sound seemed to be like a curse that echoed away in the night—he was already continuing their conversation.

"Bucharin argued that you can predict the speed of social processes," he reported. "He wanted to turn sociology into a natural science. We have to discuss that some time. By the way, most of us are already opposed to him. Many even say that he's a pessimist. They agree with Lukács, who naturally recognized what is precisely dangerous about Bucharin and clubs him down with Lenin. 'There are revolutionaries who try to prove that there is no way out of the situation. That's a mistake. There are no absolutely hopeless ways out.'"

"Did Lenin say that against Bucharin?" asked Leo.

"Oh go on, out of the question. Lukács quotes it simply from one speech or other of Lenin that has nothing at all to do with Bucharin. But it's genially quoted. Lukács always quotes genially."

He suddenly stopped walking.

"Leo," he asked, "are we in an absolutely hopeless situation?"

"On the contrary," Leo answered, "just think about all we've set into motion. With nothing but a little ruckus in the universities and with a few demonstrations. We're just getting started."

He had answered without thinking about it, and yet it seemed to him immediately as though he hadn't been completely honest, as though he had merely wanted to appease Marcel. But it really was his intent. He hadn't been talking away like that just for the sake of Marcel, on whose face the blood was already beginning to congeal. To distract him, he said while they were already walking on: "Well, leave Lukács in peace! He wrote very good stuff. Do you know 'Narration or Description?'"

When Marcel shook his head, Leo was about to hold forth on Lukács's "Narration or Description," but Carla interrupted him.

"Do you know actually," she asked, "how Bucharin died?"

"Of course we know that," answered Leo. "Stalin, the show trials and so on."

"Words," Carla said. "Empty speech bubbles: Stalin, show trials."

"What do you mean by that?"

"Bucharin described himself before the court as a criminal character. He denied Trotzki. On the morning he was shot they had to pull a whimpering piece of flesh out of his cell. He even pleaded with the firing squad for his life."

"Nonsense," said Marcel. "Read Merleau-Ponty, if you want to know how the trial against Bucharin went!"

"I have read it," said Carla vehemently.

While they were arguing, Leo began to kick a stone that lay before him in the street. He simply had to do something. This night was nothing but a catastrophe. He ran along for a while behind the stone, kicked it on and on, then he stopped and waited.

"Why are you with us actually?" he had once asked Carla, shortly after he had gotten acquainted with her, about a year before. She had been able to give very clear information. Her father, chief surgeon at a hospital in Duisburg—Carla, too, wanted to become a surgeon—in his youth had for a short time been in a concentration camp. He had taught Carla a fairly primitive but effective theory of resistance. "We all knuckled under back then," he used to say, "everybody, without an exception. We let ourselves be captured like hares. No one, I repeat, no one got the idea that you could use violence against violence. No one fought, I mean really fought, with a weapon in his hand. We all said, it's just hopeless. You're only a girl, Carla, but stick to those who fight, whenever they're confronted with violence!" The old gentleman— by the way, he was only in his fifties—also now was consistent; he wrote his daughter understanding letters but still discussed tactical questions with her to protect her from outright stupidities. Carla is a clear case, thought Leo. She has a perfect superego, her father. You can count on Carla. You can count on Carla more than on all the others who come to us because they find their parents bourgeois.

They were still walking along the Wall, but diagonally to the left of them lay the Philharmonic, Scharoun's stone tent, which Leo always admired whenever he saw it. Spun about with white light, it made the Wall just any wall.

"Excuse me," said Marcel, "but I think I've got to sit down for a minute."

He sat down on the sidewalk. Carla at once knelt beside him.

"Lie down," she said, "and take a couple of deep breaths."

He stretched out, and Carla put her arm under his head. Leo saw her wet stockings and shoes.

"Oh God, Carla, you're going to catch something," he said.

She just shook her head and watched Marcel's breathing while she propped his head up high so that the wound didn't begin to bleed again.

Leo strolled about. He was uncomfortable because he had nothing to do. After a while he discovered a graffiti on the Wall. The Wall was weakly lit by the Philharmonic.

"Man alive," he called out, "come here!"

Marcel had already sat up. Carla supported him while he stood up. They went over where Leo was standing. Together they read the inscription: JESUSKINGDUTSCHKE, which someone or other had written on the Wall with thick red crayon in one line and in capital letters. Since he had left no space between the three names, they had become a single name.

"There are crazies among us," said Leo. He laughed.

The two others remained silent. After a while Carla said, "You know, I don't find that so crazy."

Marcel stared somberly at the letters.

"All those apostles of impotence!" he said.

"Well, you can't count Dutschke among them," Leo objected.

"Stop all this Dutschke business!" said Marcel. "He always gabbles about the long march through institutions. Nothing else has occurred to him up to now."

Leo was ready to discuss power and impotence, but when he turned to walk he caught sight of the taxi that stood at Kemperplatz next to the Philharmonic.

Marcel collapsed in the car; with eyes shut he leaned back in his corner.

Leo was sitting in front next to the driver. He turned halfway around and reached out his arm, but Carla did not take his hand.

"No," she said softly, "not now."

It was dark in the Tiergarten. It was almost as though they were driving at night through an open landscape.

Leo withdrew his arm and sat up straight. He had already withdrew his arm once today.

He again saw the policeman approaching Marcel, who kept throwing rocks methodically and obliviously, even when the police attacked and everybody ran. It was quite right for them to run, and extraordinarily stupid of Marcel that he remained standing and kept throwing rocks. The policeman ran up to Marcel with his club raised, and when he was there, it would have required only a simple grab by Leo, who was standing next to Marcel, to put him out of action. Leo would have had to grab the raised forearm, ready to strike, and with a short, iron-turning motion twist the whole arm out of its shoulder socket: the man would have rolled with a roar on the ground. He hadn't done it. He had indeed stretched out his arm, but too slowly, in a calculated slow motion that he knew would come too late and that ended with his not grabbing the policeman but Marcel by the arm after the blow had struck him, that he had turned Marcel around, shoved him backward, dragged him, carried him, and by doing that the policemen left him alone. Leo was used to the policemen not attacking him. He was almost six feet tall, built like an athlete, a springy giant. He wasn't a bulldog. He was an active sportsman, had specialized in shot put and hammer throw; the trainer implored him to get involved less with politics; he said that if Leo would concentrate totally on the shot put, within a year he would be world class. Leo wore his blond, stiff hair cut short; with his crew cut, and as a result of the way his cheek muscles rimmed his face, almost everyone thought he was an American.

"It was fabulous of you," he heard Carla say, "to stay with Marcel and drag him out."

He took a breath. So she hadn't noticed what really happened. Besides it was true: he had stayed with Marcel. Only that he had then become afraid, quite normal physical fear, and not even senseless but plain fear. He had calculated exactly what would come, if he had disarmed the attacker: they would have fallen upon him fivefold, tenfold and beaten him totally. And Marcel as well. To allow the blow on Marcel's head had been the lesser evil. The whole process had run past in his mind. He was like when he sometimes did not get the shot put off but let it roll off his palm into the sand because he had realized that he had not breathed right or not weighed down powerfully enough onto his right leg.

The light towers of the Hanser quarter. The municipal train underpass. They had to convince Marcel to get out in front of the hospital. "Let me sit," he said, "it's so nice here!" Carla looked concerned.

The outpatient clinic was an almost empty room. It turned out in practice that in such a room one needed nothing more than an examination table on wheels, a medicine cabinet, three chairs. He sat next to Marcel, because Carla, when she had left, had said: "Sit next to him. He could fall over." He thought about purely functional rooms. This examination table, this medicine cabinet reminded him of nothing more than that they were an examination table, a medicine cabinet. Such things, such a room, corresponded to his conception of architecture—of buildings and spaces that defined themselves. There were no fetishes.

"I feel horribly bad!" Marcel said so obliviously that he spoke Swiss German. He said "hurrible" and the way he said *bad* came from deep in his throat. Leo saw his pale face.

Thank God Carla returned now. She brought a doctor along. Although she had been gone only a few minutes, she had managed to transform herself. She now wore a white apron and gym shoes; she had dried and combed her hair, and in addition found a doctor. Leo had never yet seen her in her work environment. Here she gave the effect of being more decisive, compact, and firm than usual. He would like to have touched her.

The doctor was a tall, asthenic man and as a result a bit bent-over in stance, about forty. He walked right up to Marcel, asked no questions, merely looked at the wound, palpated it, and observed Marcel's reactions. Leo had the impression that the doctor liked Marcel. Marcel *was* generally liked. He had been in Berlin for a year, but he still looked like he had just come from the Café Odeon in Zurich. Although he let his beard grow pretty bristly, although he took pains to look unkempt, he made a handsome impression. Even now, thought Leo, his face looks as though it had been sketched by Celestino Piatti, the face of a blossoming, pale, and glowing young man on a book cover. All the while Marcel was anything but a model for applied art; he was a methodically small antagonist, obstinate, stubborn, a Swiss with an injured sense of justice.

They had gotten to know one another in the library of the Technical University during the past autumn while Leo was writing his examination on his history of architecture. At his study place he had piled up a small reference library. Marcel always appeared between eleven and twelve, sat down to the right or left of Leo when one of the chairs was still free, and read newspapers. Occasionally he wrote something on notepaper.

"Excuse me for disturbing you," he said one day to Leo. "Please, what does *insulae* mean?"

He indicated the title of Leo's work. So it had been simple curiosity that he caused him to take a place next to Leo. He admitted it.

"The word has haunted me," he said, "since I saw it on your work. Are you simply writing about islands?"

"No," said Leo. "*Insulae* is what the tenements were called in ancient Rome."

"A remarkable name for buildings."

"The *insulae* were the first large structures for habitation. Each of these buildings was bounded by streets and free zones in order to be able to control the *plebs* that lived in them. The largest *insulae* came into existence under Nero. It's as good as certain that Nero set the fire because he wanted to get rid of the slums and the Forum that had become a jungle in which the *plebs* could no longer be kept under observation."

They spoke to one another in whispers, as was prescribed in the library.

"Were you in Rome?" asked Marcel.

"Yes, the whole summer," Leo answered. "I had an Italian fellowship for this work."

Since, like everybody, he found Marcel attractive, he asked: "And you, what do you do?" He pointed, perhaps a trace disparagingly, at Marcel's newspaper.

Marcel shoved his notepaper over to him.

"There," he said, "that's what I found today. Just today. In a single issue."

Leo took the slip of paper and in astonishment read the words that Marcel had written in a very neat, exact handwriting that swallowed up the descenders: *do-nothings—unkempt loafers—troublemakers—rabble—SA-methods—brawling radical adolescents—hooligans—ringleaders—political visionaries—political rowdyism—agitators—young muddleheads—mob—terror—rioting—*

criminals. At some distance away were the words *the decent* and *tough* and *consistent.*

"I'm working on a socio-linguistic study about hate murders," Marcel whispered. "Title: *Before the Pogrom. On the Technique of the Institution of Ghettos through Language.*"

Leo had stared at the slip of paper. "Do you see the situation so darkly?" he had asked.

"You don't?" Pointing at the slip of paper, Marcel had said: "This here will lead to murder, that much is certain."

The doctor finished with Marcel. He shrugged his shoulders. "In any case, we have to take an X ray," he said.

He asked Leo to help Marcel get undressed. "We first have to cleanse the wound," he said to Carla. "I'll see whether operating room two is free."

When he had left, Carla said to Marcel: "It'll be with only a local anesthetic. You won't feel anything." Marcel remained apathetic. In the warmth under the harsh gray light he indifferently let himself be undressed, but walked alone in his underpants and shirt to the examination table and lay down upon it. They saw that he had a skinny and delicate body. Carla spread a woolen blanket over him.

"So it *is* more than a laceration?" asked Leo softly.

"In such cases there's always suspicion of a fracture," said Carla.

She shook her head indignantly when Leo said: "You look great in your white smock."

The doctor returned and reported that the operating room would be free in ten minutes. He took Marcel's pulse rate again then sat down on a chair. Obviously he was tired.

Suddenly they heard him say: "You're reading for the candy of revolution instead of the bread of reform."

Leo had a sharp retort on the tip of his tongue but he reflected that he didn't want to get Carla into trouble. Maybe she had to get along with this medicine man. Leo had taken a seat on the window ledge because it was darkest there. In this medical room he felt too big, too huge.

It was Carla who replied without thinking about it.

"We just don't want to eat the shit of this society anymore," she said.

Leo looked over at the doctor. Would he give any sign of indignation, of disgust? But he seemed to be accustomed to the fact that girls with long-falling dark hair and pale faces who made a romantic impression unthinkingly used scatological expressions. It seemed as though he withdrew again into his weariness.

"Society," he said after a while. "It doesn't matter at all in which society you live. The only thing important about a social system is whether it is made by decent or by indecent people."

"Oh, for Heaven's sake!" said Carla.

Leo joined in. "So with a few nice people at the top," he said, "we already have a decent capitalism. Do you really believe in a thing like that?"

"Or a decent Communism," answered the doctor. "Yes, actually that's my opinion."

"A useless elite theory," said Leo. "Sounds good, like all those liberal phrases, but. . . ."

A nurse interrupted him. She reported that the operating room was ready. Together with Carla she wheeled the table out, on which Marcel was lying. The doctor smiled politely at Leo, when he followed them. Leo regretted that he had tossed the word *phrases* at his head.

His father was still up when he got home. He and his father lived in a row house in Lankwitz. His mother had died at his birth. His father had been in a concentration camp from 1933 until 1945, and when he got out he had nothing more urgently to do than have a child, from which his wife, exhausted by war and by waiting, had died. "If she knew what kind of life you lead!" Leo's father said sometimes. He himself was rather small and skinny. Now he was sixty-five and looked like he was Leo's grandfather, not his father. He had been a metalworker with Siemens; they had retired him three years before as a foreman. With the money that he had received for his years in a concentration camp he supported Leo's studies; together with the hundred and sixty marks from the *Berlin Model* it was just enough.

"I'll make up for your twelve years in Oranienburg," Leo had once said. At home, he spoke the Berlin dialect with his father.

"Never mind, don't think about it!" his father had retorted. "It hadda happen."

In reality, it wasn't his opinion that it had to happen. That in 1933 he had been a member of the Wedding District leadership of the Communist Party had cost him twelve years of his life. He used to summarize his view of the party with the sentence: "The Party was always big on theory." And he added: "Nothing but always forecasting precisely also can't fill up an evening."

Leo had to describe the demonstration in front of the Press House in detail for him. He nodded in acknowledgment.

"Great, all that you're accomplishing!" he said. "And everything just outta the crowd. Without organization, without a Party."

They were sitting in the kitchen. Leo, who had eaten nothing since afternoon, was eating a sausage and bread, drinking light beer.

"When I think about how precisely we considered everything before we risked anything," his father said.

He was smoking a bent pipe, blowing out gray clouds.

"I wonder if it's good that you reflect so little? I think you don't know who you're getting mixed up with. Rudi Dutschke didn't know it, for sure."

Leo noticed that the trauma of the concentration camp literally shook his father.

"Father," he said, "none of that is of any help. We have to get our experiences all by ourselves."

"I know that," his father replied, in control of himself again. "It's just you're heading for defeat, that's a fact."

Leo had no desire to talk about victory or defeat. His father had gotten him on an entirely different train of thought. If a great revolutionary party, he thought, had reflected too long before it risked something, then he also could possibly for once reflect, think about consequences, choose the lesser evil instead of striking out insensibly only because a friend was in danger.

Except that such a consideration, of course, changed everything.

He had to present this question to Marcel. If Marcel doesn't have a fracture, he reflected, I'll go to him tomorrow and tell him that I could have deflected the blow on him. He imagined how Marcel would react.

"But that's quite unimportant," he would probably say. "In every struggle there are changing subjective situations."

Leo would try to explain it to him as patiently as possible. "I was afraid of violence," he heard himself saying. "I can no longer speak up for the use of violence by others for which I myself lack courage. And now I can also not join those whom you call the apostles of nonviolence—be gentle because you're cowardly: no, to that!"

What would Marcel bring out against that? Leo could think of no convincing arguments that he could put in Marcel's mouth. Of course, Marcel would give a methodical lecture: on the objective significance of violence, on the subversion of revolutionary thought by psychology. And all of that not even to comfort Leo, to help him get past what was painful, but because he really believed in the power of objective cognition, believed that faced with subjective weaknesses it didn't even come into question. What did a single, split-second failure signify in the long history of revolution? Nothing.

Finally, he would quote his beloved Merleau-Ponty: "The euphoric revolutionary comes from the image factory of Epinal," he would say.

When his father had gone to bed, Leo called the hospital. It lasted an eternity before Carla got on the phone.

"Marcel is OK," she said. "He doesn't have a fracture. He has to stay two or three days in the hospital."

She told him the visiting hours. He felt how she was waiting for him to arrange something with her. She was no longer cold as before.

After he had hung up, he reflected on the fact that he still lacked some material for the *insulae* work. There were some buildings in Ostia that he had not yet researched. His father would give him the money for the trip. He didn't need much.

Translated by A. Leslie Willson

Stefan Andres

El Greco Paints
the Grand Inquisitor

It struck Master Domenikos Theodokopoulos like a bolt of lightning when the Cardinal's chaplain, who had ridden over to Toledo
from Seville expressly for that purpose, conveyed to him that the
painter El Greco was to appear before His Eminence on the first
Sunday in Advent. While he ordered that his guest be offered some
refreshment, with a ceremoniously polite phrase and a voice that
recited the words automatically and as if by rote, he measured his
inner world, not whether it was good, but whether it was impervi-
ous and inaccessible. He thought of his friends, of names unpleasant to the ears of the Inquisition; he thought of Cazalla, thought
of remarks he had made to his assistant Preboste about certain
commissions for religious portraits. He thought about his portraits
themselves. In his mind he traveled here and there to all the
churches and chapels and monasteries; the quivering beat of the
wings of his compelling anxiety fluttered over his portraits and
cast shadows across them, searching the faces of his saints and his
mortals. . . . He did not look at the hungry chaplain as he shoved
the bowl of oranges toward him; he looked only at the pale, bony
hands of the priest that grasped a piece of fruit with fingertips
alone and pierced it with long, sharp nails. El Greco saw the gleaming juice drip and in his mind still looked at his portraits, and the
juice of the orange was there on the brows of his saints, golden
sweat; and as the skin of the orange rose, quietly splitting, the fruit
came forth under the tips of those fingers.

A man can conceal himself for a long time, thought El Greco—and he felt the sweat break out in his armpits—until fame arrives. Fame is a polished burning-glass held over our work; it will burn a hole where the eyes of the world will meet. The Grand Inquisitor sends his chaplain.

"What does His Eminence wish from his servant?" he asked and raised his eyes, though just to the priestly temples that were much overgrown with hair.

"You are to bring your painting equipment; the house steward will discuss the rest with you."

El Greco coughed away his congested breath in concealed relief and smiled obligingly at his guest. One hazard gives way to another, he thought, and spoke: "I thank His Eminence for the singular honor." He wanted to say still more, wanted to pay obeisance to Seville in words; however, he added only: "I am surprised!"

The chaplain, with the slice of fruit in his hand, hesitated as with the Host before the proffered tongue of a person under suspicion; then he ate and nodded: "I am not surprised that it surprises you. Your style of painting, when viewed next to Juan del Mundo, could be called—very—," he deliberated, "—strange."

"My lineage!" El Greco interposed. "Don't forget, I am Greek!"

The priest—he might well have been past fifty—nodded as before. "Your parents were schismatics?"

"People can never be called schismatic; it is the priests, the pastors—they set up barriers and tear them down!"

The chaplain pricked up his ears. He pushed himself a little away from the table with spread hands; his chair rocked on its back legs, the wicker crackled. He repeated El Greco's words; he murmured them, meanwhile watching the artist without watching him. Then he added, somewhat more emphatically, no longer murmuring: "If a whole people breaks away from Rome, then even the youngest child who has reached the age of understanding and reason can be called to answer for it. Or do you think differently on that point?"

El Greco shook his head vigorously. "Otherwise it would be at the least barbaric to have young children burned at the stake." He arose at that and the chaplain rose too.

At this moment the boy Manuel entered the room; the appearance of his little son was pleasant for El Greco; they spoke about his talents and inclinations, and when the chaplain left after a while, he first blessed the boy, who helped him into the saddle at the doorway.

While the narrow passageway was filled with the sound of the horseshoes, El Greco stood in the middle of the room, and unconsciously with his lips he matched some iamb in his own language to the beat of the hooves—oh, it was much more like the relaxed and fading gait of the horse than were the ponderous tones of the Spanish. Then he looked around perplexed and wrote a few names on a scrap of paper—he wanted no guests today—and sent the servant to the palaces of Toledo to cancel the visits, to say that El Greco was indisposed. "Only the doctor should come, Dr. Cazalla, and he should come late."

It is better to sit with Cazalla at night in the library; then even the servants will not see that a Cazalla is a guest of El Greco by night. This family has a habit of talking loudly. Another Cazalla, the doctor's brother, the *Dr. Theologiae* in Valladolid, has paid for his full voice with his life. The Holy Inquisition does not want any full voices; but Cazalla was to come. Now what does Manuel want? His father is brooding over the portrait of the Grand Inquisitor; for the time being he cannot play with his little son. "Go on, Manuel, where is your nursemaid? Go on, Father will have to return to his studio."

But El Greco does not go back to the studio. Preboste will finish alone. Preboste only needs to glance at the fragile, gray-tinted shapes. He has made up the palette himself—he presses on his eyes, then slowly the stars ascend and circles revolve in all directions; those are El Greco's colors: in the train of the stars, in the tails of the comets that are always there whenever he presses his eyeballs until they hurt. Preboste, good fellow, discovers them first on El Greco's palette, ah, with a stealthy look over his shoulder; Preboste looks stupid now with his swift and secretive cunning. Preboste accepts the colors as the surface of the world, he looks upon the world as something painted; how wrong he is, good old Hidalgo. Preboste paints onto each El Greco when he has the palette and the pattern of colors; but His Eminence Niño de Guevara—El Greco himself must go to paint him, to Seville, on the first Sunday in Advent. And yet only men can be painted, or saints, men as they are, saints as men are not.

El Greco remembered a past encounter. In the Escorial, out of the depths of the endless corridors, there came a streak of red and one of black. The red one was tall and the black one small, the red one moved under the folds of his moiré silk as if on rollers, no steps could be seen; the black one limped and supported himself on a stick. It was Niño and Philip. They came to view his painting of the martyrdom of Saint Maurice and the Theban legion, just as he had put his name on the picture in Greek letters: DOMENIKOS THEODOKOPOULOS. The name is on a little shield with a viper stretching up toward it, as if to read the name; a painted viper that twists up from behind a stone.

Philip sat down in an armchair. El Greco could still hear the valiantly restrained groan of the King, who was constantly plagued by the gout. Or was the groan meant for the picture, which the King was seeing for the first time?

"We do owe our throne, after all, to these heroes," said Philip, but in earnest, without a smile—he would not permit any irony in a sentence that mentioned a throne.

The Cardinal turned away toward the painting, as if he wished to ignore the words of the King—so it appeared to El Greco—and then his eyeglasses flashed toward the artist.

"A snake, why a snake to lift your nameplate into the light?"

"Forgive me, Your Eminence, the viper does not support my nameplate—it is perhaps indistinct—it is only stretching up toward the writing. My name is there to prohibit all evil from entering the picture; the name is, to be sure, the entrance to the work; evil shall lie prostrate before the entrance and be in dread."

The Cardinal lowered his eyelids behind his glasses, as if he had understood; then he said: "It seems to us that the name of a man cannot banish evil, as we can see just now in all the countries of Europe. In the name of man there is conjured up pride and hence error and hence dissension and hence the weakness of the Kingdom of God."

Philip groaned, reaching toward his knees but then running his hands over his thin, blond hair.

El Greco said, "Forgive me, Eminence, but it seems to me that a man who creates such a work must be full of God, and so his name is an affirmation of God, just as the names of Your Catholic and Apostolic Majesties are—for us certainly to a lesser degree."

"The picture is finished, even if it does not please us," said Philip, intervening; he did not seem to approve of this conversation.

The servants approached at his sign, and the red and the black streaks departed; El Greco can still see the King's shabby velvet and the glittering moiré silk of the Cardinal.

That was in the Escorial with a finished picture; now it is here in Toledo with one that is newly commissioned; his heart is beating in the same manner.

In this hour El Greco cursed the thirst for glory that had driven him from the free air of Venice to the jurisdiction of the Escorial. Truly, it is not for naught that Philip has given to the sober and solemn monk's palace the shape of a gridiron in memory of the roasted martyr Lawrence, on whose day his general defeated the French. On the sharp grate of these roofs the world lies roasted, and the burned flesh stinks, and the funeral pyres throw their light on the palette. One has no need to press on one's eyeballs. So the Theban legions died for the throne, for Philip's throne . . . certainly that did not please Niño de Guevara: they died for the Apostolic stool.

El Greco laughed in his room in Toledo; his pale face turned red from laughing. The snake by my name, oh, the best conceit of my life. The snake glided into the picture without a plan. The viper shall not decipher El Greco's name! And when Niño de Guevara stands painted in his picture, there will be no more need of a snake beneath my nameplate, and he laughed again, but more quietly. He heard the servant coming. Dr. Cazalla had been in Madrid for a week, the servant reported. In Madrid? Then he must be at the Escorial; in the Escorial the gout prevails. The whole Spanish Empire has the gout: the King, the army, the navy. They all are stiff and swollen and cannot move. What a powerful illness, he thought, that can bring a whole age to its death.

Then late in the night—he was still awake—there came a knock. He went to the door himself. Wrapped in a great hooded mantle, Dr. Cazalla entered, and only when in the library did he lay aside the monk's garb. Above the platelike ruff his face was pale and ravaged. "His Majesty died the day before yesterday."

The bookshelves suddenly seemed to slant, the tables and chairs seemed to slide as if on a ship as it turned on its side; El Greco spread his legs wide for support. "Now what will become of the world?" is what he wants to say and then what he does say.

Dr. Cazalla's eyes open wide: "What did you say? Do you know, the King said those selfsame words when I was alone with him for a short time the evening before. What will become of the world?"

El Greco turned his back to his friend. He spoke thus and looked at the books as if he were reading from them through their covers: "My outcry shows how much we all, in spite of our inner reluctance, are convinced of the need for a despot. We even express in their own presumptuous words that they cannot be replaced. It is time all those who secretly know that the earth is not the center of the universe stop granting the center of humankind to a single man. We have another center. And so the land will breathe a sigh of relief at the death of a monarch, and even if he were more tolerable than Philip—it is the dismantling and the disarming, the expectation of the incredible, that swells the loins of an empire."

"What do we have to look forward to?" Cazalla murmured dismally, and then his voice rose. "I hated Philip as you do, but when you see a hated man die as a king, you leave all that aside. Philip knew how hated he was; he said to me, 'Cazalla, our gout is the hate of the whole land, but we have become accustomed to our gout; it is the true lot of the monarch.'"

El Greco laughed bitterly, "Oh, these brave kings who fight with each other for a share of the gout! No, Cazalla, those are justifications made afterward for the purpose of disguising a wasted effort. What would be left beside this comic justification to people like him who are dying except for complete despair?"

Cazalla shook his head earnestly: "You did not hear Philip's servant Diego. You did not watch as this servant stumbled when he was carrying his king to the bed; you did not see the two faces, the face of the King and the face of the servant. In that moment both faces were one in pain. And still groaning the King comforted his servant: 'Don't Diego; we are already fruit for the grave, it is good you should shake us!' This servant sat the night through with me in the antechamber. He knows more than the minister of state; he knows, too, that the last time the King signed his name was beneath the death sentence of a heretic. He groaned as he did it, then he looked at his servant: 'Diego, man is evil; if he will not learn to walk holding onto the hand of God, he must learn in the cages of the partisans'; and then he prayed with Diego and had him say the Confession of Faith. At the end he said, 'That was not for us, Diego, that was meant for you.'"

El Greco rejected this: "And he watched the death spasms of his insane son through the peephole of his cell door."

Dr. Cazalla said, "Consider the impassive sun; there it is, impassive, a greater king, and allows each thing to happen. A raving mad Infante who eats seven pounds of plums and drinks ice water and rolls around on the pavement must, according to the laws of nature and thus the divine will, certainly die!"

El Greco smiled, "According to the laws of Niño de Guevara you would have to die too, my dear Cazalla; for your new knowledge about the sun and about the Will of God, that it is accomplished only through the laws of nature, is more dangerous than seven pounds of plums and ice water in Don Carlos's stomach. I warn you, especially since your name and your blood have already gone through the purifying fire of the Holy Inquisition, do not forget that at that time Philip represented the eye of the sun that, moreover, not only watched. . . ."

Cazalla made a warning gesture and clutched at his beard; as he spoke, he pulled on it, causing his head to nod: "My brother Agostino died at Valladolid in the fire of the Inquisition, Philip died of the gout. If we were immortal, then there would not be this passion for truth on all sides. The short span of life makes a man intense, and he tries in his beliefs to make himself eternal. Happy is he who can profess his faith through all time by his death. Philip built the Escorial, the Pope St. Peter's, and for you your paintings are your profession of faith—"

"Oh, yes," El Greco rose, "I can profess it in pictures. I will profess the painful arc that stretches between the Escorial and St. Peter's; let that be the halo for the portrait of Niño de Guevara, and in the future men will find their suffering more bearable in our picture."

Cazalla's neck stretched up in its plate-shaped collar: "Are you serious?"

El Greco laughed with satisfaction: "Such times! When this pronouncement causes a serious man like you to ask such a question! Or should the Grand Inquisitor not have the courage to show himself to future ages in a picture?"

Cazalla barely smiled: "Well, why not; you have a great task and also a dangerous one, it seems to me!" And he added, still somewhat amazed: "How do you happen to be in such good favor with Niño?"

"Oh, it is the favor that a mirror has in the service of an ugly woman." El Greco's eyes twinkled in all their Cretan cunning, but his heavy eyelids veiled this cunning with the melancholy of a man who is weary from all too much and too close a view of what lies behind the faces of men.

Cazalla returned this twinkle, yet not wearily but full of contempt, rolling his eyes almost into the corners of his eyelids. "He who intends to live must learn to lie!"

El Greco made a warning motion with his lean hand while he listened at an open window. The sound of thunder stretched out like the night's repressed yawn; the air rested heavy and thick between them.

"No, Cazalla, *I* should be able to lie, for I am from Crete; I could acquire for myself a scapular from the Servites or the Carmelites and occasionally let these rags be seen by Niño. I could refer to my very devout pictures that Preboste paints with my palette, I could purse my lips like Inigo de Loyola, improvise pious Christmas verses like Lope, and I know parts of Aquinas by heart—"

Cazalla broke in: "You could even join the Brotherhood of the Holy Inquisition!" They both laughed inaudibly with motionless faces. Then Cazalla lifted his head menacingly: "You speak of Thomas! But bear in mind, even a quote from Thomas, that angelic teacher"—he said this last with earnestness and scorn together—"can deliver you up to the Holy Inquisition. One day just tell Niño frankly that according to Thomas a man must follow his conscience, that our will must cling to that which our reason recognizes as the substance of the truth! My brother Agostino died not so much following the German Luther as in emulation of Thomas."

A new clap of thunder, nearer and longer, rolling like an anchor chain out of the depths of the night, made the windows tremble. El Greco alone heard the thunder; Cazalla was too deep in his thoughts and his anger and cried out: "But the will of the faithful is supposed to conform to the Holy Inquisition—ha! Every neck, like a screw, is twisted attentively to each side; every back is bent; every dream is filled with the dance of the flames. If we want to live, we must study the lie!"

El Greco again made the same defensive gesture of warning with his hand. "Are they really living?" He smiled to himself. "These pious ants of the Church talk of nothing but eternal life in order with cunning to prolong their lives, which are not eternal!"

Cazalla pounded his hands on his knees: "Why do we stay in this place, when there is a free Venice?"

A nearby flash of lightning illuminated their faces; Cazalla was startled by El Greco's eyes.

"Crete, Crete," he murmured and rose. "No, no," he said then, icily firm, "come Cazalla, let us go out into the storm."

Cazalla pleaded weariness.

"You are afraid," said El Greco menacingly.

Then Cazalla threw on his cloak and followed with heavy steps.

The narrow streets were filled with thunder. Cazalla walked hurriedly now, as if he had a destination. Wide bands of lightning, two paces long, illuminated the crumbling stairs. They walked through the night in silence. The sky lurked in darkness until it opened its ghastly eyes again. Then each time Cazalla would cover his face, but El Greco walked on, his gaze calmly examining the white of the stonework as it blazed up.

They did not know where they were headed, their steps were so detached from all sensible aim and direction. Only when they heard the Tagus slapping against its rocky banks did they know that their course had brought them all the way down to the water. At a clap of thunder they both turned toward the hillside as if they were waiting for something, as if from the battlements above the thunder had commanded them to turn their faces toward it. But they looked into surging darkness; at their backs the rush of the turbulent waters, the wind under their crackling cloaks, touching them with a hundred hands. Then a flash of lightning traveled from behind them and away over their heads. They did not see it actually, they saw only the wavering wall of clouds, bright white, blown apart into black holes by the wind, and the thunder seemed to come out of the vaulted crest of the clouds; the crest collapsed with a roar, and the darkness enveloped it all, but now the picture was in El Greco's eyes. He still saw the narrow wall leading down to the river like a hill's backbone; the pointed tower like the hands of the earth folded in prayer; the palace, defiant and strong, but shrunken; the houses, yellow, with windows black and empty.

When the rain set in with a vigorous patter, Cazalla sighed: "I would like to know why we are standing here while other people are sleeping or praying! And that is the best: to sleep or to pray when the heavens appear so frightful!"

El Greco said: "Would you call what is happening frightful, too, if there were no danger for you or for others?"

Cazalla shook his head: "Then it would just be beautiful!"

"Oh, Cazalla," El Greco laughed in a high-pitched voice, "Oh, Cazalla, I will paint this picture, and this painted lightning of mine will not strike anyone, no one will think of death by lightning when standing before my picture, but they will still find it frightful. What is great is frightful; God is frightful, not death, not Niño and his men!"

The next day El Greco went into his studio and began to create on canvas a reflection of that nocturnal countenance of Toledo as he had seen it. Preboste was silent and could not work.

Seven days before the first Sunday in Advent El Greco set out for Seville after putting his house in order and commending his wife and son to his friend Cazalla.

The bells in the Cathedral of Seville were tolling for vespers when El Greco knocked on the Cardinal's door. In the attendants' room there stood a ceremonial hat table on which each one in the house displayed what he wore on his head. At the sight of the hats beneath the crucifix, shaded by the canopy of the Cardinal, whose hat hung on the wall like a red sun over the servants' hats, El Greco smiled, even though he had entered houses of princes of the Church so often. "He that dwelleth in the shelter of the Most High," came to his mind—it was actually time for compline. "For he shall deliver me from the snare of the fowler and from the noisome pestilence!" His hat lay among the servants' hats; that seemed to be the custom in Seville; in the name of God, we are all servants after all. "With his wings he will make shade for you and under his feathers you will gather hope again."

The biretta room that came next was barren like the soul of a penitent who no longer possesses anything of this world and has still gained nothing of Heaven. On a table with long legs in front of a black crucifix—everything here was high and narrow, the walls, the legs of the table, the cross—lay the Cardinal's red biretta, likewise high and narrow, spreading wider at the top, with four rounded projections like a wind rose—he governs the wind, the Grand Inquisitor. So he who wears the biretta is at home, all right! And El Greco prayed; "Thou shalt not be afraid of the terror by night nor of the arrow that flieth by day."

In the secretary's office the chaplain got up from a pile of documents, the same chaplain who had visited him in Toledo. He returned quickly. Domenikos Theodokopoulos was to appear early on the next morning ready to work, that was the message of His Eminence; quarters had been arranged for him with the *fratres Dominicani*. The chaplain handed him over to the servant, the servant to the porter, the porter to a boy on the street, whom he summoned to show him the way, but El Greco knew Seville and rode to his lodgings.

Niño de Guevara was wearing the violet color of Advent when he received El Greco the next morning in his library. An easel was set up close to the window; he was expected. El Greco bowed three times—at the door, in the middle of the room, and then when he kissed the Cardinal's ring. The stone was not the color of Advent; the ruby was as red as the trace of blood that remains on the rough hands of a housewife who has washed her hands too hurriedly after beheading a chicken. The wintry fabric of the Cardinal's clothing smelled of camphor; it had just come out of the chest. El Greco found this smell to be immensely harmonious with the face of Niño de Guevara. Otherwise it smelled like every library: of dust and paper and ink.

When El Greco arose from kissing the ring, he looked the Cardinal in the eye. He saw only the black frame of his glasses, like a grating, gratings over cisterns to protect children and animals, as in Crete, in his beloved Crete. In this moment he heard his mother speak, warning him fondly: "Don't raise the grating, Domenikos, or Father will come with his switch!"

"We are pleased, Theodokopoulos, to see you again in good health!" The voice of Niño de Guevara was deep, yet its sound was not located in his chest but somewhere remote in his head, sometimes around his nose, sometimes in his throat, unaccented, regular, unmoved.

"I thank your Eminence for the honor and for your kindness in allowing me to the best of my ability to present your portrait to posterity."

"To the Church," the Cardinal corrected him and sat down.

El Greco set to work. The Cardinal rang his bell; the chaplain came.

"The biretta," Niño whispered.

The biretta, El Greco thought eagerly, the crown, the wind rose, which supplies the bare head with a dangerously precise completion, the projections to all the four winds.

For the first hour the Cardinal sat in silence; he was reading. El Greco waited patiently, lurking. Light is the garment things wear; it can veil things and can expose them. A face has a thousand faces, while only one is authentic. Let Niño read! El Greco looked past his easel, as if from ambush. Sometimes he drew a line, but only with his thumbnail.

"We heard that you work very quickly," the Cardinal said without looking up.

"That's true, when we are on the right track!"

The Cardinal looked up. El Greco had spoken of himself as "we." He was looking for the right track so very hard that he had doubled himself, had made himself a multitude. Or was the Cardinal smiling about the track? Was this smile his face, after all, this furrow that pushed his gray beard up toward his cheeks a little and caused a wrinkle between the pincers that held his glasses? No, this smile was a seasoning added to the whole that had to be tasted, too, like black pepper, not like a sweet; there was not a crumb of sweetness in Niño, he was bitter wood, hard, dry, without roots, a rod! This mouth is wide, El Greco recognized, very wide; the beard conceals it; and his lower lip is narrow; the strip of flesh below the lip that the beard leaves free simulates a broad lower lip such as the dead Philip had; but Niño has no lip: The beard is deceiving.

"I would like it very much, if Your Eminence would request that someone come in to read," said El Greco. He wanted to watch Niño listening.

The Cardinal rang his bell. "The story of the blessed Count Orgaz," he ordered—and the chaplain read.

El Greco listened attentively; he was not working now. His thumbnail scratched but a few lines on the blank surface. And the chaplain read: "Now when the blessed Count Orgaz had passed away, and the noblemen had gathered at night in the cemetery chapel for his funeral, the heavens opened over those gathered there, and the Holy Church father Augustine and the holy high martyr Stephen came forth from the clouds, and they placed the body of the count gently in his grave. Pious astonishment and holy fear seized the assembled gentlemen, the priests as well as the nobles, and they all praised the outstanding virtue of the departed count, who throughout his life had served the Church with all his strength and all his fortune and who now experienced honor to his body, even such as was shown by Heaven to but few while alive."

Here the Cardinal interrupted the monotonous impact of the reader's tone. "If we remember correctly, you have painted this miracle?"

El Greco nodded. "The attention given my pictures by Your Eminence honors me."

Niño de Guevara repeated softly to himself the words from the account of the miracle. "Pious astonishment and holy fear seized the assembled gentlemen. . . ." and he added: "I confess we missed the pious astonishment and holy fear in your picture. You paint an open heaven above, put the saints among the mortals, and your assembled grandees display not even surprise!"

El Greco's thumbnail stopped scratching; instead of an answer his charcoal made the first line: a precipitous curve caught the eyes of the Grand Inquisitor, the veiled, still faint questioning in the bearing of his head, in the oblique glance of his eye. Thus El Greco spoke, his charcoal hissed and cracked along—from behind his easel, with only his right eye visible, squinting as he measured— he spoke: "A miracle does not surprise me, Eminence; our Holy Church teaches that for God everything is possible, and if angels were to come and guide my charcoal, I would not be seized by pious astonishment—"

"Not even by holy fear?" Niño de Guevara's voice seemed to clutch at him around the protective surface of the picture, but El Greco stood his ground and answered:

"Angels are good spirits and should not frighten us!"

The Grand Inquisitor, then, with a soft voice, as if he were think- ing it over himself: "The angels always say, after all: 'Do not be afraid!'"

With his charcoal El Greco firmly fixed the points for the eyes, and his answer came with the same sharp impact: "That is the more profound invitation of the Gospel, which brings the joyful tidings, Heaven's constant call to the earth: Do not be afraid!"

Then the Grand Inquisitor asked, as if for advice; "And what about the fear of God, which is, after all, the beginning of wisdom?"

El Greco, however, just as inoffensively: "Yes, the beginning of wisdom, the lowest step!"

"And the other steps?"

El Greco stood up straight, measuring, lifted his thumb and his index finger like a tongs, as if he held the head of the Cardinal, the size of a bean, between them. Then he said: "The other steps: freedom, joy, and love!"

The Cardinal gestured to the chaplain, who went out. "Now a question, Domenikos Theodokopoulos," he lifted the timepiece from the table and held its cylinder to the light, "a question: On which step are you standing?" The voice of the speaker was becoming more and more distant and less melodic: "Are you standing at the beginning of wisdom, or have you mounted higher?" When El Greco did not answer, he repeated himself tersely, almost wearily: "You are not afraid?"

El Greco's forehead dropped a little; his heavy eyelids, which seemed about to cover his eyes, made his face old and tired, but he was only fifty. And he shook his head abruptly once and then went to the box in which his paints were kept. As he pressed a ribbon of crimson and then a ribbon of vermilion onto the palette, the Cardinal spoke: "Red? But we wear violet for Advent!"

"I am painting your mozzetta and the biretta red, Eminence, blood-red; and your face pale, your collar and surplice white, and the background dark, as God dictates to me in truth!"

Niño de Guevara was genuinely astonished at this; he raised his voice: "God dictates colors?"

El Greco repeated himself and affirmed: "Yes, Eminence, and by virtue of His truth!"

"According to what truth do you paint violet red and a light-colored background dark?"

"According to that truth which the Lord pronounced when He betook himself into the shape of the lightning that burns from His ascent until His descent and reveals everything that is hidden."

The Cardinal looked at his tensely suspended hands; he said: "Black and red, what does that reveal?"

El Greco stepped forth in his entirety from behind the easel; his voice did not tremble, yet it was faint: "Fire in the night!"

The Grand Inquisitor almost imperceptibly lowered his brow; all of his motions were slow and always inconspicuous, only new forms of his inflexibility, and in this way he looked up from below him, that he might not become a traitor with this nod, and thus he spoke, trembling: "She has become a bloody fire, Eminence!"

The Grand Inquisitor rose: "Yes, the Church has many enemies," he said quietly. Then he added that he would be ready again on the morrow at the same hour.

As El Greco kissed his ring, he heard de Guevara's restrained voice far above him: "This afternoon the procession of the Holy Inquisition has its beginning at your lodgings; watch it and consider the words that are written for the world to see on the banners of the procession. Do you know those words?"

El Greco nodded and spoke: "Those two words are the two eyes of Holy Church, may she never become blind in either eye!" He bowed and moved through the door backward. If this observance had not existed, he would have invented it in this moment. But now, as he walked through the streets, he nevertheless felt those eyes on his back, those cold, uncompromising, dark eyes.

He did not go to the refectory for the midday meal; he sat in his cell, he sat on the pallet with his hands resting next to him, their palms facing upward. And he looked at his right and at his left hand and saw that they were empty. His head had fallen onto his left shoulder.

The noonday hour in a cell at the *fratres Dominicani* can be so quiet that a man can hear his own heart beating. One needed only to hold one's breath, then there came this muffled, incessant sound, but there was a ticking as well in the wood of the worm-eaten prayer stool, clearer and not so regular. El Greco leaned over the stool, listening; in that way he forgot the deep sound of his heart. There was another heart, perhaps Manuel's heart, the heart of his little son, or the old heart of his wife or the heart of Cazalla, who was afraid. Who would not be afraid, who had once been aware of the fire and the torment in his brother's body? He stood up and walked in a circle around the cell. The groaning of loose planks filled the small room. He sought out solid planks that made no noise. It was an anxious search by his feet. If in this hour I should ride out for Toledo, and if with Manuel and his mother I should ride on—Cazalla would come with me to Venice—he stopped and he smiled—he saw the city, so hushed and yet so alive. If I abandoned everything—what is everything? What would I abandon: books, many books; a house built according to my own plans, many houses built according to my own plans; carpets, tables, cabinets, all just trifles—and the paintings: in St. Thomas *The Burial,* in the Escorial *The Theban Legion,* in the cathedral chapter house *The Disrobing;* ah, the disrobing; what more does one leave behind than one's clothes; life stripped bare is all there is. So one leaves nothing behind! Perhaps I should go to Crete and let the circle be joined there? And the floor planks cracked again, and again his feet made their search. Until the singing of the Psalms arose under his window.

He stopped in the middle of the cell, he did not approach the window. He was familiar with the black-and-white checkered train of the Dominican monks, this thousand-legged singer of Psalms; he knew the words, too, on the banner that came at the head of the procession, those dangerous words that looked back on the procession like two glittering eyes: *misericordia et justitia,* the eyes of the Church, may they never become blind in either eye! He had said that to the Grand Inquisitor. He knew the pale faces of the penitent heretics, now grown weak, who came behind the monks, led on by a crucifix that, looking backward, spread its arms over them. This line was longer than the one of impenitents. Yet the faces of the impenitents, also led by a crucifix—but one that turned its back to them—these faces were not white, they were reddened "by the fire in the night." *Misericordia et justitia,* mercy and justice, flashing eyes that extend to where the Cardinal Inquisitor moves along with his chaplain, leader of the endless procession of the pious who are safe for today and are pardoned to look on; but the thousand-legger will hungrily bite at its own tail, from the supply of those who are curious and devout it will create new action. Oh, he knows this procession and will not go to the window to look at it. The curiosity of the crowd creates a following even for an executioner; he will not go to the window.

El Greco cried out. In the frame of his window, which was located on the low second-floor level of the cloister, puppets fastened on poles floated past with tall paper caps covered with black writing, puppets representing the souls of those heretics who had died in the dungeons, who had died on the rack, moving stiff and upright on a cloud made of Psalms: "Have mercy on me, O God, in Your infinite mercy, and according to the number of Your mercies, erase my sins!" El Greco counted on his fingers, as if the numbers were their names, but the sixth and the seventh to pass by the window faced straight ahead, made in the air the little curves of the thousand-legger—now submissive after their death were those who would not submit—and disappeared.

El Greco fell to his knees. He knew that many out there in the streets and the plazas fell to their knees, but not as he did. Those below who were kneeling felt threatened by the look of the living, of the black-and-white thousand-legger; but he was threatened by the motionlessness and the orderly line of the dead, of the murdered, who had become soulless puppets according to the pleasure of the Holy Inquisition. And he lay down full length on the floorboards; saliva ran from his mouth, when he fell asleep, and moistened the boards that no longer cracked.

Now he had forgotten horse, wife, son, friend, and his house in Toledo. In his dream he saw a window, a rectangle, bright and with bars; but the rectangle became round—and the bars turned into the frame of eyeglasses. And in this round window puppets with tall caps passed by unceasingly in a twitching, curving step; but he only watched and counted; and the numbers became the names of the puppets, and he continued to wait quietly for the time when he would say his own name with an incredibly high number. However, he did not speak his name.

A lay brother found him thus on the floorboards. Awakening, El Greco saw before him the black stripe of the scapular on the white abundance of the vestment; and from the grayness of the white and the depth of the black he knew the hour; it was not yet late, but it was a day in December, and the candles in the refectory were already lighted for the evening meal.

The brother was concerned as to why Señor Domenikos had not appeared for the noonday meal. "Or do you keep a fast for Advent?" El Greco nodded wearily to this. "Then you probably want to be waked for matins?" And he added to that both proudly and secretively: "The Cardinal, whom you are painting, as I have heard, always comes to us for matins, every night, dressed like an ordinary priest; he is a very austere man, and they say he is a saint!"

El Greco lifted his head abruptly and gazed at the talkative brother with a look that the latter did not understand; if the brother had looked this way at some of his own kind, they would have called the look foolish. But artists are different men, are often absentminded when they look at a person. So the brother was thinking, as he left—and he shook his head at the pious painter, who kept the Advent fast and was to be wakened for matins.

That night the Cardinal did not come to matins. The prior waited a considerable time, then he intoned the service.

El Greco sat hidden in the depths of his choir stall and waited; he waited through lauds besides; and when the assembly left the choir, he remained in his seat and waited still for the Cardinal, for the dawning day. He was afraid he would fall asleep. It is true that a rested person is strong, but also pliant and indecisive; a man forgets in his sleep; his resolves can relax—and a dream always lures him toward the earth and toward life—he did not want to sleep! "Brother, be sober and vigilant!"

His face was so pale and wasted with watching that the skin had a glassy transparency and the creases were painfully strained when in the course of the morning he entered the house of Niño de Guevara.

The chaplain informed him that the Cardinal had suffered a severe bilious attack in the night, but he still desired to receive Señor Theodokopoulos, even though lying in bed. And the chaplain led him into the Cardinal's bedchamber.

On a monk's pallet there lay, under a red carpet, the motionless shape of the sick man. The room was high, white, cold; El Greco, feeling each shadow and every corner on his own body, took pleasure in the dreariness of the room without even thinking it strange now; he needed only consider how each person chose for himself the portion of the world that was due him.

"I am dismayed, Eminence," he began, when the Cardinal had greeted him. Niño de Guevara supported himself on his elbows and slowly raised himself up. He wore a dark-gray tunic; his head without the biretta was for the most part hairless; he looked now like an old man who, abandoned in his room, is distressed. And still not like a man, in spite of the beard, El Greco sensed. He has no concern with love. His body is there only to carry his head and the scarlet robes, and he scarcely can forgive his stomach that it grows hungry and then must evacuate itself. How often can he possibly bathe, thinks El Greco, as he sits down obediently on a stool. He can smell the body of Niño de Guevara; it truly smells like bitterwood. This is a body that never grows dirty and never is washed.

The Cardinal put on his glasses and examined El Greco briefly: "You are fatigued!" he said and sighed, running his hand over his body under the covers.

Guevara's face was as yellow as saffran, sky-blue around the eyes; a remarkable effect, El Greco thought, examining him, and spoke: "Your Eminence looks much more fatigued."

The Cardinal nodded: "We need a doctor. The doctors in Seville are not good."

"Have you no faith in them?" El Greco inquired. He clasped his hands around his knees to restrain the hidden laughter in the depths of his body.

The Cardinal's spectacles flashed, one could see only glass. "We said they are not good, the doctors in Seville. You know good doctors, do you know one for us?"

El Greco covered his eyes with his hand, what was that supposed to mean? One name alone came to him. As this name had come to him, he had covered his eyes, he could only think: Cazalla, of the living and the dead, of the doctor and the *Dr. Theologiae,* of the brothers Cazalla he thought, of them both. "His Catholic Majesty called Dr. Cazalla to the Escorial shortly before his death."

There was no pause; the Cardinal asked: "You know Dr. Cazalla?"

El Greco nodded once: "We are friends!" And they looked at each other—each with a wrinkle between his brows—for a long time.

Finally the Cardinal spoke: "We thought of Cazalla, too! The Cazallas are smart and have hard heads." And then, lifting his spectacles away from his eyes, slowly drawing the loops off of his ears, he allowed himself to sink back; he sighed, handed El Greco the glasses so that he might put them on the table. "Have Dr. Cazalla come to me," he said quietly, "and come to see me again in a few weeks time."

Upon receiving El Greco's letter, Cazalla immediately came down to Seville. As El Greco was crossing the cathedral plaza with idle steps, he became aware of the sound of horses' hooves in the noonday quiet; he turned and saw a rider. He saw him from behind, and from the folds of the cloak on the high, narrow shoulders, he recognized his friend.

"Cazalla," he called softly, and the person addressed reined in his horse at the sound of his name. They stood in front of a French bakery; the rider was hungry, nevertheless he did not notice the aroma of the pastries and the seasoned meats, he only heard El

Greco's whispered words; because of people passing by they had to whisper. But Cazalla listened and looked at the dust-covered cuff of his shirt, which was hanging out of his sleeve. And he slowly ripped off the cuff and threw it onto the pavement.

"Well then, shall I not be afraid of the honor the Grand Inquisitor does me?"

El Greco spoke louder: "Above all, do not do him the honor of fear!"

At that Dr. Cazalla answered very softly: "Of course, since he puts his life in my hands!"

To that El Greco did not want to answer him there on the plaza; he took him away from there, and then in his cell he spoke: "Not so, Cazalla, not the way you expressed it in front of the pastry shop, not so! You are a doctor—and the Cardinal has faith in you. I think that your reputation, because of which you were called to the Escorial, led him to trust his life to you. And he counts on it that you will not avenge your brother's life on him, Niño counts on that!"

"He counts on a generous enemy? With what right?" Cazalla gasped for want of breath. Now El Greco smiled—in his dangerous way.

"Friend, go and cure him quickly, so that I can finish painting his portrait as God commands me through His truth." And after a while he added: "You know, it is useless to kill the inquisitors. What we can do is—to hold fast to the countenances of these True Christians!"

Cazalla scarcely listened, he could not master his feelings. "Who else would be so cunning as to make his enemy into his doctor! He adjures my pride, my honor, my duty. And he knows that in this way he holds all my powers under oath, all my knowledge, my whole art! Oh, that this night I were no Cazalla!"

That evening, before he went to the sick man, he said: "Theodokopoulos, you know, today, the fifteenth of December, my brother Agostino would have been sixty-five." And he asked, his eyes directed at El Greco from the corners of their wrinkled pouches: "How old do you imagine the Cardinal is?"

"Just that old," said El Greco and lifted his eyebrows almost threateningly.

Then Cazalla waved him away and took up his instrument bag, which clinked softly. "Have no fear, you will get your picture! For the Grand Inquisitor's calculation is correct. He knows that heretics of our kind walk in the presence of God, that we are as harmless as oxen, when we are yoked to our mission. Just look, now I am not afraid anymore!"

El Greco could hear his spurs and the sound of the glass clinking in his bag as he went down the staircase. It was a twofold sound, both warlike and peaceful, that Cazalla's great stride turned into one.

When during that night El Greco, unable to sleep, was pacing the floor of his cell, carefully stepping on places he had noted, so that the planks would not creak and no one would be awakened, Dr. Cazalla entered the room of the ailing Cardinal. Some candles were burning over the bed and on the table. The light moved in waves over the sick man's face, which seemed masklike, with large pores and yellow, as if made from limestone. The Cardinal motioned to the attendant and the chaplain to leave. And offering the doctor a seat, he talked softly; he did not need his glasses, he did not look the newcomer in the face, he talked to the air above him: "How far into the night is it, Dr. Cazalla?"

"Eminence, it struck eleven at the cathedral a little while back!"

"Eleven," he repeated from his cushion. And immediately afterwards: "So late, and when did you arrive?"

"About four hours ago, Eminence!"

"And you did not come to us right away? You were with El Greco?"

Cazalla answered in the affirmative with his deep voice, cool and firm.

Thereupon the Cardinal, without any change: "Will you make us well or not?"

Cazalla did not look over toward the bed, he looked straight ahead into the distance, as if he were outdoors. And he spoke with a voice that came from the distance: "In Valladolid your Eminence decided in favor of justice!"

"The servant of justice: We will be that again, as soon as we are well."

All that could be heard was Cazalla's breath as it passed through his nostrils, the breath of the sick man was as silent as before.

"And the servants of justice expect their enemies to be servants of mercy?"

The voice of the Grand Inquisitor became somewhat scornful. "If we knew you did not want to make us well, you would not be able to insult us by answering us with mercy in return for justice! We thank you!"

"Oh, your justice," the words hissed as they escaped the doctor's lips, "the youngest of the women in Valladolid was sixteen years old!"

The Cardinal corrected him: "Fifteen—the little Doña Elena. She was more stubborn than your brother. Even today we can still see her before us. Bear in mind that he who has the power to choose between the stake and obedience is dangerous to just the degree that the choice is hard."

"Truly spoken," Cazalla smiled, "but does the Holy Inquisition believe that voices can be burned along with bodies?"

"We will burn bodies as often as voices can be heard that contradict the truth. Besides, we know to what degree fire can cleanse. These burning stakes will become lighthouses of truth, for voices go up in smoke along with bodies; that is the experience of the Holy Inquisition." The Cardinal spoke with short pauses, his eyes were closed.

Cazalla's look passed over the man, who lay as if asleep: "This experience of the Holy Inquisition is contrary to the experience of Holy Church, which prepared its seed in the blood of the martyrs."

"The Church alone has martyrs," the Cardinal's eyes opened, he raised himself on his elbows, turned his head toward Cazalla; his eyes without glasses seemed as they gazed to have no center within their spheres, which were like the openings of a mask through which someone hidden was staring, a stranger.

Cazalla arose. "Only the Church, Eminence?" He felt the saliva rising venomously into the corners of his mouth, horror and rage were mixed on his tongue, but he swallowed and spoke calmly: "I will make you well. A man such as you must constantly have his days of grace renewed, until he does not want another day."

The Grand Inquisitor smiled: "Spain will be preserved for the Church."

Cazalla raised the sick man's blanket. "Philip is dead," he said, as he did it. His hand felt of the sick man's burning body.

"Kings never die at an improper time," said the Cardinal, who paid no heed to the doctor's actions.

"True, the Church needs each one only as long as he lives!" answered Cazalla.

Niño de Guevara's eyes rolled and then closed. He pressed his hands against his body on the sheets. "May some of this indifference of the Church come into the hands of the doctor and make them sure." He smiled weakly. And immediately thereafter: "Your hands hate our body, we can feel that."

"My hate will make you well," said Cazalla firmly and indifferently; he called the attendant and told him to prepare hot linseed plasters.

And he prepared the medicines himself: The glasses and vials clinked quietly, the liquids made whispering sounds as they were mixed.

When the attendant had gone out, Dr. Cazalla came to the bed with the potion. The Cardinal blessed the cup and tipped it up, emptied it with one draft; the harsh gulping sound filled the room along with the bitterness that arose from his mouth and from the empty cup. "One should be mindful of one's noble enemies!" Thus he spoke and stretched his body out full length.

The chaplain was ordered to come to pray the compline that had been omitted, but Dr. Cazalla forbade it. He meant to keep watch himself while the sick man slept.

"Will we fall asleep?" Niño de Guevara inquired. Did he mean: Will the pain allow it? Or did he mean something else? The chaplain came to the bed. The hand that lay on the red coverlet had beckoned feebly—really only the finger—"Don Consales, if we should die in the night, we have died from our bilious attack, from our illness, a completely natural death. Do you understand?" The chaplain nodded. "Now leave me alone with Dr. Cazalla!"

The chaplain left on tiptoe. He meant to close the doors carefully, but all his care failed in the last hand's breadth; there was a muffled thud, really loud only here in this place.

Dr. Cazalla blew out some of the candles, only the taper above the bed was still lit; it did not disturb the sick man, it was behind him, over him; by the size of the candle the hours of the night could be measured without a timepiece.

The Cardinal had put a tightly fitting red nightcap over his thinning hair. Dr. Cazalla finds the cap pleasing. He considers its quality, the manner in which it has been made. It surrounds that head like a red skin, keeps it warm, and is light. Is it made according to measure, this nightcap of a cardinal, or does the material stretch?

The breath of the sick man cannot be heard. He can watch for the breathing and examine the nightcap's fabric at the same time. He pulls a down feather from his beret; a doctor must always have a small bunch of feathers in his cap. And even if the whole bunch is used up on nights like this, the dead man, too, will still have to pay for the feathers. He steps to the bed, bends down cautiously, bends low with effort; he is getting old, is older than El Greco, or is it that much-talked-of ramrod of the harquebuses that every Hidalgo has got in the back, or—or—the feather is ruffled, well and good! He moves back and sits down. Why, after all, is he listening this way to the breathing of the sick man? He has certainly seen people die of a bilious attack before; they do not talk so much beforehand and do not lie so quietly as this one here, or does a Grand Inquisitor die differently? They say that death makes us equal. Furthermore, he has forgotten what material the cap is made out of. But he will not examine it again. Judging by the candle, an hour has burned away, maybe even two. It is surprising how time disappears when one has to think of such unimportant things as a cardinal's nightcap, his breath, his gall, his peaceful sleep. When he had gone through the library, Cazalla had seen El Greco's picture.

There was not much to see, a dark background and an empty space in the middle, a place for the torso and the head. In the place meant for the head only the eyes—really only the spectacles—were sketched in. A detestable apparatus on the face, these spectacles! Does the Cardinal agree that these spectacles should disfigure him so? Yet El Greco asks permission of no one whom he paints, he would not even consult a cardinal. Cazalla wished he knew, were El Greco keeping watch here, if he would direct his gaze at such ridiculous things as candles, nightcaps, respiration, and downy feathers. Could El Greco contemplate the sleeping man calmly? This pile of bones under the coverlet; a fly would probably look at it as someone at home would view the hills of Toledo: distant, lofty, barren. Perhaps El Greco would view him with the eyes of a fly, this sleeping Grand Inquisitor.

What is it—fear? He is afraid, but he wants to paint him. That was why he went out into the storm, too. Like a sponge would water, he absorbed the weather, was thrilled and rocked to the core by the blue-colored illumination; each flash went down his back like a cold spasm, and the thunder crashed on his skin as it did in his ear. Then: Out of his pores the colors flashed and darted onto the canvas, and afterward there stood Toledo on the hill in a storm, dreadful and brilliant, in a ghostly instant; there came the fear that the next moment would bring eternal darkness, but only the painted lightning endures and maintains the terror forever.

And Dr. Cazalla sat quietly on his chair the whole night long and thought about fear—"so that you need not be afraid," said El Greco with a quick smile when his friend informed him about the hours of his vigil.

Dr. Cazalla understood: "So I am right when I think: You paint fear so that you can become fearless."

El Greco took a pear from the breakfast basket—they were sitting in his cell, taking refreshment after the sleepless night. And as he cut up the fruit, his face became grim, and he slowly pointed with his knife to the path of a worm that marked both halves of the fruit. "Look, Cazalla, look!" And then he was silent. The doctor did not understand and regarded the worm writhing in its own filth. "You need to make sure of even the finest fruit," murmured El Greco, "you must cut it in pieces. This is my worst fear: to get a worm and its filth on my tongue."

"That is just caution," Cazalla smiled.

"That is abhorrence," El Greco assured him and cut out the core with care, "abhorrence of what is unclean, mistrust of the outside world, fear! Fear cuts the world in pieces, fear presses into the core. Do you eat mushrooms?" he asked just as deliberately.

Cazalla said yes, he did.

"You see, you could be called timid, if you did not eat mushrooms. Fear does not keep you from eating mushrooms, rather it is exactly what gives you the courage to eat this excellent dish. I tell you, Cazalla, fear gives us safety and pleasure, fear divides the world into parts, yes, truly, it is the beginning of wisdom. This knowledge was confirmed for me by the Grand Inquisitor." He smiled to himself again. "I have divided him into parts now, too," he continued, "I have seen him lying before me cut in two, that is what fear can do. But Niño knows that I am not frightened of him. A man who is frightened falls to his knees when the flag of the Holy Inquisition goes on parade. Fear goes to the stake as a sacrifice to the Holy Inquisition, it does not give up what it has espied in its view of the core of the world. So I will not paint fear, but rather my fear will paint. My pictures will cut the world into parts, yes, that is what I intend, and Niño shall be made aware of how the Grand Inquisitor appears within."

During the week of Epiphany, the day arrived on which El Greco finished the portrait of the Grand Inquisitor. Dr. Cazalla was still there, watching over the condition of the convalescent from all aspects and at all times of the day, like a man of ambition who is dissatisfied with his work. Dr. Cazalla had become the door on which in the last weeks everyone was obliged to knock who wanted to see the Cardinal, even El Greco, who came and went just as restlessly, until that day in the week of Epiphany.

The Cardinal had been docile and obedient, and even though the piles of documents accumulated in the secretary's office, he let them read light verse to him just as Cazalla considered proper for a bilious attack, and El Greco found the Cardinal ready for him every day for an hour.

"We must gather our strength anew," Niño de Guevara was given to murmuring quite suddenly into the silence, as if he wanted to offer excuses for his idleness. Then a surge would flow into his hands, as they hung over the arms of the chair, as if through a flaccid tube, and the end of the tube—his fingers—would jerk just once and then his hands hung there again as before, idle and ready.

El Greco saw this; he continued to wait for the surge in the hands whenever the Grand Inquisitor spoke of the accumulation of his responsibilities. And he waited for the brief, impatient movement of his lashes behind the spectacles.

A great variety of animals lie in the eyes of men just as in the cages of the animal parks. There are things there that smack diversely of greed, cunning, indolence, and bloodlust, yet mostly they are harmless and contained by custom and by fear. But Niño's eyes are dangerous. As in the cool darkness of the crypt, everything there is motionless and enclosed. And what some unsuspecting person might take for a rod is the most dangerous of all the animals, like Moses' rod that becomes a viper when flung down. El Greco thinks of the caves where dragons live. He also thinks that the dragons stand guard over a treasure. These are the eyes of the crypt just like mine, El Greco thinks, they are sad eyes like mine; in these eyes there are graves. Oh, this cold, stony melancholy in the eyes of the Inquisitor! It may destroy the meaning of the picture, and people will not see the serpent in the dark night of this sadness. Things that are sad belong in the realm of humanity. Then should he suppress the melancholy?

Suddenly he extends his head past the easel and stares at the Grand Inquisitor. His long look asks only one thing: What is the serpent guarding? The treasure of great melancholy, which the world has recognized? Are you sad as my saints are sad? A sorrowful executioner?

At that Niño de Guevara arose and approached El Greco slowly, came behind the easel. "Let me look," he said abruptly. It was the first time that he had viewed the picture. El Greco hesitated. At this the Cardinal waved him aside and then, as El Greco stood by with his lips compressed, with his own hand he pushed the picture halfway toward the window.

Cazalla stood there and spoke: "Eminence, think of your health!"

Niño de Guevara heard these words, a sharp motion of his head toward the window seemed to prepare for an answer, but his eyes remained fixed on the portrait; and so he stood with his gaze turned there and forgot the answer, his hands were lifted out of the folds of his robe, they intended to make a defensive gesture toward the doctor or to pull the picture still more toward the light—no one could tell, for the movement faltered as he looked at the portrait, and the index finger of his right hand scratched at the palm of his left hand. Who had ever seen the Cardinal make such a ridiculous, unconscious gesture, but he continued to scratch with this little movement, apelike and quick, in which only his index finger moved and otherwise all was frozen still.

Finally he said in a very small, husky voice: "Silk?"

"Yes, silk," El Greco answered.

At his voice Niño de Guevara seemed to awaken, he let his hands drop and said, now much more firmly: "But we are wearing our winter wool!"

"And I painted silk," El Greco repeated.

"Are you finished?" de Guevara then asked in his usual tone, and as El Greco shook his head quickly and started to turn the picture around, he gave a command: "The picture is finished! It seems to be finished—or—what is still missing?" The Cardinal was pale.

El Greco tried to gain time, and he said: "My name is still missing."

"And the serpent in front of it?" The Grand Inquisitor smiled malignantly.

Then El Greco turned pale, too, and said: "Not in front, it is missing there; to be sure, it is not missing, you can see it, but it is not as erect as it is in your eyes now, Eminence."

The Cardinal—he towered over El Greco by half a foot—shook his head; no one could know what was in his voice, scorn or coolly dispassionate faith: "Theodokopoulos, who spoke these words: 'As Moses lifted up the serpent in the wilderness'—the serpent can also represent Christ, everything can represent Him. Those who are bitten by serpents shall be healed by the likeness of serpents."

And then he turned toward Cazalla and again toward El Greco; and as if he meant to cut them down together with this look, he asked: "Have you been healed?"

El Greco did not answer. He was placing his name under the picture.

As he did so, he heard Dr. Cazalla's voice in his roaring ears. "Eminence, you are now healed, but I do not know for how long."

Thereupon the Grand Inquisitor spoke, and those were his last words, with which he dismissed the two, "Following the doctor's wishes, we should in future serve only our gall. But our gall serves to heal the world. For the doctor, as you know, dies of his cures!"

With these words in their ears they rode for a week through the desolate mountains back to Toledo; and the messenger came from the Grand Inquisitor and paid them, the painter and the doctor. And the fiery stake of the Holy Inquisition was aroused like the newly strengthened life spirits of Niño de Guevara.

As the two waited and wondered whether the other messenger of the Grand Inquisitor would come to them, they waited in vain.

But later El Greco wrote the name of the Grand Inquisitor in that list where his paintings of saints were recorded. And when Cazalla showed great surprise over that, he smiled and pointed out the considerable sum that the Cardinal had sent.

"You see, he pays ten times as much as that miserly Philip— and I wished him ten times more misfortune than the bad king. I recognized his face, and he is grateful for it. How seldom that is! He is a saint because of his melancholy, a sad, sad saint, a sainted executioner! He has the eyes of the grave," said El Greco softly, "and where their source is, in the darkness of his head and his world, we do not know."

Translated by Jeanne R. Willson

Jürgen Becker

From the Story of a Separation

In the mid-1930s Kenneth Patchen, on the first page of a kind of memoir, had figured out how often he had eaten breakfast and had lunch and dinner since he was two years old. In addition there were figures about miles traveled by subway and numbers of socks, pants, shirts, shoes worn out; the voluminous enumeration further contained detailed data about the use of Colgate toothpaste, Ogilvie hairbrushes, Herald Square razor blades, hair oil, and skin lotion and more such stuff. I was sitting in my room on the courtyard and pondering whether the man had such a fantastic memory or whether he had always written down everything exactly or perhaps just figured it out halfway, when the door flew open and Lene and Maja entered with their huge brown bags and unpacked a bottle of Gibson vodka, a bottle of Four Roses, a bottle of Beefeater, a six-pack of Schweppes, two six-packs of Miller High Life, two bottles of chablis, two bottles of Perrier, two pounds of Santa Lucia spaghetti, four cans of Heinz tomato sauce, two heads of Lattuga lettuce, three T-bone steaks, two long loaves of white bread, a carton of Lucky Strikes, and a bunch of small articles such as spices, toiletries, sweets, magazines, and candies. Maja had succeeded in one year in putting three families behind her: in the first family, she had jumped screaming out of bed because her exchange-parents had constantly stuffed her fat exchange-sister into the bed; in the second family, the fat exchange-father had tried it; in the third family, it seemed to be going fine toward the end of the exchange year—Susan, the youngest exchange-sister, had taught her a few cosmetic tricks in front of the boudoir mirror. Maja looked entirely different and had a singing accent even in her German since we had driven her a year ago to the Frankfurt air terminal for her exchange year in Toledo, Ohio. My charter flight was also supposed to take off from Frankfurt but was suddenly transferred to Brussels, for which reason about 120 sleepy backpack tourists and GI relatives had to travel to Belgium by bus, where the charter took off five hours late. Naturally, no Lene was at the airport, nor at the bus terminal on Thirty-seventh Street, but in the hall was an information booth with a lady who was just closing up and said that a blond lady from Europe had stood around five hours before, asking about a charter from Frankfurt am Main, no, she had no word from her. I did the expected thing and looked up Jeff Weisman's number, who answered quite a bit surprised. No, Lene ought to be at the Institute, in the room over the courtyard. I had forgotten the bus line that I had last used two years before and climbed into one of the bulky yellow cabs. And Lene did come after I had finally waked up the janitor with my ringing. Maja is upstairs and is quite glad. The massive elevator creaked up for an eternity, but even so, not enough time to look at Lene. We lived 150 miles apart and met again high over Eighty-second Street.

The great lobby was full of carpets on which, some distance apart, groups of seats were scattered, containing solitary figures who seemed to be waiting for nothing and hardly even looked up as we passed by on our way to the elevator. On a television set on a pedestal a film was playing that was about as old as the whole ambience of the lobby, where nobody was watching the tube. The elevator rose very slowly. A few years later Maurice and Marie were divorced, but now they looked down on Fifth Avenue satisfied and happy in the roomy suite in their hotel. From the Frigidaire Maurice got some glass containers of orange and tomato juice, and tonic, ice cubes, vodka, and gin as well. We had last sat together in Zurich and had driven to Frankfurt for table tennis. Since that time Marie had been burning for revenge, whereas Maurice took the matter with complete nonchalance and pointed to the fact that—and this reunion proved it—chance was a better organizer. We could talk another time in Europe about meeting for a grudge game. As chance would have it also, in the elevator we were suddenly standing facing Eileen, the heroine of a fairly long story that had started at the end of the 1950s in Worpswede, in a gigantic farmhouse-atelier, where Hennes kept drawing tiny pictures on tiny sheets of paper until he fell in love with Eileen and drove back with her to the Rhineland to divorce Hali-Halo and to live with Eileen before and after their marriage, until their separation and divorce because of Giulia. In those years Eileen had often turned up at Nora's and had sat next to her full of understanding after I had left the house and gone to Lene, who now was standing right next to me in the elevator when Eileen asked without further ado: And how is Nora anyway? Are you staying in this hotel too by any chance, I asked Eileen, when the elevator had stopped on the floor where Maurice and Marie had their suite, for which reason only in the following year did Eileen get around in the Café Select to telling us the still topical story of her Cuban coproducer and the film mess in which she was again involved, but with verve, she said, and repeated a couple of times, but with verve. What a town, where you can meet whomever quite suddenly: I wanted to get rid of this sentence before the first Bloody Mary, but I didn't get around to it because Maurice and Marie had already started telling about their experiences of the past months. Karsch, who was writing a novel about the life of an emigrant woman in this city, had been here, had flown over from Berlin just because he wanted to know for exact certain whether the letter box on West End Avenue was on the left or the right side of the street. Maurice was involved with the continuation of his diary. Marie had begun translating the new stories by Duck, who lived a few blocks away with his daughter in a building that his Danish wife had left shortly before. When you've tried everything, Maurice said, then you have to wonder at one time or another what you ought to try now. Lene admired the way Maurice and Marie lived, now in this and now in another city, always changing countries, from one suite to another; just don't get stuck, said Maurice, and Lene nodded. We'd rather be on a Greek island, she said; no, I said, if anywhere, then in this city. This is a complex city, said Marie; but you can live here quite simply, said Maurice. It was a time when many of us hardly lived in concord with our apartments, houses, and cities; many traveled around the country looking for old farmhouses; many moved abroad; boy, the disappointments that came along, said Maurice, there must be some reason for all that. There are no reasons, I said, but I knew no more than that either; Marie mixed me a new Bloody Mary, and I looked down at the slow current of sparkling car bodies. Maybe it's only moods, I was about to say, when Marie said: Djuna Barnes lives near here. Have you seen her, I asked. I see her sometimes when I'm shopping, said Marie. Have you talked to her, I asked. She's a little, very old lady, said Marie, and I always wanted to say something to her, but I don't dare. Djuna Barnes, I said, there were times when I dreamed about her and the women in *Nightwood;* just that one novel, said Marie, which makes so many others superfluous. I must see her, I said, but I don't think I can get a word out. I've heard, said Marie, that she won't see anyone, and I don't know either whether our publisher found out much when he was with her recently. If we want to eat fish at Sweet's, then we've got to get going, said Maurice and refilled his pipe. We drank up our cocktails and stood a while still at the windows, behind which we hardly heard the noise of the beginning rush hour.

Inga had written the word down for me on a piece of paper: *cockroaches.* They will outlive us all, said Inga, there are a couple of million more than the population of this place, and they live everywhere, in the sewers, in the elevator shaft, in the television set, in the refrigerator, in the electric wires, under the wall-to-wall carpet, behind the wallpaper, in the water pipes, in the heating system, in the garbage disposal, in the drain, and after the nuclear winter they'll still be alive, and all by themselves. They're a kind of alien bug? I inquired. Maybe with you all in Europe, said Inga, but here they are the true population. Will you get me another drink? Inga's kitchen was not a real kitchen but served in her small apartment as a corridor between the bathroom, the living room, and the building hallway; through the corridor door, which was furnished with a supplementary safety lock, a door chain, and two bolts, you could hear when somewhere in the building there was a break-in, a neighbor lady was raped, the janitor slain, or there was a cry for help somewhere else. In the ice box I found the rest of the tomato juice, a swallow of vodka, and half a lemon; Inga did not approve of my suggestion to get a couple of drinks in the shop around the block: I'd be able to shop, but that I'd get the stuff home was fairly out of the question, now at this time of evening; in the bathroom there still had to be a six-pack of Miller High Life, isn't that your beer? Inga had been living in the city for five years, working in an institute for cultural exchange, and once a week she went to a group. What do you do in the group? We seek one another out with our eyes. And then? We try touching.

Don't you talk to one another? Some can't talk, and some just want to scream. Through one wall came a radio station with rock music; through another wall came a radio station with romantic music. We have more radio stations here than we can set up transistor sets in one apartment, said Inga and put on the record with the Stylistics. Why do you keep on living here? I asked. In Europe I'd have to travel all over to find what I can find in a couple of square blocks here in Manhattan; won't you think about staying on? I just have a visitor's visa, I said. Inga opened up a can of beer. In Europe people just sit on their problems, here people take their problems to one another. And do one another in with them. You have the wrong idea, said Inga, in this town eight people at most are killed every day. And how many emigrants arrive per day? We don't ask such cynical questions, said Inga, now all the concerns are returning that years ago went to New Jersey, to Texas, to Arkansas. Behind the courtyards outside the fire trucks howled; I asked Inga if she was afraid to live here. She shrugged her white shoulders. We all live with fear, but that doesn't matter, because, well, everybody does, and so you don't notice it so much, besides, we keep talking on the phone at night. She showed me snapshots from Germany: Inga in kindergarten, in front of the Brandenburg Gate, with her relatives at a celebration. It was worse there, and the worst thing was, I felt so little, in the group they always say to me, Inga, you have to learn to feel it afterward. Do you feel it afterward, now? I've started to, said Inga and with her feet rolled a new can over to the bed, but I'm sure I'd backslide again somewhere else, you know, really slide back into this condition, I can't exactly describe it, you have to stay here and live here, then you'll soon find out. During the night I walked through empty streets in which garbage bags were stacked yards high. Inga had pretended for a long time that she couldn't find the safety lock key, but I had shown her my jackknife with a smile, whereupon Inga, grinning likewise, had said, put that thing away and instead of that held up a twenty dollar bill in her hand, you'll get by sooner with this. On Fifth Avenue the big yellow taxicabs came past in droves, but I did not have so many blocks to walk, pulled my cap over my face and walked on in high spirits against the wind into the driving snow. Somewhere nearby Chet Baker was playing again, Dusty Springfield was singing at the Plaza Hotel. Suddenly a group of young people were dancing around two men lying down. Columns of

steam hissed from the culverts. A woman walked past with a mon-
key on a leash. A battle between a gull and a rat went round and
round. In my courtyard room with a view of yellow brick façades
traces of Lene's departure lay about. Our problems had something
to do with contradictory ideas of keeping order. On the pillow lay
several polaroid pictures: Johann with his MG among pine trees;
Lene and Maja swinging in Bryant Park, 42nd Street; Johann trans-
plants a conifer on a wet meadow; Lene leans over a bridge railing
and smiles into the future; Johann and Boris bent over a record
player on which a record with Keith Jarrett is turning; Maja and
Lene on an excursion flight over Hoboken, the birthplace of Frank
Sinatra; arm in arm Maja and Johann. Our problems had something to do with children from former marriages, former marriages,
later affairs, lies in bed, and truths in intoxication. Lene had left
me a bottle of J.B.; some bottles later Gesa M. of Cornell University
called and said that the archive had to know precisely: J.B. was a
Scotch and not a Bourbon; years later, in the Berlin "Zwiebelfisch,"
I had provided such contrary information that an American female
German professor found occasion, on the basis of research on labels, to correct the fellow. Lene had landed with TWA at the Fiu-
mincino airport, drank an espresso at the bar, had a Vecchia
Romagna set before her, and leafed through her notebook for telephone numbers. On the table under the lamp lay a yellow sheet,
torn out of a notebook with yellow pages, on which American
writers wrote their short stories: please call Johanna Moore. That
was on Lake Michigan. I called up Fifty-seventh Street. You did
find your way? What are you doing now? What does a woman do
now alone in the city? Is it a complex city? The best city to be
alone in. Hey, Inga, that can't be true, say something. I suddenly
had an urge to call more people in the city and all around: Marie
and Maurice, Jeff Weisman, Duck Barthelme, Gesa M. Valk, Fred
Jordan, Mike Roloff, Gene Lettau, Viola Drath, Charles Foster,
Pyla Patterson, Johnny Jahn, Frankie Scholz, Nico Peffgen, Gesine
Cresspahl, John Lennon; I didn't call anybody. On the table under
the lamp in a house in which a person could have died now unnoticed, lay the book with the photograph of Kenneth Patchen,
bebob-haircut, thick throat, square neck. Outside in the courtyard
it was snowing. "This room is cold." Lene asked for a reservation
to Heraklion. "We can't stay here." Everything all booked? "It's
snowing out and your shoes are through." Back, where we were,

to Miami. "We must leave here." Or even better, Brindisi? "She wanted never to leave me." On my part, however, it was in the direction of Frankfurt, North End, Holzhausen Park; in the Editions office I had to display: Lanford Wilson, William Logan, Red Ryder, Joseph Papp, Kenneth Patchen, second printing. We had driven Maja to La Guardia Airport; no, you won't get me back so fast; Mike, or whatever the guy's name was, was waiting in Detroit, in the night on to Toledo, Ohio; the next night it happened; that's what you wanted, wasn't it, young woman? The books on Edward Hopper and Andrew Wyeth, the photos by Walker Evans and Edward Steichen, the records with the early Stan Kenton: you have to go back to Macy's and buy an extra Samsonite, and since you're in the vicinity, Herald Square, have breakfast again, opposite the Hotel Martinique, you know, the sixty-sixth night with Percy Sledge, and how he never stopped singing: "When a man loves a woman"; Lene said everything finally in the bus on her way to Kennedy Airport; we'll be back in Europe, will see one another again, separated by a few hundred kilometers, and the problems keep on, the war will start over. I was sitting at the table under the lamp, looking at the yellow paper. "The war lingers on." From one of the windows in the courtyard below the lead number of the Top Ten came from the darkness again: "How can I tell her that we are dead?" Snow scratched at the window. I was tired now and had to prepare a report and an interview in the morning. When I was about to go to bed, I saw a black spot run off across the bedcover. I got out Inga's piece of paper: *cockroaches.*

Translated by A. Leslie Willson

Ulla Berkéwicz

Hi, Wendy!

Wendy held onto the book, thinking of something else, rubbed her fingerprint off the shiny black jacket, held tight to the book, stuck a finger between the pages, pressed the book with the balls of her hands until her finger turned white, let her hands drop but did not let go of the book.

She was sitting on her bed, her back against the wall, her legs entwined next to her. She was waiting for Edward. She was sitting quietly, for she was willing to wait.

Edward had come. She had not expected him, had not expected anything, only the ordinary, what she could foresee because it recurred daily. Had expected no great emotion, no flights or sudden changes, just always the same, perhaps later the apartment alone without her girl friend, or another one with a balcony, or perhaps to give up her job at the university and open up a little café, for she was a good cook. Or perhaps even to marry still, even now at twenty-seven to meet someone with whom she could imagine a yard with flowers out front.

The fellows whom she had met, whom she had had anything to do with, such as when you accept an irksome invitation the ninth time that you have already refused eight times or else you won't fit into the frame of the picture that confines you but sustains you and holds you, the two or three fellows who clapped her on the shoulder in the morning and said, "Hi, Wendy," she had forgotten them.

Only seldom did a little ache burst through, pull at the two or three scars from injuries she did not want to notice, and then she had to swim far out in the ocean. And only then was she willing to imagine she had a share in what must be so rich and fervent in the world, so different that no images of it came to her.

Training in evening courses, she had gotten the job as a German professor's secretary and soon after, infected by all those who were reading on the campus lawns, who lay there with their books as if everything that they lacked was written down in them, as if they could absorb it by reading, be filled with it for all time, she had begun to read, had written down the names that appeared most frequently in the lists that she kept for the professor, had gone to the Booksmith with them, and they had sold her *Elective Affinities* by J. W. GOTHY.

And in that book was to be found what was different portrayed so differently and still richer and more fervent than she could ever have believed it existed in the world. And it lay hold of her and drove her half the nights through in a fever, and then, although Ottilie appeared strange to her and as if mad, she wanted to take on her features, put on her clothes. She walked through landscapes like those of hers, lay down on moss, looked up into the crowns of age-old chestnut trees, lost herself in the play of shadows from the leaves, in the shine of the leaves, in the sunlight, in the freshness of the earth, in the fragrance of the grass, in the stillness of a May Sunday.

And she fell fast asleep into a dream: of Ottilie's untouched, white breasts and of someone who squirted fire on her white breasts with a squirt bottle full of ketchup so that they lay charred and plastered with red tomato in the grass on the smooth campus lawn, smoking among those who lay prone reading, who went on reading and did not look at the breasts that went up in smoke in the hot sun under the blue sky, and also there was the sound of the Florida ocean.

In the morning she was awakened by Doris Day. Her girl friend had given her the alarm clock for her twenty-fifth birthday. Doris Day squawked with a Daisy Duck voice, "Hi, Wendy." There were alarm clocks with all the names in demand, all squawked by Doris Day. The friend with whom she shared the apartment had one, too, jumped up out of bed each morning as soon as it went off, got her program of aerobic exercises taken care of while Doris Day squawked, and after that toast with marmalade and off in the bus to Boca Raton Beach to do her best as a receptionist. But once or twice a month for a night or a weekend, she went off with a visitor and then came back a little dull, her chewing gum a little tough between her coated teeth, no machine-gun chewing as usual, no bubbles, only a slow, tedious, chewing survival.

When her friend stayed away on the weekend, Wendy didn't open the curtains, lighted candles, draped the room with large white bed sheets, wrapped herself in one of them, hunted on the radio for old music that seemed to come over to her from Europe, and read her book and read it again and again.

On the campus they were nice to Wendy. She was, after all, very pretty and still young, caused no problems for anyone, seemed also not to have any, helped everyone who did have. "Hi, Wendy," they clapped her on the shoulder until in the evening it hurt.

But what she really wanted to know, she didn't dare ask anyone there, because she would have been ashamed, if they had laughed when they heard that Wendy Jones was capable of reading. Ottilie—she would have liked to ask—did she really exist? Had J.W. patterned her after a real woman? Was it perhaps even J.W.'s own story? Had he become a writer really because of this story? And, finally, did he owe his writing to Ottilie, as men in truth owe everything to women and women everything to men, but only in truth, and that lay for Wendy in Europe, and in Florida there was only the sun that brought nothing to light except just the ordinary.

But then Edward had come, had come as a conqueror from Germany. Stood in Wendy's office, tall, well-built, an all-around athlete, laughed, was full of life. She did not understand; she did not comprehend. She saw him and heard him and saw that he was looking at her and waited for something that could happen any moment, suddenly or not for a while or never.

He had come to Florida for six weeks as a guest professor, and the students crowded into his lectures, fought over his office hours, stormed his seminars. They looked up from their books when he went by, followed him with their eyes, ran after him, pursued him across the green campus, and the girls would have liked to tumble in the grass with him.

He had preserved something childlike in spite of his years, something impetuous and full of anticipation that they wanted to encounter, that they wanted to share, that swept them along, transported them into their daydreams.

Wendy lay awake in the night, sat on the bed with the book in her hand, was not reading, could not, for the words and the images in her head that came from the book in her hand whirled around and flew off and mixed with her own, and Edward was Edward and she, who had seen the darkness in his eyes that seemed to her to mean that he had lost something or not found it, installed herself there where she believed she knew the lack, the renunciation, and the need. Night after night she appeared there, making the dark place bright, cherishing him, caring for him. Whatever his longings were, she sought to fulfill them, to prevent whatever would distress him. And often in the night Edward's form seemed to appear at her door so that she got up from the bed and went to it and opened it.

But in the morning, after Doris Day and her friend, in the bus with the other people, she knew: That cannot be me after all, I am much too insignificant for me to be her, I am nothing compared to all those who could be her, and if there were maps of people, one for special people as there are for mountains or mineral resources, on my place there would be a nice white spot.

After two weeks Edward invited Wendy to have dinner. Out of gratitude, Wendy said to herself, just out of gratitude. For she had taken care of his schedule, had organized his classes and arranged his office hours with everyone who spoke his language, which she did not speak, had explained the way things were done on the campus, and had given him her map of Florida because he had tried in vain and had not found one even at the Booksmith.

She was helpful and friendly to everyone, but toward him most of all, and he had noticed that and it pleased him.

He wanted to pick her up at home, but she, ready to invent a thousand reasons against it, was successful with the first one that came along: She would be in the vicinity of his hotel, had things to do there after work, could be in the lobby about seven. She, with her apartment on the south side of town where there are no trees, where the fronts of the houses are rickety, the cement cracked, and the children wither.

They had made a date to eat in the restaurant of his hotel. She had never been in this restaurant or one like it, had no clothes for anything out of the ordinary, borrowed from her friend, who had more of a wardrobe because of her weekends, a green pullover to go with a red skirt, made up her face more than usual, and still sat quietly on the bed with the book in her hand for five minutes more, and then she left.

She had taken the bus, had arrived at the hotel much too early, went up one side of the street and down the other, had pulled herself together and walked through the revolving door into the hotel, had seated herself on a colorful chair in the lobby, had ordered a Coke, had not dared to go to the john to freshen up after the hot bus and the dusty street, for he could have come, after all, and then she would not have been sitting at her place, and then he would have passed by her empty place, out onto the street, across the street, away, farther and farther away and never again.

Edward saw all that. None of her excitement and anticipation escaped him. He knew women, had gotten acquainted with each one he had known. For among those he had known, there was not one whose pleasures he had not searched out, whose happiness he had not found. For that reason he was unconcerned.

They went into the restaurant. He directed her. She felt his hand on her back at the waist.

They sat at a table; they ate and drank. He drinks wine like water, she thought, she who seldom drank, and she drank with him. He spoke pretty words, sought out and found even prettier ones because of the wine, made them up for her, words that she would have liked to embroider and frame and hang up everywhere in her room. He played with them, presented them, arranged them bright and lofty before her, and tossed them at her feet.

And she listened to him and looked at him, and words from the book entered her mind as if they were hers, as if she were the one who was being written by the words, as if she came from the words, as if she existed through the words, as if J.W. had created her from his words. "Edward," she said.

Saw him, heard him, German words, she thought, even though they are English, and then it was to her as if she were being created just from J.W.'s words, but she also seemed to take shape from Edward's and grew up toward him and took hold of his hands. "Edward," she said.

So that he stood up, placed his hand flat on her back at the waist, and guided her out of the restaurant and through the lobby and through the glass door, the revolving door where everything revolved, glass, frame, and she herself and everything in front of and behind her.

Whirled out onto the street, she heard herself say: "No, not to my place"—and felt herself being revolved back again and left standing in the lobby. The moment outside had been hot. Florida in August does not cool off even at night. Inside it was cold. A pane of ice grew before her face.

Through the ice or frosted glass she saw him go to the reception desk. He broke the ice with every step and pushed the pieces away. She saw herself go after him through the swaying pieces, saw him go before her, step into the elevator, no flat hand on her back at the waist, saw him go before her until they were in his room.

He locked the door. He poured wine for her. They sat in two easy chairs and drank. Wendy walked through glass doors, turned around, there was a grating noise.

"Edward," she said.

There came a hand; it was small, became larger, came near. She could see the pores in the skin of the hand. They were so close together that Wendy could get no air, they whirled in confusion, they rushed toward her. The huge hand turned over, lay on its back, and opened up before her. The pulse was beating before her. She saw the lines on the hand meet and separate. The pulse beat faster and faster. A second hand came, whirled itself through the revolving door, was doubly reflected in the glass, and rested next to the first. Two hands, different, German, Wendy thought, are lying before me on their knees and questioning me. And when she answered with yes, she was whirled out of the revolving door by the hands, she was taken in hand by the hands, she could feel how the pulse of the hands increased, how the pores beat and the lines of the hands wrapped around her, closer and closer, stronger and stronger, until they ripped.

Then there was a streak of light, then there were voices passing, then her tongue moved through her mouth and found no gums and found her teeth coated and the moist membrane of the mouth dry, and then she heard him sleeping.

Then the light was constant on her eyelids, then she placed her feet on the cool floor next to the bed, with her hand located a wall that was solid and did not give way when she pulled herself up on it. Then she saw him sleeping on the bed.

Then she looked for her red skirt and her friend's green pullover and found the pullover on a rug with an intertwining pattern whose intricacies she traced dizzily and could not discover in what way they were entwined. Then the red skirt lay there wrinkled.

Then she dressed and went to the door, stopped, stood silently, listened to him sleeping, counted his breaths, could not stop, had to count until he paused in breathing, turned over in bed, and continued to breathe in a different rhythm.

Then she opened the door, went out, found her way to the elevator, found her way to the street.

She followed a footpath step by step that led her home, even though there was water flowing under the bridge, even though the streets intersected each other.

The apartment was empty, her friend was away with a visitor. The book lay on the bed. Wendy lay down on the floor.—Was he still sleeping? Will he still know, when he wakes up after so much wine? She searched, dug into her memory, and became dizzy, for the revolving door was always between the images, there was frosted glass in front of the images, and the images did not extend beyond his hands.

Doris Day gave the alarm and with her voice clove the glass of the revolving door. It broke into pieces then, and Wendy washed and dressed, looked at herself in the mirror. "I am not pretty," she said, "I am not at all pretty, and I am nothing," ate a piece of toast and jelly, left the house, got on the bus, got out at the campus, went to her office.

She sat on her chair at her desk and was aware of herself and was aware that she was different, was beyond herself—where, she did not know. She remained in her chair, kept still. And only when the first people came in, clapped her on the shoulder, and said, "Hi, Wendy," could she become part of herself again. Then she did what she did every day, gave out information, wrote things down, filled things out. But sentences from the book constantly kept occurring to her, appeared to her as fixed as formulas, as an evocation of her story by the one she had read in the book. And when the doors opened and she was startled, she looked for, and immediately found, a sentence that stood so solidly before her that she did not need to ask anymore whether she hoped he would come in or whether she feared it.

Then late in the afternoon she had found a sentence that she recited to herself like a guiding principle, like a verification, which she took with her on the way home, and which she continued to recite to herself when she had arrived home. "And it seemed to her as she looked up and all around," she said to herself, "as if she were and were not, and as if she were aware of herself and not aware, as if all this was sure to disappear for her and she for herself."

She walked through the apartment, was moving in a different way, stumbled, had lost her rhythm, could no get back into the old rhythm, could not find a new one. She followed her usual routine; but a glass fell out of her hand, she mashed her finger in the door, something red got into the wash.

She lay down on the bed. She was still there. She took the book in her hand and was about to read, but then it turned over and she could not hold onto the words and the images and not onto Ottilie's feelings either, and she went and fell back over and over again to her own feelings, about which she scarcely knew that she felt them.

And then she fell asleep and sank into a dream, was walking through Ottilie's wooded meadows. Edward's words were hanging in the branches, ivy angels stood threateningly in her path, and blood flowed over stones on which the names of Edward and Ottilie, of herself and Edward, were intertwined with each other to form powerful symbols. She gave Edward her hair, she adorned him, and the two of them stood hand in hand by the ocean under which she was sleeping so deeply, ready to perish ceremoniously in the dream wave. Her arms were snatching at the leafy towers, in which the evening was already suspended, and broke off the green and wove for him a cover for tomorrow. And here the dream persisted and she began to weave it from the beginning again and again, but always according to a new pattern.

When next morning Wendy went into her office, Edward came, clapped her on the shoulder, had gotten tan, had been swimming in Palm Beach, and then had eaten at Charley's Crab. "And what is little Wendy doing today?"

She went with him. He came to her place. He liked her apartment. He liked to experience a bit at firsthand the lives of women, of those women whom he loved with a total longing for the one single love and a total desire for all the others, short and tall, large and small. His five senses raced unceasingly in every direction.

He came in the evening and brought the wine, and she cooked. Her friend was still gone with her visitor, a card came from the

Bahamas: "Hi, Wendy, don't forget to feed the cat." She had forgotten the cat. It had disappeared. She had not thought of the cat anymore for two weeks.

She went with Edward and sat with him and lay with him and was small when she stood next to him and leaned on him and still had no hope of ever being able to lean on him.

At night and with the wine—he was accustomed to enhance his talkativeness, his enjoyment, and his desire by drinking wine—his discourses were intensified greatly, and with glowing eyes he made the whole world known to her. His imagination ranged into all possibilities: She was to be happy, and even if he had to leave in two weeks. perhaps even with someone else. Or she might remain his, and he would come again, once a year or twice. Women climb up to the widow's walk, watch the ship sail away, climb up again and again tearfully to the walkway, see that the ship does not return. Women sit by the fireside, sing weaving songs. But men sail out to sea and ride off to war.

In the morning, when he had spent the night with her, they often sat silently together. He said nothing and did not look at her, and she tried and tried and found nothing to say and kept her eyes glued to his face, which was completely aloof.

In Germany, Edward was married and had a child. The story was not enlarged upon, and she did not dare to question further. She imagined his wife, tall and blond, German and haughty, saw her at festivities. People grew silent when she entered the room. People followed her with their eyes. Edward kissed her hand.

But she had not made the darkness in his eyes bright, she told herself; and Ottilie was willing to die for Edward, but would Charlotte have died for Edward?

Edward came every evening, came to her in the office in the daytime, too, and she saw that he enjoyed seeing her. He brought her little gifts, little chains and rings and glorious, huge bouquets, for which she had no vases. She had emptied out a drawer in her lingerie chest. There lay everything that he had given her, everything that he had touched and used. And when she was waiting for him or when he had gone in the night, she sat before the open chest and became lost in her thoughts of the stories that linked the objects in the drawer with Edward.

As often as she could get away from the office, she went to Edward's lectures. He spoke about J.W. and also and again and again about Edward and Ottilie, but with a background that was not familiar to her and in connections that she did not understand. She sat in the last row and was ashamed because she understood so little of what Edward knew how to say, watched him as he spoke with expansive gestures about great things, and listened to him speak about his language in her language with his beautiful voice and its foreign tone.

She never told him how well she knew the book and did not ask him the questions that had occurred to her. For whether Ottilie was invented by J.W. or whether she had existed for him, and whether J.W. had become a poet through her or not was not important anymore. The story was to be found, after all, in the world and occurred here and there and now and then, and J.W. had perhaps only picked it out of thin air where these stories perhaps hang eternally as if they were written, black on white, in an ancient chronicle.

"We'll go to Acapulco for five days, the Princess Hotel," he said with a bouquet of roses in his hand. And she knew: Two days more after the five days, then he would be gone, and no day would bring him back to her.

Five days in Acapulco!—He pulled roses from the bouquet and fixed them in her hair. In my hair, she thought. The roses are much too beautiful for my hair. My hair is thin. So that it will look thicker, I get a permanent. For that reason the ends are split and the color of ashes.

She took five days of vacation. She couldn't imagine it. She was not happy, she was not sad. She waited for him, otherwise nothing.

In the airplane she would have been afraid—for she had never flown before—if he had not been sitting next to her and if, because of the wine he had given her, she had not wanted to think that the airplane could fall, plunge through space with him and her, how they would hold onto each other and embrace each other, sink into one another, not out of fear, no, only so that the rending wind would not rip them apart, so that, dissolved by the heat from their plunge into one light being, made of nothing, and gathered up by a wind and lifted high above all limitations, they could fly away over their dark stars, God knows where to.

Would they have one room in the hotel or two? Would he sleep next to her for the five nights? She had never yet stayed in a hotel, and when Edward was standing at the reception desk in order to check in, she did not know if she should stay with him or stand apart from him, if she should stand up or sit down.

He took her into a large room with two beds and a balcony overlooking the ocean. "That's your bed, that's mine," he said and unpacked his things. "That's your chest, that's mine," he said and put his things away. He was restless and forbidding, as if he wanted to reproach her for the intimacy that she would have with him now for five days.

Later, when they stepped into the brilliant room, with piano music and the light laughter of women's voices that were not localized but murmuring amorously throughout the room, ablaze with candles, he placed his hand flat on her back at the waist and guided her to a table and seated her on the chair that he had pulled out for her. And she felt ashamed because he was appearing with her as if with a tall woman, blond and haughty, who doesn't bend down when he drops something.

"Youth has an end," the man at the piano played the old song. "Youth has an end: the end is here. It will never be. You know that well," Edward said slowly and meaningfully, but it was just a quotation, and he did not mean to say more by it. Nevertheless, Wendy believed the poet's every word.

And when she stood up, he stood up, too, pulled her chair out, and only sat down again when she had left the table. And when she looked at the pretty little face in the dressing table mirror where she saw, after all, that it could express none of all those things that were true within her—where then?—as J.W. had written it down in her book, she thought of the dog at the crossroads, hit by a car, sitting upright in the headlights of four autos, its eyes open, blood running out of its mouth, no expression on its face. It tips over with open eyes.

They ate and drank. He drank a lot and still came no closer to her. In the night he slept far away from her in his own bed. She slept only in little, disconnected, frightened, confused fragments of sleep, and when she was awake she tried in the darkness to make out his still-darker body and listened to his breath and in spite of the distance thought she could inhale it. And inhaled when he exhaled, as if to store up his breath so that on into all the inconceivable future she might daily have her day's ration of it. And before light came into the room, she had already gotten up twice, quietly, so that she would not rouse him from his deep sleep.

She washed and combed her hair and put on make up repeatedly. And lay still and looked over at him and watched him become distinct. And saw the sunlight spread over his naked legs, over his naked arms, and over the back of his head, for he lay turned away from her. But his one hand, whose arm lay under his head, lay open turned toward her.

When he woke up, he saw that she was watching him and came to her.

Then when they were sitting on the balcony and having breakfast and looking at the ocean, and then when she lay her head in his hand, he pulled his hand away and stood up and said he had to call Germany. She understood him and heard herself say, "Yes," a small, resonant, echoing word, and had nothing more to say and saw his relief through the glass pane when she shut the balcony door behind him tightly after he had gone into the room to the telephone.

She stood with her back to the room where he was, her hands around the railing, and looked at the ocean again. He did not come back right away and not for a long time and did not draw her away from the railing. She stood there and stood there, the light was blinding and the sun burned where she stood. She could not hope and she could not wish, for she was hopeless and knew that wishes do not come true.

When he came back and ran his hand over her head without looking into her face, and when they were sitting again at the breakfast table and again looking out over the ocean, the silence was precarious and the words and the gestures became entangled, came to a standstill. Each one kept to himself and did not reach out beyond himself to the other. And when she looked at him, she could see that the image of his wife had re-established itself in him, the image that had been scattered in a puzzle perhaps, the nose here, there the fragrance, somewhere else entirely the voice, a puzzle that someone in an airplane on the trip home can gather and put together, that always remains complete no matter how thoughtlessly the player handles it, no matter how long he does not play with it, no matter what game he has played meanwhile.— And here in a room with me and now five days and four nights before us, he is thinking of her ever more lovingly. She understood him well. And thought of the book in the dresser and would like to have disappeared with the book in her hand, not to anyplace at all, just to no place at all.

But even then and till the end of the trip, Wendy did not take the book out of the dresser for fear that Ottilie's fate could spread over her completely, and with the unknowing hope that she could still take hers in hand, with whatever strength there was, with his, pull them away from Ottilie's fate and race out of the world with Edward as if the airplane had crashed yesterday after all.

After this breakfast and for five days and through four nights they forgot. He went far with her, and she went with him as if she came from there and belonged there, as if she had always been there and never had to leave.—Does he love me, she asked herself and never him, and twice she could say yes and nothing more. And when he said it to her, it happened at the end of the time and from a desperation that arose briefly and fiercely in him and originated in the knowledge of the approaching loss.

He had photos made: They gazed into each other's eyes, he placed his hand flat on her back at the waist, she rested her head on his shoulder. At noon before their return flight the photos were ready, one set for her, one set for him.

He did not need to say: No tears, please, for she made her face cheerful. He did not need to say: It was lovely, for she lay her hand on his mouth. She lay her hands on his face, he did not need to see anything or say anything.

They took their clothes out of the dressers and packed them in their suitcases, and when she picked up the book, it opened up, and there she was forced to read: "But Ottilie lost everything, it might easily be said everything: For in Edward she had found life and love for the first time, and under the present circumstances she felt an infinite emptiness such as she had scarce been able to imagine previously."

On the trip to the airport he sat silently and kept his distance from her, so that her hand did not reach him, and he leaned far out of the window and did not want to show her his face.

They walked along next to each other, past those who were welcoming each other and those who were saying goodbye. He looked straight ahead and he moved quickly, and she could not see meanwhile how he avoided looking at her, and she did not look at him anymore and had to run because she had to take three steps for each one of his.

At the last gate to the airplane a woman was kissing a man and the man kissed the woman and they both were crying, as Wendy would have liked to cry with Edward. They had to stand and watch the other two, and when he saw that she saw that he had to watch, he had to say, "I know the scene of course: In one city she cries at parting from the one man who brings her to the plane so that you think she will never survive it, and when the other man in the other city picks her up at the airplane, she cries so that you think she has scarcely survived the separation."

In the airplane they sat silently next to one another. And she did not look at him anymore, for when she looked at him, just to see him, he indicated to her with a movement of his head that she should look straight ahead. She did not know whether his rejection was sorrow or boredom, and at the end of the flight she no longer knew if it was still him. An abrupt determination came, an angry one, to live her life without him.

They made a date for the evening in his hotel, for she did not want to see him in her apartment anymore and said her friend was back again. He got in the taxi and waved abruptly. She got in the bus, transferred twice, and got back to her apartment at four o'clock in the afternoon.

She did not open the window and did not unpack her suitcase and took the book out of her handbag and sat down on a chair— lightning has struck me and scorched me and now it is burning through my breast.

She opened the book and read, but neither Edward nor Ottilie became real for her anymore. They were only marks that she knew how to decipher in her book. And when she read the sentence that Ottilie writes to her friend: "I have stepped out of my orbit, and I shall not return," she closed the book.

Went to the bathroom, washed, dressed, not without care, but forgot to put on makeup.

She came too early. He was not there yet. She looked at the chairs for a place to sit where she could impress upon herself: This is the last evening. Tomorrow I will go to the office. Tomorrow evening in connection with his course he will give a party for students, colleagues, and friends. I am invited, too. And in the morning, day after tomorrow, he will fly away.—But she did not comprehend what she told herself. She only knew it, sat on her seat in the lobby of the hotel and said it to herself again and again, and never did comprehend it.

"Hi, Wendy," said Edward and laughed more than he knew how to do. They went through the revolving door into the restaurant. Nothing revolved. Everything stayed in its place. They ate and drank, and the wine drove his laughter back to the point where he knew how to do it.

She was completely engulfed by her tears and could not see him and could not hear him. And he spoke about his students and spoke about the last lecture and talked himself out of his misery and twice followed with his eyes the women who passed by.

And then the tears came from her throat. I'm howling and I'm not ashamed of myself.

He paid the bill. They rushed out of the place. He placed his hand flat on her back at the waist and guided her to his room.

They made love once more, two equals, two who both wanted to carry out the other's wishes, two who pressed together to the point where the pain that was so firmly bound was freed by the violent union that shattered all resistance. Then they could cry out.

He slept and she lay awake.

When it got light, she gazed at him all over once more, calmly and carefully. He awoke at that and tried to embrace her, alarmed by the clarity of her look, but she shoved his arms away, got up, and took three steps.

She could see that he did not know how to help himself and still could not help him, for she could not help herself. And left.

In the evening she did not go to his lecture and not to the party. He wanted to call her and wanted to go to her and then didn't want to and then wanted to and at last, sluggish because of the wine, stayed where he was or, later, in his hotel where he could be easier than with her in her apartment, about which he then dreamed that he stood in front of it and the door was locked and, as he shook it, it collapsed and the whole building with it. and not even dust from it remained at his feet with his dusty street shoes on the street.

The next morning, when she was not at the airport either, he called her up, but she was not answering anymore.

Then he tried again and again to reach her from Germany and finally called the professor, who could only tell him that Wendy Jones had not reported to him again, that a few days after Edward's departure she had sent a written notice and in the same letter had asked that her papers be sent to a post office address in the state of Iowa.

Translated by Jeanne R. Willson

Elisabeth Borchers

Murder; or, This Story Is No Proof

Henry has gone to court. Mr. and Mrs. Mills occupy the house on Seventeenth Street. It slices a triangle out of Henry's hill. It is the only triangle that does not belong to Henry. It has been leased by the Mills and is a thorn in Henry's side. Henry says, When they finally die, the triangle will belong to me. He says, They are due. Within one of the three sides of the triangle a path leads uphill from Henry's road, makes a dogleg along the hill, and leads down to the Chagrin River. Henry's road between the country house and Seventeenth Street is broad, smooth, and black-topped. Mills's path with the dogleg is narrow, bumpy, and stony. The lessors of the triangle, says Henry, are supposed to see to it that the path is in good condition. If the rain washes out the only path in the triangle, the lessors are responsible for putting it in order again, and for seeing to it that no future rain brings about a condition that will again necessitate its repair. The deed taken over from the former owner of Chestnut Hill provides that the owner of Chestnut Hill has the right to use the path on the leased land for his horses, which are led on this path to the river. The horses of the owner of Chestnut Hill can hardly be expected to use a path that, washed out by rain, has become bumpy and stony. I ask the court to provide that my client's petition be granted, and the accused be required to put the path in order. The cost of putting the path in order is one thousand dollars. Mr. and Mrs. Mills have an annual income of one thousand dollars. Toward evening they sit on the wooden bench in front of the house. They are between seventy and eighty. They seldom talk, together they look off into the distance somewhere. At the sky for example or at the tree directly ahead on the other side of Henry's road or at the tree farther to the left. I don't want you to speak to them, says Henry. When the path is fixed, you can speak to them. When Henry has driven into town I go to them and ask, How are you, Mr. and Mrs. Mills?

Do I have to pay the admission charge, says Henry. I can't understand why people want to see an egg. I can't understand why people want to see an egg, even if it does cost money. I can have a golden egg made for myself any time, if I pay for it. I have two golden dogs for example. But I won't pay for an egg. Henry pays and says, I'm going into the exhibition hall. Tropical trees circle the round hall, it is sultry beneath the trees. There are three alligators lying under a glass dome in the center of the round hall. Henry sits down on a nice white chair and watches what they are doing. I am watching the egg. Henry's eyes grow smaller. The egg contains my shadow. Henry falls asleep. The egg is located at the level of my head. The alligator's head soundlessly pushes in the glass dome. The egg is soundless. It is standing on a right-angled marble pedestal. Feet are shuffling all around the pedestal. The feet of the alligator move ahead sluggishly. The egg is holding its own against the stares. The alligator's head has a target. The stares are aimed at the egg. The egg does not move. Henry is sitting on a nice white chair. The egg does not know that someone would like to steal it. It is steadfast. Henry knows nothing. The sultriness beneath the tropical trees has numbed him. The appearance of the insensible egg numbs the eyes of the observers. The alligator has its eye on Henry, it draws close to his left shoe, it pulls, the leg tautens. Henry slips slowly out of his chair as the alligator moves backward. The observers of the egg take a step back to be able to observe the egg better. They take two steps forward and are closer to the egg than before. Henry is fast asleep. The observers crowd into the egg from all sides. The egg closes. The glass dome closes. The observers in the interior of the egg start to scream. The alligator is a deadly animal.

I hear noises. They are not coming through the walls and not through the doors. They are not airplane noises, nor are they furniture being moved on the floor above. Above me is the space beneath the roof. The short passage between the workroom and the dancing room is woodpaneled. The ceiling is lower than in the other hallways. They are not the sounds of mice or rats. I hear shuffling sounds, clicking sounds, rustling sounds above the ceiling. The ceiling doesn't have a hole or a crack. Someone is scurrying, pushing, shoving. Between the ceiling and the roof there is space for thieves. Henry is afraid of thieves. He makes locks, protective gratings, burglar alarms, hiding places in defense of thieves. Henry is well protected. He knows nothing about the noises. I extinguish the light in the passage and squeeze into the corner. I squat down and do not move anymore. I wait for an end to the noises. They are alternating, they are taking turns. The darkness is full of noises. The thieves are cleaning out everything, they are carrying the house away, they are stealing wealth. They are stealing Chestnut Hill and Chagrin River. They are stealing the horses and Henry. He lies in chains. He cannot cry out. No one sees him. They are taking Henry along. No one will see Henry anymore. He is a bundle. I hear a noise that is growing more distinct. The beam of a flashlight falls through an opening in the ceiling. Someone is sliding a section of the ceiling farther open. Two legs are hanging down from the ceiling. The beam of light is making circles. The circles place themselves around a gleaming ladder. Someone is pushing it effortlessly onto the rug on the floor. The legs and feet turn and search for a step. Someone comes down three steps, stops, gropes with one hand in the hole, lifts out a square panel, and puts it up easily, so the hole in the ceiling is filled in. Someone climbs down, folds up the ladder easily, approaches the workroom by the beam of the lamp, opens the door so it gets light, and clicks off the flashlight. Before he closes the door again, Henry puts the ladder against the wall. Henry is a thief.

Henry has worked long and hard. He has gritted his teeth. He has gotten his hands dirty. He got little sleep. He didn't take a moment's rest. He made progress. He didn't take a break. He frequently took his bearings. He followed many good examples. He didn't let up. He made himself a list. For example, land, open parenthesis water, trees, uncultivated and cultivated close parenthesis, family, horses, God, house open parenthesis ten times as big close parenthesis, in sixteenth place: Chinese porcelain. Henry counts the plates, cups, platters, bowls between ceiling and roof. He keeps a list on him. The date for checking is predetermined. Henry will stick to it.

Chestnut Hill has a hundred and sixteen kinds of trees, says Henry, for example: oak, maple, poplar, linden, chestnut. Or fir, beech, ash. Or cinchona, sequoia, tree of heaven. Or apple tree, gall-nut tree. In spite of wind, snow, lightning, and frost my trees are not sick. They do not suffer from blight, canker, scab, mange, mildew. They have neither consumption nor dropsy. They have no strumae, witch's broom, or galls. If a tree gets sick, it is cut down. I have a gardener for lawns, one for shrubs, one for trees. If a gardener gets sick he is fired.

Henry says loudly, Of course I have friends. Georgy, for example. Georgy lives south of here. He's got a paunch, he's expecting us. Georgy, says Henry very loudly. Georgy's car is in front of the garage in the yard. The doors are open, the hood is up. Georgy comes out from under the hood, then he goes back under the hood. He throws a screwdriver in the gravel at our feet. Beaming, Henry looks around and rocks on his feet. That's Georgy, says Henry very loudly. Georgy rattles on and kicks the gravel. How's Thea, asks Henry very loudly. Georgy grinds his teeth again and says, Go on in. The large room lies in darkness behind closed shutters. Thea gets stale cookies. I bite off a piece. The crumbs fly off left and right. I begin collecting the crumbs on the left. That's Thea, says Henry very loudly in the dark. Thea watches how I shake the crumbs from my right hand into my left. Georgy comes in and wipes his sleeve across his forehead. I've got to get back to the car, says Georgy. Then we'll be off, says Henry very loudly. Thea walks behind us as far as the door, then she turns away.

The mirrors hang in Detroit. In the hall of high mirrors three hundred and twenty Lords of the Manor and three hundred and twenty Mistresses of the Manor gather each year. Those Lords of the Manor and Mistresses of the Manor who have been taking part for twenty years or more wear a sash and a cap with the colors red and gold. Some of them wear medals. The president has five medals and is saying, Another year has passed. He calls Henry's name. Henry is wearing a white suit, and he walks past the chairs to the front. There he stands still. The president puts a sash around him and places a cap on his head. He pins a medal on him, This is the Order for Merit in Manorial Tranquility. The Lords of the Manor and the Mistresses of the Manor applaud. They rise from their seats and crowd forward. They push the chairs out of place and cry, Lord Henry, Lord Henry. They crowd farther forward and clap, arms raised, above their heads. They do not stop crowding. The president cries, Back to your places. The president bends over Henry and listens. He asks the doctors present among the Lords of the Manor and the Mistresses of the Manor to come forward. Sixteen doctors, among them four women, move toward Henry. They all take hold of Henry.

Translated by James A. Hayes

Gisela Elsner

The Engagement

The children didn't feel like kissing one another, in any case not yet. That it was she, Ellikins (also called Elli and, only in rare instances when she went to extremes, called Elizabeth), who had lured Bobbikins into violating the rules of the game this way, showed in the facial expression with which she (completely inadequate to her starring role and just short of her majority and far from as slender as would have suited her years) pretended to be the naughty little girl that she stubbornly wanted to be and to remain forever in an almost antinatural way.

We feel so silly, she said.

Although the circle of guests at the table was to be dispersed so that the first part of the celebration (which, as so often happened at the Leiselheimers, had become just a bit too formal) could make way for the second part with music and dancing, Mr. Leiselheimer (while his wife cast a warning glance at her daughter) asked the photographer to wait a bit before he had the waiter who had been hired for the engagement dinner refill the couple's glasses.

Children, children, I wish I had such worries, he said a bit too cheerfully, because he sensed that the conversation had lost momentum and, thanks to Ellikins's having declined to exchange the engagement kiss, was threatening to stop entirely; and then, not without discomfort, he kissed the hand of Ellikins's future mother-in-law, because he had the strong suspicion (not, indeed, founded on so much as a wrinkle in her face) that Mrs. Wiegenstein (whose figure was almost exciting from a distance whenever and wherever he saw her approaching, and who against his better judgment was able momentarily to arouse in him a purely sexual interest) was older than his wife or the graying Mrs. Ockelmann across from him, who was considered well preserved.

What, pray tell, are worries? asked Bobbikins (also called Bobbi, Bob, and, only in rare instances when he went to extremes, called Robert), to whom coyness was more becoming by far than to his fiancee; and, as Ellikins (from jealousy, apparently) thrust herself in front of him (Now let's kiss, she shouted, and the photographer raised his camera), he made the entire party laugh, even both sets of parents, for whom the joy of their children's having found one another was by no means without consequence.

Children, children, what a kiss, called Mr. Leiselheimer no less than anyone else turning his eyes toward Ellikins, who, because of the continuing applause, leaned back her head as if from an uncontrollable fit of passion, threw her fair-skinned bare arms around Bobbikins, and shut her eyes (which had turned out to be a little too close together) so that her eyelids (painted with a subtle pale-blue crescent that matched her pale-blue ankle-length dress and even her pale-blue engagement ring and the gems in the chain around her neck) were completely visible.

What Ellikins was wearing at her engagement party matched in a way that revealed taste, indeed even lengthy fashion consultation.

Only one thing matched neither the original dress, which had cost a small fortune, nor the antique engagement ring, nor the necklace, which had been made especially by a foreign jeweler just in order to go with the ring: namely, Ellikins, whose congenital coarseness never could be entirely concealed despite all attempts at refinement.

Only when she didn't feel well did Ellikins seem almost pretty or at least cute; mostly, as on this evening (after hours of attention by the hairdresser and the cosmetician who had cleverly made her up for the engagement party so that her face looked not narrow but decidedly less wide and flat than usual, an effect that the skin, increasingly red as a result of the alcohol and the excitement, had long since destroyed) she looked, to put it gently, quite healthy, especially at the moment in which her hair fell back from her prominent right ear (which she had inherited from Leiselheimer) as she turned from the guests toward the photographer during this long kiss, which, had it not been a bit exaggerated, might have indicated a degree of being-in-love that bordered on enslavement.

But no matter how carried away she pretended to be, Ellikins by no means ignored the crowd. She loosened her hand from around Bobbikins' neck and, with her subtly tinted ash-blond hair that curled away from the face, covered the ugly, dark-red ear.

Oh, to be able to fall in love, said Mrs. Wiegenstein, smiling in Leiselheimer's direction without straining her face.

What's to prevent it? asked Leiselheimer.

She's suffering from temporary indifference, Mr. Wiegenstein answered in his wife's stead.

Oh, no, my senses are getting dull, my dear, said Mrs. Wiegenstein.

I'm awfully sorry about that, said Mr. Leiselheimer.

I'm incapable of any excitement, said Mrs. Wiegenstein (while Mrs. Leiselheimer left the room and the three-man combo in the den struck up the first notes right afterward) like everyone else turning her eyes toward Bobbikins, who, in order to whisper something to her, laid bare Ellikins's ear (the left one now) without suspecting what he was doing to her by doing this.

You're tickling me, Ellikins shouted so loudly that she drowned out the dance music, which, growing wilder and wilder, proved what privileges Leiselheimer granted to the young, even though at this point they were numerically inferior to the older people.

However, except for Ellikins dancing out of the room with Bobbikins (gorgeous Bobbikins; no matter how much she sometimes envied him and how often she fought regular contests with him for compliments, she couldn't be angry with Bobbikins for long; a bit too lively now, she seemed more poorly coordinated than she actually was despite her ballet lessons), youth was represented only by Bobbikins's older brother Conni, a girl cousin of Ellikins, as well as two of Bobbikins's girl cousins who had felt more than out of place without male dinner partners all through the meal.

Ostensibly because of these two unescorted girl cousins (but mainly so that she, Ellikins, although engaged and thus spoken for, might seem still to be sought after), Ellikins had invited for the second part of the celebration a handful of young gentlemen, the first of whom, known as Ellikins's showpiece, arrived at the moment when, since the two waiters were leaving the house, the only available servant was Mrs. Loos in the kitchen.

Briefly he stood, with a cardboard tube under his arm, in the gigantic entry hall (in the middle of which was a marble stairway that led to the upstairs bedrooms of the villa that looked very modest from the outside in order not to arouse the envy of Mr. Leiselheimer's employee immeasurably) almost vouched (as he stood there bearded and casually dressed, although he felt uneasy between the men in tuxedos) for the openminded sophistication of the Leiselheimers, at whose house one could appear unceremoniously in a turtleneck sweater for the engagement of their only child.

How nice that you've come, called Leiselheimer and (because on the one hand he sensed the other's discomfort and on the other because he himself recently had begun to value the fact that even artists were entertained at his house) greeted his guest with an over eagerness that the other would not have anticipated in his wildest dreams, let alone would have considered to be due him; indeed, Mr. Leiselheimer even went so far as to call this guest, who had long been quite unwelcome, the only free man among slaves (among us slaves, he said, plucking and picking at his stiff shirt front) before he turned him over to Ellikins, who grabbed the cardboard tube from him with a poorly pretended greediness and (while even Leiselheimer himself now found his favorite intolerable) swung this cardboard tube over her head as she dashed to the gift table in the gigantic, just a tiny bit too expensively furnished den, where the three-man combo (a pianist, a bass player, and a clarinettist) obviously was giving its all, just in case somebody sometime might be overcome by the desire to dance.

That's me, shouted Ellikins, unrolling the gift, a watercolor that bore witness to an above-average artistic sensitivity in so far as it did not show Ellikins as she lived and breathed but as fitted Ellikins's a bit vague and a bit elevated image of herself.

This image, no bigger than a thumb, dancing on a balustrade that formed a dividing line between the pale-blue cloudless sky and the earth, showed Ellikins's elevated but vague image of herself so far away and tiny that, because of the lack of individualizing traits (only the color of the hair shown matched Ellikins's albeit unnatural hair color) one could not say it was like or unlike Ellikins, whether, like Ellikins, one held the watercolor very close to the eyes, or, like Leiselheimer, looked for some distinguishing feature with the help of a reading glass.

What a gift, said Mrs. Wiegenstein, smiling in the artist's direction without straining her face; and then (perhaps in order to hide a little twitching at the corner of her mouth) she helped Ellikins flatten the watercolor on the gift table, as it constantly kept rolling up automatically, while (to the amusement of the whole company, yes, even the four young gentlemen who had just arrived and hadn't had a drop to drink yet) she weighed down the left edge of the picture with a gilt fork and the right with a gilt knife from the gift chest full of equally valuable place settings that had been made for the children, who had no objection to gold and even thought it very pretty and had merely objected to the customary old-fashioned design, being against grandfather's curlicues and grandmother's little roses.

With one exception the other gifts on the gift table also were appropriately restrained, if one ignored the fact that Ellikins's less wealthy relatives and childhood friends had taken the easy way out by sending flowers or telegraphed greetings; for none of the friends, business friends, or acquaintances of the Leiselheimers would willingly have been deprived of contributing his bit to the household of these two so-called children, who, even if their connection seemed at first to be only an instance of good sense, had playfully come to love one another, not overnight, it's true, but little by little, until now they were affectionate toward one another in a way that everyone found charming.

While Ellikins and Bobbikins introduced the young gentlemen to the girl cousins, Leiselheimer stood for a moment longer by the gift table and looked at what had been given to his daughter (to be more exact, to him, the financier Leiselheimer) feeling satisfied, by and large, before he involuntarily found fault with this and that as he had already done in the morning.

It was not, by the way, the flowers and the telegraphed greetings from have-nots that aroused Leiselheimer's objections—on the contrary, Leiselheimer would have been the last to expect anybody to deprive himself of necessities for something useless on his daughter's (that is to say on his) account—what Leiselheimer objected to (more than that: interpreted as downright attempts at extortion) were the disproportionately expensive gifts from some people (nobodies, as Mr. Leiselheimer generally called them) who used the engagement of his daughter in an almost deceptive way to make the financier Leiselheimer feel indebted to them.

Especially he would have liked to return a Venetian glass bowl, the gift of Mr. Miche, his only recently promoted sales manager (with whom neither he nor Ellikins, unless she had lied to him, had cultivated the slightest social contact), to this not especially appealing but comparatively young man (who was rising in his career and could sell him sand by the seashore, as he put it) in order to put him in his place.

But, while, standing there by the gift table smiling somewhat absentmindedly at the children as they cuddled up all the more affectionately under his gaze, he would have called this Venetian glass bowl the most embarrassing gift, something else (which he, who seldom failed to consider possibilities, would have forestalled had he foreseen it)—namely, six silverplated napkin rings, the gift of Mrs. Loos—occupied him anew, as it did every time he came near the gift table or Mrs. Loos came into view in the den as at this moment, in her homemade black silk dress and her little white apron, passing around a tray with champagne glasses, embarrassed and overjoyed without the slightest reason.

For, like it or not, these shabby napkin rings (hard come-by for Mrs. Loos with the hourly wages of a serving woman and practically useless for Ellikins, who at his behest had cleared a place of honor for them where they more than ever had the effect of a bad joke; but it was too late to change that) stood out so among the expensive gifts that had been paid for with casually written checks and moved and shamed the not very delicate sensibilities of Leiselheimer (who had meanwhile given in to the idealists in theory; but, he asked, of what use would it be to humanity if I gave away my business? None, he said) so much that he had forced himself to look away from the napkin rings which caught the eye (and not just his; the reactions ranged from his being moved to Mrs. Wiegenstein's cleverly overplaying curiosity to his friend Ockelmann's being sarcastic) as nothing this inconspicuous had ever done before, as far as he could recall.

Less from calculation than from impulse (he could not, try as he might, separate the two; he found more and more that what he thought he was doing for humanitarian reasons helped him in business too) Leiselheimer was momentarily on the point of acknowledging Mrs. Loos by inviting her (she got the salary of a serving woman but at the same time had the trusted position of a housekeeper) to a glass of champagne.

However, when he saw her approaching with the tray (not just overjoyed for some accountable reason, as has been said, but beyond that so embarrassed that, in the effort to be as little noticed as possible, she walked on the front half of her shoe soles) it became clear to him how this well-meant gesture would confuse the world as it existed in the mind of Mrs. Loos, who was already serving the same champagne to the musicians as to Ellikins with mental reservations that could indeed not be proved, but could be sensed.

And so he simply helped himself, nodded to her, a bit annoyed (as he always was when he, the financier Leiselheimer, who went fishing with fishermen, who argued with taxi drivers, who let street-cleaners treat him to beer, failed in overcoming a social barrier for at least a few hours) put aside the matter for now as, once and for all, he turned his back on the gift table when he sat down by the older gentlemen in the club chairs during the now truly earsplitting solo of the clarinetist (who had still not succeeded in yanking the young people out of their lethargy and into the dance) and began to joke harmlessly with Mrs. Wiegenstein (just like Ockelmann with Mrs. Leiselheimer and Wiegenstein with Mrs. Ockelmann) because this was what good taste dictated.

Only they didn't stay alone that way for long. While Mrs. Leiselheimer and Mrs. Ockelmann (in contrast to Mrs. Wiegenstein, by the way, who accepted compliments in an almost insultingly relaxed way) burst out laughing as if they had been tickled, the children (not knowing what to do about the young people, at least for the moment) came running up hand-in-hand to those who, more than they themselves, had helped provide them their happiness in order to kiss and embrace Mommy and Daddy and Mom and Dad on the one hand and Mommy and Daddy and Mom and Dad on the other (Ellikins with a charm that seemed to have been pounded into her; Bobbikins with a seemingly innate one), both, indeed, to the sorrow of Mrs. Wiegenstein, who, during the demonstrations of devotion from the children, held her oversized evening bag before her as if for protection, because her face (which had cost a small fortune) had, like so many another valuable, been intended more for looking at than for touching.

Don't you want to dance? Mrs. Leiselheimer asked.

If we have to because of the band, then naturally we'll dance, said Bobbikins.

We feel so silly, Ellikins said.

They play excellently, said Wiegenstein.

Heavenly is how they play, insisted Mrs. Wiegenstein, although she too did not in the least want to dance. Maybe later, she said (as if incidentally answering that question of Leiselheimer's, because what she was mainly concerned with was rooting around in her oversized evening bag), but not just now.

That nobody wanted to dance was clearly disturbing to Mrs. Leiselheimer, who, stemming from modest circumstances, always felt great uneasiness when people did not avail themselves immediately or did not avail themselves at all of something that was available; she—who constantly wanted to prove what all but she took for granted: that the Leiselheimers could afford heaven-knows-what-all—had to restrain herself from urging her guests to dance, too, having already urged them to drink, to switch rooms, to eat, drink, switch rooms, and so forth; yes, she had to restrain herself from standing up and dancing so that somebody would "make use of the band," as she had been phrasing it in her thoughts for some time while sitting there as if on a bed of coals, for she danced with neither skill nor pleasure.

Even after the practice she had had meanwhile and the arguments she had had year in and year out with Leiselheimer every time she had thrown herself almost pathologically into demonstrating what she considered to be an elegant life style and luxury, Mrs. Leiselheimer showed (albeit not with dexterity and not without lapses but, at any rate, with an advanced degree of skill) how capable she was in what was accepted as an endearing or at least an amusing foible.

Go into the bar for a while, she proposed to the children, urging, even almost begging, despite Leiselheimer's glances.

Maybe later, said Ellikins, just as unyielding as her father.

If we have to, said Bobbikins, then we'll do it, naturally.

Nobody has to do anything here, children, said Leiselheimer, while next to him Mrs. Wiegenstein emptied the contents of her oversized evening bag on the carpet.

Or go into the summer house, his wife requested, her discomfort becoming visible only because the veins on her temples were a bit more prominent than before as well as because of the slightly fixed smile with which she acknowledged Ellikins's headshaking and the torturously affable "maybe-later-but-not-just-now" that followed nearly every entreaty and was adopted from Mrs. Wiegenstein by Ellikins, who, like everyone else, turned to where Mrs. Wiegenstein knelt on the carpet before the heap of cosmetics from the evening bag.

Good Lord, she shouted, I've forgotten my comb.

Are you sure? asked Wiegenstein.

For Heaven's sake, said Bobbikins and brought his hands together in front of his face.

If that's all, shouted Leiselheimer while his wife arose, not just relieved, but yes, ridiculously intent.

Unfortunately, said Wiegenstein, urging her with a gesture to sit down, there is a lot more to it than that.

It brings me luck, said his wife, suddenly so disconsolate that even Leiselheimer, who thought he had long since seen through Mrs. Wiegenstein, would not have been able to say what he thought of that.

The chauffeur will fetch your comb immediately, Wiegenstein silenced her.

Does he know my comb? his wife inquired.

Everybody knows your comb, my child, said Wiegenstein, who was a much better father to the mother of his sons than to his sons in any case, already underway with Leiselheimer, who as host felt likewise duty-bound to pursue this puzzling matter personally.

I only hope she hasn't lost it, said Wiegenstein, who was quite obviously worried.

What's it all about, asked Leiselheimer, if I may ask?

How should I know, said Wiegenstein, for goodness' sake.

A secret, said Leiselheimer.

I only know, said Wiegenstein, that her hair has been combed with it ever since she was a child.

A talisman then, said Leiselheimer.

Possibly, said Wiegenstein, mostly to himself.

At the moment when the gentlemen, surprised by the heaviness of the snowfall, stepped outside, Wiegenstein's chauffeur (although it was the duty of only Leiselheimer's chauffeur to stir the fire in the hearth every quarter hour in case somebody sometime might after all be overcome with a wish to have a short sojourn in the summer house at the other end of the quite extensive estate) also held in his arms an armful of firewood, which he laid down close to the lighted silver fir, which annually provided a bigger Christmas tree, before he, careless in his excessive zeal, more slid than ran on the sleet under the cover of snow in the direction of the gentlemen, who, because of their dress suits, stopped under the overhang of the roof.

You see, you see, Director, it's a good thing I stayed, he called as soon as he knew what was to be done, with a self-righteous obstinacy that Wiegenstein would not have allowed himself, if it had not been so selfless. Because the chauffeur, having slid immediately in the direction of the snowed-in line of cars, was now stopping again and warning Wiegenstein in a reproachful tone of voice; you'll catch cold, Director, he said, still acting superior by no means for his own good but solely for the good of his employer.

What enviable zeal, said Leiselheimer.

He stays content only as long as one keeps prodding him, said Wiegenstein and stepped into the house, on the one hand a bit repelled although on the other he did know how much such over-zealousness was to be valued.

He has taken on so much, he added, that he and his wife and child would starve without his bonuses.

What was his latest demand? asked Leiselheimer.

His own new car, said Wiegenstein, and then he joined in Leiselheimer's ringing laughter, even though meanwhile he didn't consider the story funny anymore.

When they came back into the den, Mrs. Wiegenstein was holding shut Bobbikins's mouth (so that he couldn't give away any information about the comb), for from it was issuing for the first time in the evening some conversational material that went beyond platitudes and included everyone but Mrs. Leiselheimer, who, with her fixed smile, was clearly pretending to listen; did the chauffeur change the candles in the bar? she asked.

Even Ellikins, however, who, since she had discovered how important the world of emotions was to Mrs. Wiegenstein and she to it (it is true, it was far more to Mrs. Wiegenstein than bread winning was to others), tried to compete with her future mother-in-law, being so much impressed by this foible that she, despite her almost primitive naturalness, managed to bring forth something like a hysterical giggle.

Will it really bring you bad luck? she asked.

She has proof, said Wiegenstein.

It occurs to me, his wife called, that he won't be able to find the comb.

Where did you hide it? inquired Wiegenstein.

In the left snakeskin boot, said his wife.

My chauffeur will get it for you right away, proposed Leiselheimer.

Does he know it? Wiegenstein asked.

I'll go along, called Bobbikins.

We'll all go along, called Ellikins, apparently without knowing what she was doing to her mother by saying this.

While suddenly, high spirited because of the upset in the plan of the formal engagement party, which had been so strictly followed up to now, the young people left the den as the sounds of several motors starting and then dying again penetrated from outdoors, Mrs. Leiselheimer got up and slowly went out, because she sensed that she wouldn't be able to control herself for more than a few minutes more.

Don't you want to dance with me? she suddenly heard Leiselheimer ask.

Maybe later, she let slip out, but not just now.

After glancing to check through the leaded-glass window in the cloakroom whether the young people had truly driven off in the middle of the party (and some had probably even run away, because the Wiegensteins' villa was at most five minutes' walking distance from the Ockelmanns's, since there was only one fashionable area in the town), Mrs. Leiselheimer went resolutely on a kind of patrol of the house, because she thought the correctness of the engagement party she had planned for her daughter was still in question; but no matter how thoroughly she checked details, her instructions seemed to have been carried out perfectly—in the bar, to which the music was carried by loudspeaker (although it penetrated through the door anyway) the candles had been replaced, just like the ice cubes in the buckets; the first crock stood directly under the tap of the barrel in the wine cellar; in the ping-pong basement the celluloid balls lay just as carefully arranged next to the net as the freshly cleaned caftans lay on the divan and the hookahs lay on the camel-leather cushions around the dice cup in Ellikins's Moroccan room, which (no less than the camel-leather cushions, the hookahs, the caftans, the ping-pong table, the crocks with wine on tap, the bar) Ellikins said she had "up to here," making a gesture as if to cut her throat—To be honest, Mommy, Ellikins had admitted to her mother before the engagement party began, I've had the whole engagement "up to here."

Knowing quite well how bitterness spoiled her appearance, Mrs. Leiselheimer avoided glancing into the wall-sized mirror next to the front door as she left the house before she went (through the snow, past the illuminated silver fir and the likewise illuminated swimming pool full of snow) to the summer house, where during parties one occasionally took care of the sudden (yes, even almost spasmodic) needs of some guests with a rather bucolic simplicity.

But the fireplace was just being stirred by the chauffeur, who had already returned because the young people had suddenly decided halfway there to go the rest of the way on foot.

Should he go on stirring? he asked Mrs. Leiselheimer.

Why, of course, she said, more or less incidentally, because she was mainly seeing about the bottles of beer that had been kept cool for hours and the cooker, where for hours the hot sausages had been kept warm.

Did you do that? she asked, pointing to the burst sausages, which had been kept much too hot.

Not I, insisted the chauffeur.

Then it must have been Mrs. Loos, said Mrs. Leiselheimer, and then, despite the warning of her family doctor, she waded back through the snow with the pot of sausages, through the cold wetness next to the trail the chauffeur had made running back and forth every quarter hour and on the often enough but less often trod path left by Mrs. Loos; she was exclusively concerned with the question of what would have happened if somebody sometime had been overcome with the desire for hot sausages.

Did you do that? she repeated, so convinced that she would find Mrs. Loos alone in the kitchen that she really gave a start at the sight of Bobbikins's brother Conni, who was squatting on the refrigeraor in a tuxedo, eating chocolate pudding.

We're just discussing art, he said, jumped down from the refrigerator (gallant toward Mrs. Leiselheimer and affable toward Mrs. Loos) and, taking the pot before either woman could prevent it, took a burst sausage and dunked it, as one usually does in mustard, in the chocolate pudding and devoured it without changing his expression.

Have you ever tried that? he asked Mrs. Leiselheimer.

Didn't you say I could depend on you? she asked Mrs. Loos.

How could I have forgotten that? asked Mrs. Loos, herself again; and then, embarrassed as she was by the presence of a Wiegenstein in the kitchen (because Mrs. Loos had so much admired the Wiegensteins ever since, as she put it, she had "known them," that she had expressed the wish to be allowed to clean at their house sometime; I'd simply love to do that, she said afterward repeatedly), she carried the pot with the burst sausages, murmuring, I'll put new ones out right away.

I think she thinks I wanted to make fun of her, said Conni, while he accompanied Mrs. Leiselheimer (who was thinking he had had the same intentions toward her) into the den, where she saw just then Mrs. Ockelmann with Ockelmann and Wiegenstein and her husband suddenly dancing wildly.

Why don't you say we should dance? asked Ockelmann.

All you had to do was say the word, said Leiselheimer breathlessly and stretched out his arms toward his wife.

Please leave me alone, she said and then sat down by Mrs. Wiegenstein.

Just imagine, I really feel like dancing, Mrs. Wiegenstein admitted, and I can't risk a single step.

Without a comb, you mean? inquired Mrs. Leiselheimer.

When every step can be a misstep, said Mrs. Wiegenstein, who actually permitted her fingertips, with which she constantly drummed on the black leather arm of the club chair, a certain freedom of movement. During the again ear-splitting clarinet solo she even refused the champagne being served by Mrs. Loos, who made not only an arc around the dancing group but also bent her entire body away in an arch in her efforts to be as little noticed as possible.

It was probably mostly because of this clarinet solo that even Mrs. Loos didn't hear the children ring the doorbell, that is to say the chimes that more pleasingly served the same purpose at the Leiselheimers; but, though the solo lasted only a few minutes, the children, even Ellikins, felt locked out and, finger on the doorbell, felt so silly that they climbed over the fence and approached the den from the other side to the alarm of the two women who sat very close by the terrace door on which the children pounded with their fists; for, what these children, who could do so many things other people's children couldn't, could do least was wait.

It wasn't in the snakeskin boot at all, said Bobbikins, and (am the laughter of the young people who, in their high spirits, we grinding the lumps of snow into the carpet with their shoes) hand his mother the comb, an almost toothless little rose-colored baby comb.

It was simply too much, said Ellikins.

The chauffeur is still looking for it, called Bobbikins.

Did you really not tell him? Wiegenstein inquired.

A little searching won't hurt him, Ellikins shouted.

He bet his life, said Bobbikins.

It was simply too much, said Ellikins.

Somebody has to call him, said Wiegenstein, already on the way to the telephone.

Tell him the matter took care of itself, said his wife, who sat there caressing her baby comb.

Don't you want to comb your hair in the bathroom? asked, almost begged Mrs. Leiselheimer, who for a moment envisioned Mrs. Wiegenstein standing before the mirrored walls which made the indisputably imposing room like a salon, tiled as it was with pastel green, leaf green, and bottle green and which had floor and ceiling covered with algaelike and fishlike ornaments.

But she doesn't need the comb, Ellikins shouted with irritation, as if she couldn't muster any understanding for the lack of understanding on her mother's part.

I simply have to have it, said Mrs. Wiegenstein, whose rose-blond coiffure artistically piled on the back of her head needed grooming just as little as did the symmetrical little curls on both sides of her cheekbones, as, smiling without straining her face (which always began to decay a bit about midnight), she put the almost toothless baby comb in her oversized evening bag and then stood up, debilitated, as though the matter of the comb (though she hardly seemed relieved now that she had it) had brought her to the end of her endurance.

Don't, for Heaven's sake, think I'm awful, she said primarily to Mrs. Leiselheimer, but I have to go.

While in the immense entryway (which, like everything at the Leiselheimers', was a bit too expensive) Mrs. Loos (who had to stand on tiptoe because she was shorter, but with self-righteous obstinacy would not let Leiselheimer deprive her of doing this) helped her slip into her coat, Mrs. Leiselheimer, trying to save face, smiled with a warmth bordering on hate, ready for a moment to wager any amount that all evening she had been made a fool of as never before.

But the next moment this suspicion, hingeing on the way she kissed Mrs. Wiegenstein goodbye, seemed to her far fetched; you just don't know how sweet you are, she said.

Mrs. Wiegenstein kissed all the other ladies after her in exactly the same way she wanted to be kissed: tenderly but quickly. She didn't even leave out Mrs. Loos, who blushed. Mrs. Wiegenstein wasn't the way people said she was, at least not the way those who knew her only by sight or by reputation said she was.

You will come to my house sometime, won't you? she said to Mrs. Loos, in a way that anyone who didn't know anything about Mrs. Loos's wish to be permitted to clean as extra help at the Wiegensteins' would have taken to be a completely normal invitation.

I'd love to do that, said Mrs. Loos.

Translated by Minetta Altgelt Goyne

Hubert Fichte

The Garden

"You may not play in the street!" said his grandfather to Detlev. "There could be an air-raid alarm. Remember once and for all! You're just eight years old. When you get to be a big boy later on, then you may also play in the street."

Detlev turned his tricycle around at the garden gate. He took the ash-hardened path through the front yard, where ordinary and leaf lettuce grew to the right and the left. He heaved the tricycle up two steps and drove over the concrete slab to the house, past the picturesque lump of rock and the juniper bush, the birch, the laburnum, and the rose borders. At the rhododendrons he turned into the sandy path and stopped at the walnut tree and the morello cherry. His grandmother knocked against the upstairs window and said: "Your grandfather just raked the sand path. Stay on the hard ways."

Detlev rode back, drove around the house, and with his legs stretched out forward coasted down the small rise at the terrace and came to the larkspurs and to the spinach and to the strawberries. He pedaled the tricycle and reached the garden house, from the roof of which sometimes drops of tar fell down. He drove to the hydrangea and turned at the chicken-stall mesh. He drove to the garden toilette, to the rain barrel, to the balls of peat, to the compost heap. He drove around the three apple trees and drove between the neighbor's yard and his grandfather's yard, past raspberries and blackberries and past the neighbor's chicken pen, to the gate.

His grandfather walked up behind him and said : "I told you not to do that! You ought not to play in the street. What if there was suddenly an air-raid alarm?!"

Detlev rode back to the garden house and put the tricycle next to the chaise. He took the shield and feather headdress and played Indian by himself.

At supper—as Detlev was shaking sweetener into the cup and tossing the foam tablet onto the surface of the peppermint tea—Herr Wiesen came. His grandfather and Herr Wiesen called one another by their first names. Herr Wiesen talked softly to his mother, his grandmother, and his grandfather. Detlev heard: ". . . razed to the ground.—Ground-level bunker, ground-level bunker!—It's safer!"

Grandmother and grandfather answered nothing. Grandfather shook his head and said: "No. No."

Herr Wiesen said: ". . . talk to your other neighbors," and left.

After supper, because it was summer, Detlev was allowed to go outside into the yard again.

"Don't get dirty, if you want to go with us to the Schlesners'!" she called after him.

Detlev pulled his scooter out of the garden house and rode on it down the middle path and over the concrete slab. He lifted the scooter down the concrete steps, rode it to the gate, turned, let it whiz down the slight rise, at the garden house turned the corner.

Aunt Irma was walking past the gooseberry bushes. Next to her walked a young woman whom Detlev had never seen before, and a sailor in a real, blue sailor suit. He had a white hat on, from which two long, dark ribbons were hanging. Around his neck lay a quadrangular, white collar with blue stripes.

"Put the scooter in the garden house now!" said his grandfather. "I want to lock it up. Go into the house and wash your hands!"

Detlev dropped the scooter in a corner of the garden house. The handlebar struck the floor.

"Be a little careful with your things! We don't know when we'll be able to buy another scooter. If your scooter is broken, you won't be content then, either.—Go and wash your hands! We want to go to the Schlesners'."

Detlev obeyed. When he was washed and combed, his mother hugged him hard. His grandmother gave him a wet kiss on the mouth, and then they walked—grandfather ahead—to the Schlesners' garden house.

Frau Schlesner, Herr Schlesner, and Aunt Irma were sitting with the sailor outside. From the garden house came a smell of shell parakeets. Cats were rubbing their backs against the legs of wicker chairs.

The sailor stood up. Frau Schlesner said: "This is our nephew Paul. He's the same age as our Ernest, from whom we've had no news for three months now."

Frau Schlesner wept. Detlev had to shake hands and make a bow to everyone. When he stood in front of the young woman, he saw that she had a very big belly. He shook hands with the sailor last. He made a particularly nice bow and sat down on the footstool next to the sailor. The grown-ups scooted their wicker chairs together and talked fast and softly. Once the sailor turned to look at Detlev. He took his white sailor hat with the two long, dark ribbons, gave it to Detlev, and continued talking to the grown-ups about terror attack and ground-level bunkers, and thousands and thousands of dead. Detlev put on the sailor hat. It slipped down onto his nose. The two long ribbons fell over his face. The grown-ups didn't notice. They didn't laugh at him. Detlev took the hat off again and looked it over on all sides. The grown-ups were talking very loudly. Detlev didn't listen to them. He whirled the white sailor hat on his index finger.

"Our little cellars offer us no protection anymore!" his grandfather shouted. His face was red.

Detlev wrapped the dark ribbons around his wrist. Then he straightened them out again.

The grown-ups couldn't agree.

"We've got to come together again. We have to talk to the other neighbors. There's no time to lose!"

They all shook hands. Detlev started to go to the sailor first, but his mother shoved him to Frau Schlesner. Detlev had to bow several times. When he got to the sailor, he gave him back the white hat with the two long, dark ribbons.

During the night the grandfather, grandmother, mother, and Detlev went with woolen blankets and suitcases and candles and valerian into the small cellar under the house. The air raid was soon past.

The next day Detlev rode from one garden gate to the other and around the hydrangeas.

Behind the raspberry bushes the dark ribbons on the white hat fluttered past. Detlev let the tricycle stand and sprang through the prickly branches. He ran to Paul, the sailor, and held out his hand.

"But Detlev, you say hello to the lady first!" said the young woman with the big belly.

Detlev shook her hand and made his bow.

"Detlev, come here!" his grandfather called. "You left your tricycle standing in the middle of the path."

"Do you hear, Detlev?" said the young woman.

"Your grandfather called you," the sailor said.

Detlev went back and put his tricycle away.

After supper they were all sitting at the Schlesners' again. The footstool next to the sailor's wicker chair was missing. Detlev found it in the garden house. He sat down again next to Paul, the sailor.

One of the grown-ups said: "Every night we have to be prepared for the worst!" They were again talking very softly.

The sailor said: "I don't know anything about being on land. I can't give you any advice."

He scooted his wicker chair back a little. He again took his hat off his head. But Detlev didn't want it a second time. He said: "Come into my yard, and play with me. I have a scooter and a tricycle and Indian stuff."

The sailor said: "I'll definitely come some time."

"You mustn't forget. At our house are a lot of fruit trees and pretty, straight paths. We can take turns pushing one another on the tricycle."

"We can also climb the trees."

Detlev looked up at his grandfather. He had laid his face in his hands and was breathing deeply. He had heard nothing.

"Yes, we can climb all the trees. We can pick plums and built a big pirate's nest in the apple tree. I'll show you our chicken pen and the rabbits. When you come to play with me, we'll let out the chickens, and the rabbits, too."

"Do you have cherries?" said the sailor.

"Morellos. We'll pick some. We'll build a hollow in the hydrangeas. We'll strew peat in it. Next to our garden house is a big ball of peat. When our hollow is finished, we'll eat cherries and plums and currants."

"We'll definitely do that."

"You'll have to come early, and you have to bring your sailor suit along."

"But early in the morning it's cold!"

"That doesn't matter. I'll put on my red overcoat. Then I don't get cold."

"When shall we meet?"

"On Sunday. It'll have to be real early!"

"Yes, it gets light early. Three o'clock in the morning!"

"Yes! Then we'll make a big fire by the compost heap, and we'll both of us build a hollow."

Detlev lay in his bed. He was thinking about the black cloths that were spread in the church over long blocks—often—when he had been sent away. He thought about the cannon shots, about the women with black veils. He thought about a yellowish face in thick heaps of flowers in the cemetery chapel. He thought about *Seafaring Is Necessary,* by Gorch Fock, where he had read about the sailor who swims and swims, alone on the ocean, and who then doesn't want to swim anymore, but lets himself go under. Finally, he thought about how it had looked in the garden at three o'clock in the morning. He had never walked through the garden so early. He thought that the trees would stand there very large and black, that thick, white, cold fog would well out from between the branches, and birds would be sitting on all the twigs and now and then fly away; but the leaves wouldn't be moving at all, from them would drip only the fog, almost like rain, on the larkspurs, the shallots, the spinach, the gooseberries, and the daisies, the buttercups, and the roses; the blossoms would not be open, they would be closed, and teensy-tiny and black.

Then Detlev went to sleep—in the house with the shattered walls.

Translated by A. Leslie Willson

Günter Bruno Fuchs

Confessions of an Elderly Cane Maker

For Willi Heepe,
Doctor of Medicine
and Cane Making,
His Wife, His Children

1

So, I repeat: The walking cane is an invention beyond compare. And still, the invention is misused. It has been the victim of a thick-headed stupidity through the centuries. On the other hand, as I suspect, the victim of an underhanded cover-up. For ever since the walking cane came into existence, the one-sided appreciation of the walking cane has also existed. I will illustrate that by way of an example.

2

Schneeberg is a town with few inhabitants. I live here well situated scenically. The windows show me the Devil's Pulpit. That is a mighty rock monstrosity that was left behind by the Devil up on the highest peak of the Schneeberg Mountain range when he was on his way one time or another through this region with his grandmother. At a weak moment the grandmother supposedly challenged her grandson. Probably she said: "Fine, then for all I care take this piece of cliff on your shoulder and be happy with it!" The old woman could laugh pretty loud. She laughed along behind her grandson when he took off with the rock on his shoulder. After a hundred and sixty two years, the Devil was already tired and sullen, and dropped the monstrosity from his shoulder. Hardly had the rock lay on the highest peak of the Schneeberg Mountain range than happiness rushed into the Devil's horns. He began to dance and stomp. With his dancing and his stomping he created the beautiful Schneeberg Valley. He had a bladder full to the top and with his stream created a sharp-edged bed for the Schneeberg River called the *Stoneroller.* The Stoneroller flows past Schneeberg, flows into the chambers and the troughs of the cane maker, and purifies into the beer lines of the Schneeberg Tavern *The Merry Satan,* that is, for the purpose of cleaning the beer lines once every two months. But the inhabitants of Schneeberg don't drink without reason; they are world famous, their walking canes unsurpassed. A cane maker who becomes an apprentice and finishes his apprenticeship, carries it on and can set his clock by it. And still I can't refrain from reproaching the Schneeberg cane makers. I'll explain that with my example.

3

Someone from our family came to Schneeberg during the Thirty Years' War of the previous century. I don't want to harp on something, but still I believe the man must have had a handicraft, perhaps as a mason. While going for walks he most certainly looked around in the busy woodlands around Schneeberg. He discovered aspen, birch, oak, and other wood. He shook his head in disbelief and established a new trade. My talented ancestor is the first Schnee-berg cane maker. There is a mayor here who questions that. Unfortunately, that mayor hasn't the slightest idea about making canes. He has a soft spot for processions in folk costume, likes very much to take a seat on a rostrum, waves with both hands, no, he has bad manners, claps his hands—it sounds like a shot. Now, in the autumn, the popping is going on again. The Schneeberger put on costumes and build a rostrum for the mayor. Years ago once, I said to him: "Why do you pop and clap like that? Is that supposed to be a greeting? There are many ways of giving greetings, just remember that! There is a country whose inhabitants take the foot or the hand of those they wish to honor and rub their faces with it. There is a country, Mr. Mayor, where the inhabitants push their nose firmly into the face of the one they wish to greet.

There is a country where they lay leaves on the head of the one they wish to greet. There is a country whose inhabitants take off a shoe when they wish to greet another inhabitant. If these people meet at home, then each takes off his socks, puts his hands on his cheeks, and bows very deeply. Later they mutually press their middle fingers three times." At the time the mayor breathed faster and faster, then interrupted me and said: "I sure hope you're a rat!" The mayor raised his head, a red one. Then he suddenly held his breath with fury about the lesson he had received. Gently I poked the crook of my walking cane against his belly. That was liberation for the mayor, the air could escape. Then he said nothing more. What can someone say, anyway, who can't be told anything? If we meet by chance on the street, each of us looks at some swallow or other. Our gazes look for the closest street sign, as though we didn't know the right path for our legs. The whole thing is ridiculous. I, too, am a walking cane in the hand of my ancestry. Sometimes I remain standing before these round clay ovens that are gradually weathering and crumbling. These days the cane maker works with centrally heated ovens. I'm an old clay oven in which a small fire glows. The older I become, the more often I say: "Your ancestor, who came to Schneeberg back then, was a mason. He built the first clay oven!" I seldom use the exclamation mark that cannot be left out right here. In what follows, when I get to speak about a particular example, the exclamation mark will return a few times.

4

In the frame of my window at evening appears not only the rock monstrosity surrounded by clouds, shortly before dark I also see the first cane maker building the clay oven. The man has a horse's head, he keeps saying "haw" to himself. He drives himself on, he whinnies and snorts, he shoots steam from both nostrils over the bricks, he sets the foundation out of bricks, the bottom of the oven. He's in a hurry every evening—he has to be finished with his work before it gets dark. So, hastily and grinding his teeth, he devours a trough empty and drinks himself smashed with liquid, watered-down corn schnapps. Now he has the bottom of the oven finished; now he's building the framework for the clay vault. He digs the clay out of the Schneeberg loamy soil; he bends down, farts—the meal tasted good to him—he pounds the unwieldy, greasy clay, he adds water, very often his own, to the clay, he makes it malleable, he feels good in the mire, in his hands he carries the clay to the oven frame. When the vault is finished he wipes out his finger prints with watery clay. That's how his evenings passed, and one evening the clay had set, the framework can be chopped apart, the horse's head whinnies a song into shape, the vault is finished, the first fire of brushwood burns the oven dry and for a topping-out ceremony. Here the raw wood will lie, the oven warmth peels off the bark of the stick or makes the cane-maker's work of peeling off the bark easy. There he stands all day long before two wooden stakes, lays the untreated stick between the stakes, bends it straight, puts it back in the oven. The stick is peeled and dead straight and like a heating magic wand is clamped on one end in the iron winch, the man with the horse's head pulls the semicircular crook into shape. He has bound more than fifty sticks. He bares his teeth, with a handsaw he saws the bundle at a specific length. Now someone helps him carry off the bundle. They drop the bundle into the staining trough in the board shed like the Devil dropped the rock. The sticks can rest in the liquid. They get their color for life. Then they get acquainted with the rasp and part from their bumps. accept pointed or flat iron caps, there is no argument, and shortly before dark I see the first cane maker leave Schneeberg. On his back the baptized clubs peer from the sack. This one time they are being supported, then they will support. But with this sentence begins the one-sided appreciation of which I spoke at the beginning. I will illustrate it with the following example.

5

The son of the present mayor had spoken about it in the parish hall. The newspapers that reached Schneeberg from outside were full of headlines, and in the newspapers, too, there was talk about it. In the Schneeberg Tavern *The Merry Satan* the beer glasses were full of it. We wanted to know something about it, but none were able to know anything about it. Nevertheless, the mayor's son spoke so loudly and high-spiritedly about it that even the Schneeberg cane makers let their clay ovens go out and for weeks were fed by people who, with a helmet on their heads, covered long sheets of paper with the names of Schneeberger who still knew nothing about it. At the time a rostrum was also built—there was still a bit of work for the unemployed cane makers, who were already known for their work in the neighboring countries. The Schneeberger knew about it but capped their reason quickly under their hats, ran and strutted strangely around in front of the rostrum, began to don broad leather belts. At their sides dangled a kind of hunting knife. The mayor's son suddenly has visitors, nothing but men in folk costumes. They talk about it and haven't merely heard about it. Maybe there's a clap, it sounds like a shot. The Schneeberg men leave the village. There are flowers, a drum, voluntary eschewing of work at the clay ovens; a small fire goes out. I picked up a well-wrought walking cane and strolled in the opposite direction through Schneeberg. "You," said a fellow in the proximity of the parish hall, "what are you doing?" "I'm telling myself," I said to him, "you ought to take a better look." "What does that mean?" he said, "what are you up to? Don't you want to know anything about it?" "That means," I said, "you know something about it? Well, tell me about it!" The son of the present mayor came down from the rostrum. They have all moved very tensely out of Schneeberg, now he, too, asked, looking at me, but not directly, no, with his right eye past his nose, he asked: "What are you doing standing around?" "I'm leaving," I said and took a step. "Stop!" both shouted, "where are you headed? Anyone who wants to register, has to do it here, the office is here." "They all disappeared long since behind the Devil's Pulpit," I said, "and will soon be coming back, or do you know something about that, Mayor?" Then they both looked at one another, each made a fist, raised it to the height of their brows, and twisted their fists around in front of their brow as though they were trying to make themselves dizzy with the circling fist." "You know," said the mayor's son, "you're cuckoo. How do I know whether they're coming back soon, since they just left, you cuckoo!" "Yes," I said, "I thought you know something about it, because you were talking about it when you were up on the rostrum. After all, you're a mayor who knows that walking canes are made here. You weren't talking about something you know anything about! You forgot to tell what you know about a walking cane. Or don't you know anything about it? Then you could and should have let someone else talk about it, for all I care some cuckoo, one like me, you should have done it wrong."The mayor's son and his companion twisted their fists in front of their brows again, only faster. So much for the first part of my example. There's a continuation.

6

The Schneeberger, about whom no one knew for certain where they were and what they were doing there, should have felt a general affection for the matter behind which they had wandered away out of Schneeberg. Individual letters are written in a full chord of enthusiasm. Others, which arrived somewhat later, contained throughout the complaint because of lacking foodstuffs. "The walking cane," I said at the time, and again got to see circling fists, "the walking cane is a foodstuff when you handle *it* and not something else!" The exclamation point can't be omitted here, because I really became very loud at the time and more screamed than shouted. When the disturbing signs arrived in Schneeberg, my utterances were held to be disturbing. I, a horse from the stall of the cane makers, should once and for all, as they said, keep my mouth shut, which I also did. For years I kept it shut while sniffing within the burning proximity of the clay oven, bundled up and stacked up the sticks of ash, birch, oak, and other wood. I kept it shut while strolling through the Schneeberg bushy woods in the direction of the Devil's Pulpit. Gradually I no longer was enraged by the children, who sometimes ran along beside me, yelling "Cuckoo!" At first my hands jerked, I wanted to tear into the children with a high-raised cane, then sometime or other I gave a start and felt momentarily the warm, smooth inner curve of the cane handle. At once I listened more closely to the mockery of the children, which suddenly sounded like a bird cry. In any event, the number of the circling fists declined as well as did the number of the returning Schneeberger. And most of them didn't have a lot to say; they needed walking sticks by the dozens. Lucky for me I was able to fall back upon my supply. The hobbling son of the present mayor chose a cane made of ash, the crooked handle of which I had smoothed for a long time with sandpaper. This example requires still a short epilogue.

7

The array of defensive weapons that should protect the whole body or single parts of the body against the effects of hostile firearms, thrusting weapons, and cutting weapons, that array is very large and at first expansive. There were thick wooden shields as tall as a man, there was an entire steel armor for man and horse, there were head pieces out of metallic scaled webbing, there was armor with riveted steel springs to ward off striking balls, there was leather padding and stuffed canvas. I'm not a silly person, but at this listing I have to laugh. I laugh like a goat that has taken a wolf for a ride. From my window I see the Devil's Pulpit. I wish for the Schneeberger just as clever a grandmother as the Devil had or has. For here I am covering my yellowish paper with my writing, while outside a rostrum is being hammered together. Now and again I have the impression that quite suddenly I was getting a slap or a cuckoo. At certain moments I see the first cane maker looking into my room. So the thing has meanwhile reversed. Earlier I saw him working hurriedly and watched him at his hasty work. Now he's looking into my room and gurgling with joy about the old guy who would like to complete a treatise for young people and doesn't even know where he should begin and what must be contained in it. The previous enumeration, the enumeration of defensive weapons, could be at the beginning. Of course, I would have to complete it, oh yes, make it up to date. This section alone is endless. And then there follows the examples for what I would like to say, examples for what I would like to say something against. And a more extensive history of cane making cannot be left out, naturally. Because from this viewpoint I base a lot. But I can only talk about what I know something about. Nevertheless an example, even if it comes at twilight, can be useful. What I know is the walking cane. What I am faced with is thick-headed stupidity or underhanded covering up. But if I get cuckoo, then the thing gets complicated. For that reason, at the end of the enumeration of defensive weapons I will set the sentence: Strolling is a matter that moves us forward. The second sentence will say: The walking cane is an invention beyond compare. The third sentence: And still, the invention is misused.

Then the examples follow.

Translated by A. Leslie Willson

Max von der Grün

Shorthand Text

On Sunday, February 16, 1969, a white VW left the road on an icy hairpin curve on Highway 13, two miles south of Ochsenfurt between Ansbach and Wurzburg. It collided with a roadside tree.

The collision was so violent that the tree trunk tore into the car. A doctor and his wife were in the wrecked car. They had been returning from an urgent house call to which they had been summoned in the early morning by telephone.

The doctor had responded to this call immediately, since he had been on emergency duty during the weekend. In an outlying village the doctor had treated a child suspected of having diphtheria. The accident occurred at exactly 10:30 A.M.

10:35 A.M.

Coming out of the curve a green Mercedes with three occupants approached the wrecked car at a moderate rate of speed. At the wheel sat a middle-aged man, in the back seat was a young woman, next to her an older woman, her mother-in-law. In her lap the young woman was rocking a child about three years old. The young woman cried out: Ewald, you've got to stop. My God, something has happened.

The man shook his head irritably.

Nonsense, he said, that's nothing for the child.

The older woman agreed with him. Just keep on driving, she mumbled, he's right, you know, he's right.

But we just can't . . . the young woman said precipitately.

Calm down now, her mother-in-law said. The man at the wheel added: And we can't go to the police in Ochsenfurt and report the accident either. I forgot my registration papers. You think I want to get into a mess because of that VW? As they drove on past, the man looked straight ahead, the young woman looked hesitantly at the wrecked car, her mother-in-law lit a cigarette. Her hands trembled.

When they had driven about a mile farther, the young woman said: We really ought to go to the police.

The man at the wheel and the older woman remained silent, only the child in his mother's lap cheerfully whirred like a siren: Mommy . . . rrrh . . . rrrh.

10:42 A.M.

A black VW with four occupants came hard out of the curve. The driver of the car saw the wrecked car, attempted to brake, then let the car roll to a stop some fifty yards farther on.

A man about forty years old left the car. The man looked around cautiously, down the road. His wife, who was reading a newspaper in the seat next to the driver's, looked up in astonishment and asked: What's going on? Don't drink so much coffee in the morning. You wouldn't have to go to the bathroom so often. The two little girls in the back, the daughters of the couple, giggled. One of the girls called out: Daddy's our waterfall.

A VW ran into a tree back there, the man said. He started to walk over to it, but his wife called him back.

Mind your own business, she yelled. Drive on. People shouldn't always be racing around on the road anyway. The girls yelled: Where, where, where, where? Oh wow, that car's really wiped out.

The man hesitated. The woman leaned out the window and said softly: Emil, get back in; don't be childish. You'll have to stay as a witness, and maybe they'll even want to see your driver's license. What'll you do then? Do you want to cause such a stir the last month before you get it back again? You see? So get in the car.

The man nodded agreement, got in, and slowly drove on. The girls in the back seat pressed their faces against the rear window until the wrecked car was out of sight.

Well, drive a little faster, the woman hissed, we'll get there too late anyhow. What do you think my father bought you the studded tires for anyway? You see?

10:53 A.M.

A canary-yellow Fiat eased into the curve, skidded anyway. The young woman at the wheel had trouble keeping the vehicle under control. She drove slowly out of the curve. She noticed the car against the tree. She closed her eyes for a moment. She cried out softly.

Her mother, who was sitting next to her, crossed herself, and whispered: Elsa, for heaven's sake, keep going, quick, before someone comes. We don't want anything to do with something like this. Elsa, honey, I just can't stand to see anything like this, you know that, honey; it just makes me feel awful.

We have to report it to the police, Mother.

Police? Honey, just keep going. We don't want a big hassle. We've never had anything to do with the police before. Just keep going, we simply haven't seen anything. Somebody else will come along behind us anyhow.

The mother crossed herself again. She was mumbling to herself.

10:58 A.M.

A car came from the direction of Ochsenfurt. It had met the canary-yellow Fiat leaving the area. The man drove past the wrecked car as if it were not there at all.

That's all I'd need, thought the man, to get held up now and maybe even end up with my name in the papers, that's all I'd need.

He was met in the curve by a diesel Mercedes at. . . .

10:59 A.M.

At the wheel of the beat-up, black diesel sat a white-headed man. The man gave a momentary start when he saw the VW wrapped around the tree, then he slowly drove on, toward the wrecked vehicle, and stopped a few meters in back of it.

The man got out. He was about sixty years old, very fat, and somehow he looked as if he hadn't grown tall enough. The fat man went around the VW, looked in horror for a few seconds through the splintered windshield at the two lifeless people, whispered: Terrible. . . .

Then, when he saw, as if by chance, his own worn-out tires, he got back in his car and drove away. I don't want to have any trouble when the police come, he thought.

The rattling of his loose tailpipe could be heard for some time.

11:08 A.M.

A jazzily painted Citroen 2CV crept into the curve. The four young people, two boys, two girls, were singing a pop tune. They were boisterous and playful in spite of the icy road, as if they were coming from a party.

The man at the wheel yelled: Be quiet for a minute. Look up ahead. Somebody's really wrapped around a tree.

The girls kept on singing, and the young man yelled even louder: Shut up! Damn it, you silly chicks, can't you quiet down for once!

He stopped the car. He and his companion got out. They stopped a few meters in front of the VW. They moved their arms helplessly. Then they walked nearer.

Oh boy, he must have really been moving. Nothing you can do now though, they're long gone.

What'll we do now? asked the other fellow, should we wait until the police come? Or should we go to the police in Ochsenfurt?

Man, are you nuts? I've been doing some heavy drinking. I'm still high from last night. My breath still smells like booze. They'd notice it for sure. You know they're no hicks from the sticks. If they give me the baggie test, I'm done for. I can't afford that.

They went back, got in the car, and drove away. One of the girls asked: Are they dead?

No, said the man at the wheel, and he gripped the steering wheel so hard that his knuckles turned white, they're only playing cards, they're waiting for the third man for a game of skat.

Wow, that's funny, the other girl said, and both began to sing another pop song.

11:15 A.M.

A red VW with a fox tail on the antenna made an extremely risky entrance into the curve and came out of it sharply. The bald-headed man alone in the car whistled sharply through his teeth when he saw the accident.

Damn, he murmured, damn, that's all I needed. He stepped down on the gas cautiously. The wheels spun anyway. The car skidded for a few seconds, then straightened out again on a dry section of the road.

The bald-headed man started to sweat. His palms became moist.

I hope nobody comes toward me and gets my license number, he growled to himself. Damn, if the police stop me now, with a stolen car . . . that would be too much . . . leave them lie . . . leave them lie . . . they're through the Pearly Gates anyway.

11:28 A.M.

A beige BMW comes into the curve, at the wheel a blond, very pretty woman. The man next to her is sleepy. He yawns constantly.

Don't drive so carelessly, he says to the blond woman. Then he sees the accident, and he says: Do you see that over there? Do you want to end up the same way?

The woman was about to stop. The man yelled: Are you crazy? We'd have to be witnesses later.

Well, so what? asked the woman.

Tell me something, the man gasped, are you a little slow, maybe? What'll happen if my wife gets hold of the subpoena; your name'll be on it, too . . . what then, huh? . . . get it?

The woman slowly drove on, but she no longer looked at the man next to her.

11:35 A.M.

The highway department sanding truck slowly approached the wrecked car from the curve, its yellow light rotating.

The man next to the driver yelled: Franz! Stop . . . there . . . look! I told you right off that we'd find another one wrapped around a tree today. We should've made a bet.

They stopped behind the wrecked car. Both men got out. They looked briefly at the lifeless occupants, looked at each other, shrugged their shoulders. The driver of the highway sanding truck wordlessly got in and reported the accident to the dispatch station on his two-way radio.

They waited for a quarter of an hour without exchanging a word until the police came, and then ten minutes more until the arrival of the ambulance with a doctor.

When the doctor saw the dead man at the wheel, he gave a soft cry.

Something wrong, doctor? one of the policemen asked.

No, no, nothing. They've been dead for at least an hour, the doctor said.

An hour? one of the other policemen asked. Odd they weren't found earlier.

How could they have been, answered the doctor. Who would go out in this stinking weather on these roads and on a Sunday morning, if he absolutely didn't have to? And who absolutely has to on a Sunday morning?

Yeah, you're right again, the first policeman said, and the three policemen began to write up their reports.

Report in all Wurzburg newspapers on January 17, 1969: On Highway 13, just outside of Ochsenfurt yesterday afternoon, Dr. Wilhelm Altmann, a general practitioner, and his wife suffered a fatal accident. The police assume the car went out of control in a curve on the extremely slick road because of excessive speed and then collided with a tree. Both occupants were killed instantly, according to the doctor who rushed to the scene.

All the people who passed the site of the accident on Sunday, February 16, 1969, between 10:30 A.M. and 11:35 A.M. read the newspaper on Monday morning.

Translated by John Derrenberger

Peter Handke

The Goalie's Anxiety at the Penalty Kick

"The goalie watched the ball roll over the line. . . ."

When Joseph Bloch, a construction worker who had once been a well-known soccer goalie, reported for work that morning, he was told that he was fired. At least that was how he interpreted the fact that no one except the foreman looked up from his coffee break when he appeared at the door of the construction shack, where the workers happened to be at that moment, and Bloch left the building site. Out on the street he raised his arm, but the car that drove past—even though Bloch, hadn't been hailing a cab— was not a cab. Then he heard the sound of brakes in front of him. Bloch looked around: behind him there was a cab; its driver started swearing. Bloch turned around, got in, and told the driver to take him to the Naschmarkt.

It was a beautiful October day. Bloch ate a hot dog at a stand and then walked past the stalls to a movie theater. Everything he saw bothered him. He tried to notice as little as possible. Inside the theater he breathed freely.

Afterward he was astonished by the perfectly natural manner of the cashier in responding to the wordless gesture with which he'd put his money on the box-office turntable. Next to the movie screen he noticed the illuminated dial of an electric clock. Halfway through the movie he heard a bell; for a long time he couldn't decide whether the ringing was in the film or in the belfry outside near the Naschmarkt.

Out on the street, he bought some grapes, which were especially cheap at this time of year. He walked on, eating the grapes and spitting out the skins. The first hotel where he asked for a room turned him away because he had only a briefcase with him; the desk clerk at the second hotel, which was on a side street, took him to his room himself. Even before the clerk had gone, Bloch lay down on the bed and soon fell asleep.

In the evening he left the hotel and got drunk. Later he sobered up and tried calling some friends; since most of these friends didn't live in the city and the phone didn't return his coins, Bloch soon ran out of change. A policeman to whom Bloch shouted, thinking he could get his attention, did not respond. Bloch wondered whether the policeman might have misconstrued the words Bloch had called across the street, and he remembered the natural way the movie cashier had spun around the tray with his ticket. He'd been so astonished by the swiftness of her movements that he almost forgot to pick up the ticket. He decided to look up the cashier.

When he got to the movie, the theater's lights were just going out. Bloch saw a man on a ladder exchanging the letters of the film for tomorrow's title. He waited until he could read the name of the next film; then he went back to the hotel.

The next day was Saturday. Bloch decided to stay at the hotel one more day. Except for an American couple, he was alone in the dining room; for a while he listened to their conversation, which he could understand fairly well because he'd traveled with his team to several soccer tournaments in New York: then he quickly went out to buy some newspapers. The papers, because they were the weekend editions, were very heavy; he didn't fold them up but carried them under his arm to the hotel. He sat down at his table, which had been cleared in the meantime, and took out the want-ad sections; this depressed him. Outside he saw two people walking by with thick newspapers. He held his breath until they had passed. Only then did he realize they were the two Americans. Having seen them earlier only at the table in the dining room, he did not recognize them.

At a coffeehouse he sipped for a long time at the glass of water served with his coffee. Once in a while he got up and took a magazine from the stacks lying on the chairs and tables designated for them; once when the waitress retrieved the magazines piled beside him, she muttered the phrase "newspaper table" as she left. Bloch, who could hardly bear looking at the magazines but at the same time could not really put down a single one of them before he had leafed through it completely, tried glancing out at the street now and then; the contrast between the magazine illustrations and the changing views outside soothed him. As he left he returned the magazines to the table himself.

At the market the stalls were already closed. For a few minutes Bloch casually kicked discarded vegetables and fruit along the ground in front of him. Somewhere between the stalls he relieved himself. Standing there he noticed that the walls of the wooden stands were black with urine everywhere. The grape skins he had spat out the day before were still lying on the sidewalk. When Bloch put his money on the cashier's tray, the bill got caught as the turntable revolved; he had a chance to say something. The cashier answered. He said something else. Because this was unusual the girl looked up. This gave him an excuse to go on talking. Inside the movie, Bloch remembered the cheap novel and the hot plate next to the cashier; he leaned back and began to take in the details on the screen.

Late in the afternoon he took a streetcar to the stadium. He bought standing room but sat down on the newspapers, which he still hadn't thrown away; the fact that the spectators in front of him blocked his view did not bother him. During the game most of them sat down. Bloch wasn't recognized. He left the newspapers where they were, put a beer bottle on top of them, and went out of the stadium before the final whistle, so he wouldn't get caught in the rush. The many nearly empty buses and streetcars waiting outside the stadium—it was a championship game—seemed strange. He sat down in a streetcar. He sat there almost alone for so long that he began to feel impatient. Had the referee called overtime? When Bloch looked up, he saw that the sun was going down. Without meaning anything by it, Bloch lowered his head.

Outside, it suddenly got windy. At just about the time that the final whistle blew, three long separate blasts, the drivers and con-ductors got into the buses and streetcars and the people crowded out of the stadium. Bloch could imagine the noise of beer bottles landing on the playing field; at the same time he heard dust hitting against the windows. Just as he had leaned back in the movie house, so now, while the spectators surged into the streetcar, he leaned forward. Luckily, he still had his film program. It felt as though the floodlights had just been turned on in the stadium. "Nonsense," Bloch said to himself. He never played well under the lights.

Downtown he spent some time trying to find a phone booth; when he found an empty one, the ripped-off receiver lay on the floor. He walked on. Finally he was able to make a call from the West Railroad Station. Since it was Saturday, hardly anybody was home. When a woman he used to know finally answered, he had to talk a bit before she understood who he was. They arranged to meet at a restaurant near the station, where Bloch knew there was a jukebox. He passed the time until she came putting coins in the jukebox, letting other people choose the songs; meanwhile. he looked at the signed photos of soccer players on the walls. The place had been leased a couple of years ago by a forward on the national eleven, who'd then gone overseas as coach of one of the unofficial American teams; now that that league had broken up, he'd disappeared over there. Bloch started talking to a girl who kept reaching blindly behind her from the table next to the jukebox, always choosing the same record. She left with him. He tried to get her into a doorway, but all the gates were already locked. When one could be opened, it turned out that, to judge from the singing, a religious service was going on behind an inner door. They found an elevator and got in; Bloch pushed the button for the top floor. Even before the elevator started up, the girl wanted to get out again. Bloch then pushed the button for the second floor; there they got out and stood on the stairs; now the girl became affectionate. They ran upstairs together. The elevator was on the top floor; they got in, rode down, and went out on the street.

Bloch walked beside the girl for a while; then he turned around and went back to the restaurant. The woman, still in her coat, was waiting. Bloch explained to the other girl, who was still at the table next to the jukebox, that her friend would not come back, and went out of the restaurant with the woman.

Bloch said, "I feel silly without a coat when you're wearing one." The woman took his arm. To free his arm, Bloch pretended that he wanted to show her something. Then he didn't know what it was he wanted to show her. Suddenly he felt the urge to buy an evening paper. They walked through several streets but couldn't find a newsstand. Finally they took the bus to the South Station, but it was already closed. Bloch pretended to be shocked; and in reality he was shocked. To the woman—who had hinted, by opening her purse on the bus and fiddling with various things, that she was having her period—he said, "I forgot to leave a note," without knowing what he actually meant by the words "note" and "leave." Anyway, he got into a cab alone and drove to the Naschmarkt.

Since the movie had a late show on Saturdays, Bloch actually arrived too early. He went to a nearby cafeteria and, standing up, ate a croquette. He tried to tell the counter girl a joke as fast as he could; when the time was up and he still hadn't finished, he stopped in the middle of a sentence and paid. The girl laughed.

On the street he ran into a man he knew who asked him for money. Bloch swore at him. As the drunk grabbed Bloch by the shirt, the street blacked out. Startled, the drunk let go. Bloch, who'd been expecting the theater lights to go out, rushed away. In front of the movie house he met the cashier; she was getting into a car with a man.

Bloch watched her. When she was in the car, in the seat next to the driver, she answered his look by adjusting her dress on the seat; at least Bloch took this to be a response. There were no incidents; she had closed the door and the car had driven off.

Bloch went back to the hotel. He found the lobby lit up but deserted. When he took his key from the hook, a folded note fell out of the pigeonhole. He opened it: it was his bill. While Bloch stood there in the lobby, with the note in his hand, looking at a single piece of luggage next to the door, the desk clerk came out of the checkroom. Bloch immediately asked him for a newspaper and at the same time looked through the open door into the checkroom, where the clerk had evidently been napping on a chair he'd taken from the lobby. The clerk closed the door, so that all Bloch could see was a small stepladder with a soup bowl on it, and said nothing until he was behind the desk. But Bloch had understood even the closing of the door as a rebuff and walked upstairs to his room. In the rather long hall he noticed a pair of shoes in front of only one door; in his room he took off his own shoes without untying them and put them likewise outside the door. He lay down on the bed and fell asleep at once.

In the middle of the night he was briefly awakened by a quarrel in the adjoining room; but perhaps his ears were so oversensitive after the sudden waking that he only thought the voices next door were quarreling. He slammed his fist against the wall once. Then he heard water rushing in the pipes. The water was turned off; it became quiet, and he fell back to sleep.

Next morning the telephone woke Bloch up. He was asked whether he wanted to stay another night. Looking at his briefcase on the floor—the room had no luggage rack—Bloch immediately said yes and hung up. After he had brought in his shoes, which had not been shined, probably because it was Sunday, he left the hotel without breakfast.

In the rest room at the South Station he shaved with an electric razor. He showered in one of the shower stalls. While getting dressed, he read the sports section and the court reports in the newspaper. Afterward—he was still reading and it was rather quiet in the adjoining booths—he suddenly felt good. Fully dressed, he leaned against the wall of the booth and kicked his foot against the wooden bench. The noise brought a question from the attendant outside and, when he didn't answer, a knock on the door. When he still didn't reply, the woman outside slapped a towel (or whatever it might be) against the door handle and went away. Bloch finished reading the paper standing up.

On the square in front of the station he ran into a man he knew, who told him he was going to the suburbs to referee a minor-league game. Bloch thought this idea was a joke and played along with it by saying that he might as well come too, as the linesman. When his friend opened his duffel bag and showed him the referee's uniform and a net bag full of lemons, Bloch saw even those things, in line with the initial idea, as some kind of trick items from a novelty shop and, still playing along, said that since he was coming too, he might as well carry the duffel bag. Later, when he was with his friend on the local train, the duffel bag in his lap, it seemed, especially since it was lunchtime and the compartment was nearly empty, as though he was going through this whole business only as a joke. Though what the empty compartment was supposed to have to do with his frivolous behavior was not clear to Bloch. That this friend of his was going to the suburbs with a duffel bag; that he, Bloch, was coming along; that they had lunch together at a suburban inn and went together to what Bloch called "an honest-to-goodness soccer field," all this seemed to him, even while he was traveling back home alone—he had not liked the game—some kind of mutual pretense. None of that mattered, thought Bloch. Luckily, he didn't run into anyone else on the square in front of the station.

From a telephone booth at the edge of a park he called his ex-wife; she said everything was OK but didn't ask about him. Bloch felt uneasy.

He sat down in a garden café that was still open despite the season and ordered a beer. When, after some time, nobody had brought his beer, he left; besides, the steel tabletop, which wasn't covered by a cloth, had blinded him. He stood outside the window of a restaurant; the people inside were sitting in front of a TV set. He watched for a while. Somebody turned toward him, and he walked away.

In the Prater he was mugged. One thug jerked his jacket over his arms from behind; another butted his head against Bloch's chin. Bloch's knees folded a little, then he gave the guy in front a kick. Finally the two of them shoved him behind a candy stand and finished the job. He fell down and they left. In a rest room, Bloch cleaned off his face and suit.

At a café in the Second District he shot some pool until it was time for the sports news on television. Bloch asked the waitress to turn on the set and then watched as if none of this had anything to do with him. He asked the waitress to join him for a drink. When the waitress came out of the back room, where gambling was going on, Bloch was already at the door; she walked past him but didn't speak. Bloch went out.

Back at the Naschmarkt, the sight of the sloppily piled fruit and vegetable crates behind the stalls seemed like another joke of some kind, nothing to worry about. Like cartoons, thought Bloch, who liked to look at cartoons with no words. This feeling of pretense, of playing around—this business with the referee's whistle in the duffel bag, thought Bloch—went away only when, in the movie, a comic snitched a trumpet from a junk shop and started tooting on it in a perfectly natural way; all this was so casual that it almost seemed unintentional, and Bloch realized that the trumpet and all other objects were stark and unequivocal. Bloch relaxed.

After the movie he waited between the market stalls for the cashier. Some time after the start of the last show, she came out. So as not to frighten her by coming at her from between the stalls, he sat there on a crate until she got to the more brightly lit part of the Naschmarkt. Behind the lowered shutter in one of the stalls, a telephone was ringing; the stand's phone number was written in large numerals on the metal sheet. "No score," Bloch thought at once. He followed the cashier without actually catching up with her. As she got on the bus, he strolled up and stepped aboard after her. He took a seat facing her but left several rows of seats between them. Not until new passengers blocked his view after the next stop was Bloch able to think again. She had certainly looked at him but obviously hadn't recognized him; had the mugging changed his looks that much? Bloch ran his fingers over his face. The idea of glancing at the window to check what she was doing struck him as foolish. He pulled the newspaper from the inside pocket of his jacket and looked down at the letters but didn't read. Then, suddenly, he found himself reading. An eyewitness was testifying about the murder of an imp who'd been shot in the eye at close range. "A bat flew out of the back of his head and slammed against the wallpaper. My heart skipped a beat." When the sentences went right on about something else, about an entirely different person, with no paragraph, Bloch was shocked. "But they should have put a paragraph there," thought Bloch. After his abrupt shock, he was furious. He walked down the aisle toward the cashier and sat diagonally across from her, so that he could look at her; but he did not look at her.

When they got off the bus, Bloch realized that they were far outside the city, near the airport. At this time of night, it was a very quiet area. Bloch walked along beside the girl but not as if he were escorting her or even as if he wanted to. After a while he touched her. The girl stopped, turned, and touched him too, so fiercely that he was startled. For a moment the purse in her other hand seemed more familiar to him than she did.

They walked along together awhile, but keeping their distance, not touching. Only when they were on the stairs did he touch her again. She started to run; he walked more slowly. When he got upstairs, he recognized her apartment by the wide-open door. She attracted his attention in the dark; he walked to her and they started in right away.

In the morning, wakened by a noise, he looked out the window and saw a plane coming in for a landing. The blinking lights made him close the curtain. Because they hadn't turned on any lights, the curtain had stayed open. Bloch lay down and closed his eyes.

With his eyes closed, he was overcome by a strange inability to visualize anything. He tried to tell himself the names he knew for each thing in the room, but he couldn't picture anything, not even the plane he had just seen landing, though he might have recognized in his mind, probably from earlier experience, the screeching of its brakes on the runway. He opened his eyes and looked for a while at the corner where the kitchen was: he concentrated on the tea kettle and the wilted flowers drooping in the sink. He had barely closed his eyes again, when the flowers and the tea kettle were unimaginable. He resorted to thinking up sentences about the things instead of words for them, in the belief that a story made up of such sentences would help him visualize things. The tea kettle whistled. The flowers had been given to the girl by a friend. Nobody took the kettle off the hot plate. "Would you like some tea?" asked the girl. It was no use: Bloch opened his eyes when he couldn't stand it anymore. The girl was asleep beside him.

Bloch grew nervous. If the pressure of everything around him when his eyes were open was bad, the pressure of the words for everything out there when his eyes were closed was even worse. "Maybe it's because I just finished sleeping with her," he thought. He went into the bathroom and took a long shower.

The tea kettle was actually whistling when he came back. "The shower woke me up," the girl said. Bloch felt as if she were addressing him directly for the first time. He wasn't quite himself yet, he replied. Were there ants in the teapot? "Ants?" When the boiling water from the kettle hit the bottom of the pot, he didn't see tea leaves but ants, on which he had once poured scalding water. He pulled the curtain open again.

The tea in the open canister seemed—since the light reached it only through the small round hole in the lid—oddly illuminated by reflection from the inner walls. Bloch, sitting with the canister at the table, was staring fixedly through the hole. It amused him to be so fascinated by the peculiar glow of the tea leaves while inattentively talking to the girl. Finally he pressed the cap back on the lid, but at the same time he stopped talking. The girl hadn't noticed anything. "My name is Gerda," she said. Bloch hadn't even wanted to know. He asked whether she had noticed anything, but she'd put on a record, an Italian song with electric-guitar accompaniment. "I like his voice," she said. Bloch, who had no use for Italian hits, remained silent.

When she went out briefly to get something for breakfast—"It's Monday," she said. Bloch finally had a chance to study everything carefully. While they ate, they talked a lot. Bloch soon noticed that she talked about the things he'd just told her as if they were hers, but when he mentioned something she had just talked about, he either quoted her exactly or, if he was using his own words, always prefaced the new names with a hesitant "this" or "that," which distanced them, as if he were afraid of making her affairs his. If he talked about the foreman, say, or about a soccer player named Dumm, she could say, almost at once, quite familiarly, "the foreman" and "Dumm"; however, when she mentioned someone she knew called Freddy or a bar called Stephen's Dive, he invariably talked about "this Freddy?" and "that Stephen's Dive?" when he replied. Every word she uttered prevented him from taking any deeper interest, and it upset him that she seemed so free to take over whatever he said.

From time to time, of course, the conversation became as natural for him as for her: he asked a question and she answered; she asked one and he made the obvious reply. "Is that a jet?"—"No, that's a prop plane."—"Where do you live?"—"In the Second District." He even came close to telling her about the mugging.

But then everything began to irritate him more and more. He wanted to answer her but broke off in mid sentence because he assumed that she already knew what he had to say. She grew restless and started moving about the room; she was looking for something to do, smiling stupidly now and then. They passed the time by turning records over and changing them. She got up and lay down on the bed; he sat down next to her. Was he going to work today? she wanted to know.

Suddenly he was choking her. From the start his grip was so tight that she'd never had a chance to think he was kidding. Bloch heard voices outside in the hall. He was scared to death. He noticed some stuff running out of her nose. She was gurgling. Finally he heard a snapping noise. It sounded like a stone on a dirt road slamming against the bottom of a car. Saliva had dripped onto the linoleum.

The constriction was so tight that all at once he was exhausted. He lay down on the floor, unable to fall asleep but incapable of raising his head. He heard someone slap a rag against the outside doorknob. He listened. There had been nothing to hear. So he must have fallen asleep after all.

It didn't take him long to wake up; as soon as his eyes were open, he felt exposed; as though there was a draft in the room, he thought. And he hadn't even scraped his skin. Still, he imagined that some kind of lymph fluid was seeping out through all his pores. He was up and had wiped off everything in the room with a dish towel.

He looked out the window: down below, somebody with an armful of coats on hangers was running across the grass toward a delivery truck.

He took the elevator, left the building, and walked straight ahead for a while. Then he took the suburban bus to the streetcar terminal; from there he rode back downtown.

When he got to the hotel, it turned out that his briefcase had already been brought downstairs for safekeeping, since it looked as if he wouldn't be back. While he was paying his bill, the bellboy brought the briefcase from the checkroom. Bloch saw a faint ring on it and realized that a damp milk bottle must have been standing on it; he opened the case while the cashier was getting his change and noticed that the contents had been inspected: the toothbrush handle was sticking out of its leather case; the portable radio was lying on top. Bloch turned toward the bellboy, but he had disappeared into the checkroom. The space behind the desk was quite narrow, so Bloch was able to pull the cashier toward him with one hand and then, after a sharp breath, to fake a slap against his face with the other. The cashier flinched, though Bloch had not even touched him. The bellboy in the checkroom kept quiet. Bloch had already left with his briefcase.

He got to the company's personnel office in time, just before lunch, and picked up his papers. Bloch was surprised that they weren't already there ready for him and that some phone calls still had to be made. He asked to use the phone himself and called his ex-wife; when the boy answered the phone and immediately launched into his rote sentence about his mother not being home, Bloch hung up. The papers were ready by now; he put the income-tax form in his briefcase. Before he could ask the woman about his back pay, she was gone. Bloch counted out on the table the money for the phone call and left the building.

The banks were also closed for the lunch break by now. Bloch waited around in a park until he could withdraw the money from his checking account—he'd never had a savings account. Since that wouldn't take him very far, he decided to return the transistor radio, which was practically brand new. He took the bus to his place in the Second District and also picked up a flash attachment and a razor. At the store they carefully explained that the goods couldn't be returned, only exchanged. Bloch took the bus back to his room and also stuffed into a suitcase two trophies—of course, they were only copies of cups his team had won, one in a tournament and the other in a championship game—and a gold-plated pendant in the shape of two soccer boots.

When no one came to wait on him in the junk shop, he took out his things and simply put them on the counter. Then he felt that he'd put the things on the counter too confidently, as though he'd already sold them, and he grabbed them back off the counter and hid them in his bag; he would put them back on the counter only after he'd been asked to. On the back of a shelf he noticed a china music box with a dancer striking the familiar pose. As usual when he saw a music box, he felt that he'd seen it before. Without haggling, he simply accepted the first offer for his things.

With the lightweight coat he had taken from his room across his arm, he had then gone to the South Station. On his way to the bus stop, he had run into the woman at whose newsstand he usually bought his papers. She was wearing a fur coat while walking her dog. Even though he usually said something to her, staring all the while at her grimy fingernails, when she handed him his paper and his change, here, away from her stand, she seemed not to know him; at least she didn't look up and hadn't answered his greeting.

Since there were only a few trains to the border each day, Bloch spent the time until the next train sleeping in the newsreel theater. At one point it got very bright and the rustling of a curtain opening or closing seemed ominously near. To see whether the curtain had opened or closed, Bloch opened his eyes. Somebody was shining a flashlight in his face. Bloch knocked the light out of the usher's hand and went into the men's room. It was quiet there; daylight filtered in. Bloch stood still for a while.

The usher had followed him and threatened to call the police. Bloch had turned on the faucet, washed his hands, then pushed the button on the electric dryer and held his hands under the warm air until the usher disappeared.

Then Bloch had cleaned his teeth. He had watched in the mirror how he rubbed one hand across his teeth while the other, loosely clenched into a fist, rested oddly against his chest. From inside the movie house he heard the screaming and horseplay of the cartoon figures.

Bloch remembered that an ex-girlfriend of his ran a tavern in some town near the southern border. In the station post office, where they had phone books for the entire country, he couldn't find her number, there were several taverns in the village, and their owners weren't listed; besides, lifting the phone books—they were all hanging in a row with their spines out—soon proved too much for him. "Face down," he suddenly thought. A cop came in and asked for his papers.

Looking down at the passport and then up at Bloch's face, the cop said that the usher had lodged a complaint. After a while Bloch decided to apologize. But the cop had already returned the passport, with the comment that Bloch sure got around a lot. Bloch didn't watch him go but quickly tipped the phone book back into place. Somebody screamed; when Bloch looked up, he saw a Greek workman shouting into the phone in the booth right in front of him. Bloch thought things over and decided to take the bus instead of the train; he turned in his ticket and, after buying a salami sandwich and several newspapers, finally made it to the bus terminal.

The bus was already there, though of course the door was still closed; the drivers stood talking in a group not far away. Bloch sat down on a bench; the sun was shining. He ate the salami sandwich but left the papers lying next to him, because he wanted to save them for the long ride.

The luggage racks on both sides of the bus remained quite empty; hardly any of the passengers had luggage. Bloch waited outside until the back door was closed. Then he quickly climbed in the front, and the bus started. It stopped again immediately when there was a shout from outside. Bloch did not turn around; a farm woman with a bawling kid had got on. Inside, the kid quieted down; then the bus had taken off.

Bloch noticed that he was sitting on a seat right over a wheel; his feet slipped down off the curve the floor made at that point.

He moved to the last row, where, if necessary, he could comfortably look out the back. As he sat down, his eyes met the driver's in the rearview mirror, but there was nothing important about it. The movement Bloch made to stow away the briefcase behind him gave him a chance to look outside. The folding door in the back was rattling loudly .

While the passengers in the other rows of seats all faced the front of the bus, the two rows directly in front of him were turned around to face each other; therefore, most of the passengers seated behind one another stopped talking almost as soon as the bus started, but those in front of him started talking again almost immediately. Bloch found the voices of the people nice; it relaxed him to be able to listen.

After a while—the bus was now on the road leading to the highway—a woman sitting next to him showed him that he had dropped some change. "Is that your money?" she asked as she fished a single coin out from between the seat and the backrest. Another coin, an American penny, lay on the seat between them. Bloch took the coins, explaining that he'd probably lost them when he'd turned around. But since the woman had not noticed that he had turned around, she began to ask questions and Bloch went on answering; gradually, although the way they were sitting made it uncomfortable, they began to talk to each other a little.

Between talking and listening, Bloch did not put the change away. The coins had become warm in his hand, as if they had been pushed toward him from a movie box office. The coins were so dirty, he said, because they had been used a little earlier for the coin toss before a soccer game. "I don't understand those things," the woman said. Bloch hastily opened his newspaper. "Heads or tails," she went on, so that Bloch had to close the paper again. Earlier, when he had been in the seat over the wheel, the loop inside his coat collar, which had hung over a hook next to him, had been ripped off when he had abruptly sat down on the dangling coattails. With his coat on his knees, Bloch sat defenseless next to the woman.

The road was bumpier now. Because the back door did not fit tightly, Bloch saw light from outside the bus flash intermittently into the interior through the slit. Without looking at the slit, he was aware of the light flickering over his paper. He read line by line. Then he looked up and watched the passengers up front. The farther away they sat, the nicer it was to look at them. After a while he noticed that the flickering had stopped inside. Outside, it had grown dark.

Bloch, who was not used too noticing so many details, had a headache, perhaps also because of the smell from the many newspapers he had with him. Luckily, the bus stopped in a district town, where supper was served to the passengers at a rest stop. While Bloch took a stroll, he heard the cigarette machine crashing again and again in the barroom.

He noticed a lighted phone booth in front of the restaurant. His ears still hummed from the drone of the bus, so the crunch of the gravel by the phone booth felt good. He tossed the newspapers into a trash basket next to the booth and closed himself in. "I make a good target." Once in a movie he had heard somebody standing by a window at night say that.

Nobody answered. Out in the open, Bloch, in the shadow of the phone booth, heard the clanging of the pinball machines through the drawn curtains of the rest stop. When he came into the bar, it turned out to be almost empty; most of the passengers had already gone outside. Bloch drank a beer standing up and went out into the hall: some people were already in the bus, others stood by the door talking to the driver, and more stood farther away in the dark with their backs to the bus. Bloch, who was getting sick of such observations, wiped his hand across his mouth. Why didn't he just look away? He looked away and saw passengers in the hall coming from the rest rooms with their children. When he had wiped his mouth, his hand had smelled of the metal grips on the armrest. "That can't be true," Bloch thought. The driver had got into the bus and, to signal that everybody else should get aboard, had started the engine. "As if you couldn't understand him without that," Bloch thought. As they drove off, sparks from the cigarettes they hastily threw out the window showered the road.

Nobody sat next to him now. Bloch retreated into the corner and put his legs up on the seat. He untied his shoes, leaned against the side window, and looked over at the window on the other side. He held his hands behind his neck, pushed a crumb off the seat with his foot, pressed his arms against his ears, and looked at his elbows in front of him. He pushed the insides of his elbows against his temples, sniffed at his shirtsleeves, rubbed his chin against his upper arm, laid back his head, and looked up at the ceiling lights.

There was no end to it anymore. The only thing he could think of was to sit up.

The shadows of the trees behind the guard rails circled around the trees themselves. The wipers that lay on the windshield did not point in exactly the same direction. The ticket tray next to the driver seemed open. Something like a glove lay in the center aisle of the bus. Cows were sleeping in the meadows next to the road. It was no use denying any of that.

Gradually more and more passengers got off at their stops. They stood next to the driver until he let them out in front. When the bus stood still, Bloch heard the canvas fluttering on the roof. Then the bus stopped again, and he heard welcoming shouts outside in the dark. Farther on, he recognized a railroad crossing without gates.

Just before midnight the bus stopped at the border town. Bloch immediately took a room at the inn by the bus stop. He asked the girl who showed him upstairs about his girlfriend, whose first name—Hertha—was all he knew. She was able to give him the information: his girlfriend had rented a tavern not far from town. In the room Bloch asked the girl, who was still in the doorway, about the meaning of all that noise. "Some of the guys are still bowling," the girl answered, and left. Without looking around, Bloch undressed, washed his hands, and lay down on the bed. The rumbling and crashing downstairs went on for quite a while. But Bloch had already fallen asleep.

He did not wake up by himself but must have been roused by something. Everything was quiet. Bloch thought about what might have wakened him; after a while he began to imagine that the sound of a newspaper opening had startled him. Or had it been the creaking of the wardrobe? Maybe a coin had fallen out of his pants, hung carelessly over the chair, and had rolled under the bed. On the wall he noticed an engraving that showed the town at the time of the Turkish wars; the townspeople strolled outside the walls; inside them the bell was hanging in the tower so crookedly that it had to be ringing fiercely. Bloch thought about the sexton being yanked up by the bell rope. He noticed that all the townspeople were walking toward the gate in the wall; some, with children in their arms were running; one child apparently was stumbling because of the dog slinking between his legs. Even the little auxiliary chapel bell was pictured in such a way that it almost tipped over. Under the bed there had been only a burned-out match. Out in the hall, farther away, a key crunched again in a lock; that must have been what had roused him.

At breakfast Bloch heard that a schoolboy who had trouble walking had been missing for two days. The girl talked about this to the bus driver, who had spent the night at the inn before. As Bloch watched through the window, he drove back in the almost-empty bus.

Later the girl also left, so that Bloch sat alone in the dining room awhile. He piled the newspapers on the chair next to him; he read that the missing boy was not almost crippled but had trouble talking. As soon as she came back, the girl, as though she owed him an explanation, told him that the vacuum cleaner was running upstairs. Bloch didn't know what to say to that. Then empty beer bottles clinked in the crates being carried across the yard outside. The voices of the delivery men in the hall sounded to Bloch as though they came from the TV set next door. The girl had told him that the innkeeper's mother sat in that room and watched the daytime shows.

Later on Bloch bought himself a shirt, some underwear, and several pairs of socks in a general store. The salesgirl, who had taken her time coming out of the rather dim storage room, seemed not to understand Bloch, who was using complete sentences in speaking to her; only when he told her word for word the names of the things he wanted did she start to move around again. As she opened the cash register drawer, she had said that some rubber boots had also just arrived; and as she was handing him his things in a plastic shopping bag, she had asked whether he needed anything else: handkerchiefs? a tie? a wool sweater? At the inn Bloch had changed and stuffed his dirty clothes in the plastic bag. Almost nobody was around in the yard outside and on his way out of town. At a construction site a cement mixer was just being turned off; it was so quiet now that his own steps sounded almost out of place to Bloch. He had stopped and looked at the tarpaulins covering the lumber piles outside a sawmill as if there were something else to hear besides the mumbling of the sawmill workers, who were probably sitting behind the lumber piles during their coffee break.

He had learned that the tavern, along with a couple of farmhouses and the customs shed, stood at a spot where the paved street curved back toward town; a road between the houses, which had once also been paved but recently was covered only with gravel, branched off from the street and then, just before the border, turned into a dirt path. The border crossing was closed. Actually Bloch had not even asked about the border crossing.

He saw a hawk circling over a field. When the hawk hovered at one spot and then dived down, Bloch realized that he had not been watching the hawk fluttering and diving but the spot in the field for which the bird would presumably head; the hawk had caught itself in its dive and risen again.

It was also odd that, while he was walking past the cornfield, Bloch did not look straight down the rows that ran through to the end of the field but saw only an impenetrable thicket of stalks, leaves, and cobs, with here and there some naked kernels showing as well. As well? The brook which the street crossed at that point roared quite loudly, and Bloch stopped.

At the tavern he found a waitress just scrubbing the floor. Bloch asked for the landlady. "She's still asleep," the waitress said. Standing, Bloch ordered a beer. The waitress lifted a chair off the table. Bloch took the second chair off the table and sat down.

The waitress went behind the bar. Bloch put his hands on the table. The waitress bent down and opened the bottle. Bloch pushed the ashtray aside. The waitress took a beer coaster from another table as she passed it. Bloch pushed his chair back. The waitress took the glass, which had been slipped over the neck of the bottle, off the bottle, set the coaster on the table, put the glass on the coaster, tipped the beer into the glass, put the bottle on the table, and went away. It was starting up again. Bloch did not know what to do anymore.

Finally he noticed a drop running down the outside of the glass and, on the wall, a clock whose hands were two matches; one match was broken off and served as the hour hand. He had not watched the descending drop but the spot on the coaster that the drop might hit

The waitress, who by now was rubbing paste wax into the floor, asked if he knew the landlady. Bloch nodded, but only when the waitress looked up did he say yes.

A little girl ran in without closing the door. The waitress sent her back to the entryway, where she scraped her boots and, after a second reminder, shut the door. "The landlady's kid," explained the waitress, who took the child into the kitchen at once. When she came back, she said that a few days ago a man had wanted to see the landlady. "He claimed that he was supposed to dig a well. She wanted to send him away immediately, but he wouldn't let up until she showed him the cellar, and down there he grabbed the spade right away, so that she had to go for help to get him to go away, and she . . . " Bloch barely managed to interrupt her. "The kid has been scared ever since, that the well-digger might show up again." But in the meantime a customs guard came in and had a drink at the bar.

Was the missing schoolboy back home again? the waitress asked. The customs guard answered, "No, he hasn't been found yet."

"Well, he hasn't been gone for even two days yet," the waitress said. The guard replied, "But the nights are beginning to get quite chilly now."

"Anyway, he's warmly dressed," said the waitress. The guard agreed that, yes, he was dressed warmly.

"He can't be far," he added. He couldn't have got very far, the waitress repeated. Bloch noticed a damaged set of antlers over the jukebox. The waitress explained that it came from a stag that had wandered into the minefield.

From the kitchen he heard sounds that, as he listened, turned into voices. The waitress shouted through the closed door. The landlady answered from the kitchen. They talked to each other like that awhile. Then, halfway through an answer, the landlady came in. Bloch said hello.

She sat down at his table, not next to but across from him; she put her hands on her knees under the table. Through the open door Bloch heard the refrigerator humming in the kitchen. The child sat next to it, eating a sandwich. The landlady looked at him as if she hadn't seen him for too long. "I haven't seen you for a long time," she said. Bloch told her a story about his visit here. Through the door, quite far away, he saw the little girl sitting in the kitchen. The landlady put her hands on the table and turned the palms over and back. The waitress brought the drink Bloch had ordered for her. Which "her"? In the kitchen, which was now empty, the refrigerator rattled. Through the door Bloch looked at the apple parings lying on the kitchen table. Under the table there was a bowl heaped full of apples; a few apples had rolled off and were scattered around on the floor.

A pair of work pants hung on a nail in the door frame. The landlady had pushed the ashtray between herself and Bloch. Bloch put the bottle to one side, but she put the match box in front of her and set the glass down next to it. Finally Bloch pushed his glass and the bottle to the right of them. Hertha laughed.

The little girl had come back and was leaning against the back of the landlady's chair. She was sent to get wood for the kitchen, but when she opened the door with only one hand, she dropped the logs. The waitress picked up the wood and carried it into the kitchen while the child went back to leaning against the back of the landlady's chair. It seemed to Bloch as if these proceedings could be used against him.

Somebody tapped against the window from outside but disappeared immediately. The estate owner's son, the landlady said. Then some children walked by outside, and one of them darted up and pressed his face against the glass and ran away again. "School's out," she said. After that it got darker inside because a furniture van had pulled up outside. "There's my furniture," said the landlady. Bloch was relieved that he could get up and help bring in the furniture.

When they were carrying the wardrobe, one of its doors swung open. Bloch kicked the door shut again. When the wardrobe was set down in the bedroom, the door opened again. One of the movers handed Bloch the key, and Bloch turned it in the lock. But he wasn't the owner, Bloch said. Gradually, when he said something now, he himself reappeared in what he said. The Landlady asked him to stay for lunch. Bloch, who had planned to stay at her place anyway, refused. But he'd come back this evening. Hertha, who was talking from the room with the furniture, spoke while he was leaving; anyway, it seemed to him that he had heard her call. He stepped back into the barroom, but all he could see through the doors standing open everywhere was the waitress at the stove in the kitchen while the landlady was putting clothes into the wardrobe in the bedroom and the child was doing her homework at a table in the barroom. Walking out, he had probably confused the water boiling over on the stove with a shout.

Even though the window was open, it was impossible to see into the customs shed; the room was too dark from the outside. Still, somebody must have seen Bloch from the inside; he understood this because he himself held his breath as he walked past. Was it possible that nobody was in the room, even though the window was wide open? Bloch looked back: a beer bottle had even been taken off the windowsill so that they could have a better look at him. He heard a sound like a bottle rolling under a sofa. On the other hand, it was not likely that the customs shed had a sofa. Only when he had gone farther on did it become clear to him that a radio had been turned on in the room. Bloch went back along the wide curve the street made toward the town. At one point he started to run with relief because the street led back to town so openly and simply.

He wandered among the houses for a while. At a café he chose a few records after the owner had turned on the juke box; he had walked out even before all the records had played. Outside he heard the owner unplug the machine. On the benches sat schoolchildren waiting for the bus.

He stopped in front of a fruit stand but stood so far away from it that the owner behind the fruit could not speak to him. She looked at him and waited for him to move a step closer. A child who was standing in front of him said something, but the woman did not answer. When a policeman who had come up from behind got close enough to the fruit, she spoke to him immediately.

There were no phone booths in the town. Bloch tried to call a friend from the post office. He waited on a bench near the switchboard, but the call did not go through. At that time of day the circuits were busy, he was told. He swore at the postmistress and walked out.

When, outside the town, he passed the public swimming pool, he saw two policemen on bicycles coming toward him. "With capes," he thought. In fact, when the policemen stopped in front of him, they really were wearing capes; and when they got off their bicycles, they did not even take the clips off their trousers. Again it seemed to Bloch as if he were watching a music box; as though he had seen all this before. He had not let go of the door in the fence that led to the pool even though it was closed. "The pool is closed," Bloch said.

The policemen, who made the usual remarks, nevertheless seemed to mean something entirely different by them; at least they purposely mispronounced phrases like "got to remember" and "take off" as "goats you remember" and "take-off" and, just as purposely, let their tongues slide over others, saying "whitewash?"

instead of "why watch?" and "closed, or" instead of "close door." For what would be the point of their telling him about the goats that, he should remember, had once, when the door had been left open, forced their way into the pool, which hadn't even been officially opened yet, and had soiled everything, even the walls of the restaurant, so that the rooms had to be whitewashed all over again and it wasn't ready on time, which was why Bloch should keep the door closed and stay on the sidewalk? As if to show their contempt for him, the policemen also failed to give their customary salutes when they drove away—or, anyway, only hinted at them, as though they wanted to tell Bloch something by it. They did not look back over their shoulders. To show that he had nothing to hide, Bloch stayed by the fence and went on looking in at the empty pool. "Like I was in an open wardrobe I wanted to take something out of," Bloch thought. He could not remember now what he had gone to the public pool for. Besides, it was getting dark; the lights were already shining on the signs outside the public buildings at the edge of town. Bloch walked back into town. When two girls ran past him toward the railroad station, he called after them. Running, they turned around and shouted back. Bloch was hungry. He ate at the inn while the TV set could be heard from the next room. Later he took a glass in there and watched until the test pattern came on at the end of the program. He asked for his key and went upstairs. Half asleep, he thought he heard a car driving up outside with its headlights turned off. He asked himself why he happened to think of a darkened car; he must have fallen asleep before he figured it out.

Bloch was wakened by a banging and wheezing on the street, trash cans being dumped into the garbage truck; but when he looked out, he saw that the folding door of the bus that was just leaving had closed and, farther away, that milk cans were being set on the loading ramp of the dairy. There weren't any garbage trucks out here in the country; the muddle was starting all over again.

Bloch saw the girl in the doorway with a pile of towels on her arm and a flashlight on top of it; even before he could call attention to himself, she was back out in the hall. Only after the door was closed did she excuse herself, but Bloch did not understand her because at the same time he was shouting something to her. He followed her out into the hall; she was already in another room.

Back in his room, Bloch locked the door, giving the key two emphatic turns. Later he followed the girl, who by then had moved several rooms farther on, and explained that it had been a misunderstanding. While putting a towel on the sink, the girl answered yes, it was a misunderstanding; before, from far away, she must have mistaken the bus driver on the stairs for him, so she had started into his room thinking that he had already gone downstairs. Bloch, who was standing in the open door, said that that was not what he had meant. But she had just turned on the faucet, so she asked him to repeat the sentence. Then Bloch answered that there were far too many wardrobes and chests and drawers in the rooms. The girl answered yes, and as far as that went, there were far too few people working at the inn, as the mistaken identification, which could be blamed on her exhaustion, just went to prove. That was not what he meant by his remark about wardrobes, answered Bloch, it was just that you couldn't move around easily in the rooms. The girl asked what he meant by that. Bloch did not answer. She replied to his silence by bunching up the dirty towel—or, rather, Bloch assumed that her bunching up of the towel was a response to his silence. She let the towel drop into the basket; again Bloch did not answer, which made her, so he believed, open the curtains, so he quickly stepped back into the dim hallway. "That's not what I meant to say," the girl called. She came into the hall after him, but then Bloch followed her while she distributed the towels in the other rooms. At a bend in the hallway they came upon a pile of used bed sheets lying on the floor. When Bloch swerved, a soap box fell from the top of the girl's pile of towels. Did she need a flashlight on the way home? asked Bloch. She had a boyfriend, answered the girl, who was straightening up with a flushed face. Did the inn also have rooms with double doors between them? asked Bloch. "My boyfriend is a carpenter, after all," answered the girl. He'd seen a movie where a hotel thief got caught between such double doors, Bloch said. "Nothing's ever been taken from our rooms!" said the girl.

Downstairs in the dining room he read that a small American coin had been found beside the cashier, a nickel. The cashier's friends had never seen her with an American soldier, nor were there many American tourists in the country at this time. Furthermore, scribbles had been discovered in the margin of a newspaper, the kind of doodles someone might make while talking. The scribbling plainly was not the girl's; investigations were being made to determine whether it might reveal anything about her visitor.

The innkeeper came to the table and put the registration form in front of him; he said that it had been lying in Bloch's room all the time. Bloch filled out the form. The innkeeper stood off a little and watched him. Just then the chain saw in the sawmill outside struck wood. To Bloch the noise sounded like something not allowed.

Instead of just taking the form behind the bar, which would have been natural, the innkeeper took it into the next room and, as Bloch saw, spoke to his mother; then, instead of coming right back out again, as might be expected since the door had been left open, he went on talking and finally closed the door. Instead of the innkeeper, the old woman came out. The innkeeper did not come out after her but stayed in the room and pulled open the curtains, and then, instead of turning off the TV, he turned on the fan.

The girl now came into the dining room from the other side with a vacuum cleaner. Bloch fully expected to see her casually step out on the street with the machine; instead, she plugged it into the socket and then pushed it back and forth under the tables and chairs. And when the innkeeper closed the curtains in the next room again, and his mother went back into the room, and, finally, the innkeeper turned off the fan, it seemed to Bloch as if everything was falling back into place.

He asked the innkeeper if the local people read many newspapers. "Only the weeklies and magazines," the innkeeper answered. Bloch, who was asking this while leaving, had pinched his arm between the door handle and the door because he was pushing the handle down with his elbow. "That's what you get for that!" the girl shouted after him. Bloch could still hear the innkeeper asking what she meant.

He wrote a few postcards but did not mail them right away. Later, outside the town, when he was about to stuff them into a mailbox fastened to a fence, he noticed that the mailbox would not be emptied again until tomorrow. Ever since his team, while touring South America, had had to send postcards with every member's signature to the newspapers, Bloch was in the habit, when he was on the road, of writing postcards.

A class of schoolchildren came by; the children were singing and Bloch dropped in the cards. The empty mailbox resounded as they fell into it. But the mailbox was so tiny that nothing could resound in there. Anyway, Bloch had walked away immediately.

He walked cross-country for a while. The feeling that a ball heavy with rain was dropping on his head let up. Near the border the woods started. He turned back when he recognized the first watchtower on the other side of the cleared no-man's-land. At the edge of the woods he sat down on a tree trunk. He got up again immediately. Then he sat down again and counted his money. He looked up. The landscape, even though it was flat, curved toward him so firmly that it seemed to dislodge him. He was here at the edge of the woods, the electric power shed was over there, the milk stand was over there, a field was over there, a few people were over there, he was there at the edge of the woods. He sat as still as he could until he was not aware of himself anymore. Later he realized that the people in the field were policemen with dogs.

Next to a blackberry bush, half hidden beneath the blackberries, Bloch found a child's bicycle. He stood it upright. The seat was screwed up quite high, as though for an adult. A few blackberry thorns were stuck in the tires, though no air had escaped. The wheel was blocked by a fir branch that had been caught in the spokes. Bloch tugged at the branch. Then he dropped the bicycle, feeling that the policemen might, from far away, see the sun's reflections off the casing of the headlight. But the policemen and their dogs had walked on.

Bloch looked after the figures running down an embankment; the dogs' tags and the walkie-talkies glinted. Did the glinting mean anything? Was it a signal? Gradually it lost its significance: the headlight casings of cars flashed where the road curved farther away, a splinter from a pocket mirror sparkled next to Bloch, and then the path glimmered with mica gravel. The gravel slid away under the tires when Bloch got on the bicycle.

He rode a little way. Finally he leaned the bicycle against the power shed and went on on foot.

He read the movie ad stapled on the milk stand; the other posters under it were tattered. Bloch walked on and saw a boy who had hiccups standing in a farmyard. He saw wasps flying around in an orchard. At a wayside crucifix there were rotting flowers in tin cans. In the grass next to the road lay empty cigarette boxes. Next to the closed window he saw hooks dangling from the shutters. As he walked by an open window, he smelled something decayed. At the tavern the landlady told him that somebody in the house across the street had died yesterday.

When Bloch started to join her in the kitchen, she met him at the door and walked ahead of him into the barroom. Bloch passed her and walked toward a table in the corner but she had already sat down at a table near the door. When Bloch was about to talk, she had started in. He wanted to show her that the waitress was wearing orthopedic shoes. But the landlady was already pointing to the street, where a policeman was walking past, pushing a child's bicycle. "That's the mute kid's bike," she said.

The waitress had joined them, with a magazine in her hand; they all looked out the window together. Block asked whether the well-digger had reported back. The landlady, who had understood only the words "reported back," started to talk about soldiers. Bloch said "come back" instead, and the landlady talked about the mute schoolboy. "He couldn't even call for help," the waitress said, or rather read from a caption in the magazine. The landlady talked about a movie where some hobnails had been mixed into cake dough. Bloch asked whether the guards on the watchtowers had field glasses; anyway, something was glinting up there. "You can't even see the watchtowers from here," answered one of the two women. Bloch saw that they had flour on their faces from making cake, particularly on their eyebrows and at their hairlines.

He walked out into the yard, but when nobody came after him, he went back inside. He stood next to the jukebox, leaving a little room beside him. The waitress, who was now sitting behind the bar, had broken a glass. The landlady had come out of the kitchen at the sound but, instead of looking at the waitress, had looked at him. Bloch turned down the volume control on the back of the juke box. Then, while the landlady was still in the doorway, he turned the volume up again. The landlady walked in front of him through the barroom as though she were pacing it off. Bloch asked her how much rent the estate owner charged for the tavern. At this question Hertha stopped short. The waitress swept the broken glass into a dustpan. Bloch walked toward Hertha, the landlady walked past him into the kitchen. Bloch went in after her.

Since a cat was lying on the second chair, Bloch stood right next to her. She was talking about the estate owner's son, who was her boyfriend. Bloch stood next to the window and questioned her about him. She explained what the estate owner's son did. Without being asked, she went on talking. At the edge of the stove Bloch noticed a second Mason jar. Now and then he said, Yes? He noticed a second ruler in the work pants on the door frame. He interrupted her to ask what number she started counting at. She hesitated, even stopped coring the apple. Bloch said that recently he had noticed that he himself was in the habit of starting to count only at the number 2; this morning, for instance, he'd almost been run down by a car when he was crossing the street because he thought he had enough time until the second car; he'd simply not counted the first one. The landlady answered with a commonplace remark.

Bloch walked over to the chair and lifted it from behind so that the cat jumped down. He sat down but pushed the chair away from the table. In doing this, he bumped against a serving table, and a beer bottle fell down and rolled under the kitchen sofa. Why was he always sitting down, getting up, going out, standing around, coming back in asked the landlady. Was he doing it to tease her? Instead of answering, Bloch read her a joke from the newspaper under the apple parings. Since from where he sat the paper was upside down, he read so haltingly that the landlady, leaning forward, took over the job. Outside, the waitress laughed. Inside, something fell on the floor in the bedroom. No second sound followed. Bloch, who had not heard a sound the first time either, wanted to go and see; but the landlady explained that earlier she had heard the little girl waking up; she had just got out of bed and would probably come in any minute now and ask for a piece of cake. But Bloch then actually heard a sound like whimpering. It turned out that the child had fallen out of bed in her sleep and couldn't figure out where she was on the floor next to the bed. In the kitchen the girl said there were some flies under her pillow. The landlady explained to Bloch that the neighbor's children, who, because of the death in their family, were sleeping over here for the duration of the wake, passed the time by shooting the rubber rings from Mason jars at flies on the wall; in the evening they put the flies that had fallen on the floor under the pillow.

After a few things had been pressed into the girl's hand—the first one or two she dropped again—she gradually calmed down. Bloch saw the waitress come out of the bedroom with her hand cupped and toss the flies into the garbage can. It wasn't his fault, he said. He saw the baker's truck stop in front of the neighbor's house and the driver put two loaves on the doorstep, the dark loaf

on the bottom, the white one on top. The landlady sent the little
girl to meet the driver at the door. Bloch heard the waitress running
water over her hand at the bar; lately he was always apologizing,
the landlady said. Really? asked Bloch. Just then the little girl came
into the kitchen with two loaves. He also saw the waitress wiping
her hands on her apron as she walked toward a customer. What
did he want to drink? Who? Nothing right now, was the answer.
The child had closed the door to the barroom.

"Now we're alone," Said Hertha. Bloch looked at the kid standing by the window looking at the neighbor's house "She doesn't
count," she said. Bloch took this as a hint that she had something
to tell him, but then he realized that what she had meant was that
he should start talking. Bloch could not think of anything. He said
something obscene. She immediately sent the child out of the room.
He put his hand next to hers. She told him off, softly. Roughly he
grabbed her arm but let go again immediately. Outside on the street
he bumped into the kid, who was poking a piece of straw at the
plaster wall of the house.

He looked through the open window into the neighbor's house.
On a trestle table he saw the corpse; next to it stood the coffin. A
woman sat on a stool in the corner and dunked some bread into
a cider jar; a young man lay asleep on his back on a bench behind
the table; a cat lay on his stomach.

As Bloch came into the house, he almost fell over a log in the
hallway. The woman came to the door; he stepped inside and
talked with her. The young man had sat up but did not say anything; the cat had run out. "He had to keep watch all night," the
woman said. In the morning she had found him quite drunk. She
turned around to the dead man and said a prayer. Now and then
she changed the water in the flowers. "It happened very quickly,"
she said. "We had to wake up our little boy so that he could run
into town." But then the kid hadn't even been able to tell the priest
what had happened, and so the bells hadn't been tolled. Bloch
realized that the room was being heated; after a while the wood
in the stove had collapsed. "Go get some more wood," said the
woman. The young man came back with several logs, some under
each arm, which he dropped next to the stove so hard that the
dust flew.

He sat down at the table, and the woman placed the logs into
the stove. "We already lost one of our kids; he had pumpkins

thrown at him," she said. Two old woman came by the window and called in. On the windowsill Bloch noticed a black purse. It had just been bought; the tissue paper stuffing had not even been taken out yet. "All of a sudden he gave a loud snort and died," the woman said.

Bloch could see into the barroom of the tavern across the street; the sun, which was quite low by now, shone in so deeply that the bottom part of the room, especially the surfaces of the freshly waxed floorboards and the legs of the chairs, tables, and people, glowed as though by themselves. In the kitchen he saw the estate owner's son, who, leaning against the door with his arms across his chest, was talking to the landlady, who, presumably, was still sitting farther away at the table. The deeper the sun sank, the deeper and more remote these pictures seemed to Bloch. He could not look away; only the children running back and forth on the street swept away the impression. A child came in with a bunch of flowers. The woman put the flowers in a tumbler and set the glass at the foot of the trestle. The child just stood there. After a while the woman handed her a coin and she went out.

Bloch heard a noise as if somebody had broken through the floorboards. But it was just the logs in the stove collapsing again. As soon as Bloch had stopped talking to the woman, the young man had stretched out on the bench and fallen back to sleep. Later several women came and said their beads. Somebody wiped the chalk marks off the blackboard outside the grocery store and wrote instead: oranges, caramels, sardines. The conversation in the room was soft; the children outside were making a lot of noise. A bat had caught itself in the curtain; roused by the squeaking, the young man had leaped up and rushed toward it instantly, but the bat had already flown off.

It was the kind of dusk when no one felt like turning on the lights. Only the barroom of the tavern across the street was faintly lit by the light of the juke box; but no records were playing. The kitchen was already dark. Bloch was invited to stay for supper and ate at the table with the others.

Although the window was now closed, gnats flew around the room. A child was sent to the tavern to get coasters; they were then laid over the glasses so the gnats wouldn't fall in. One woman remarked that she had lost the pendant from her necklace. Everybody started to look for it. Bloch stayed at the table. After a while he was seized by a need to be the one who found it, and he joined the others. When the pendant was not to be found in the room. they went on looking for it in the hall. A shovel fell over—or, rather Bloch caught it just before it fell over completely. The young man was shining the flashlight, the woman came with a kerosene lamp. Bloch asked for the flashlight and went out in the street. Bent over, he moved around in the gravel, but nobody came out after him. He heard somebody shout in the hall that the pendant had been found. Bloch refused to believe it and went on looking. Then he heard that they were starting to pray again behind the window. He put the flashlight on the outside of the windowsill and went away.

Back in town, Bloch sat down in a café and looked on during a card game. He started to argue with the player he was sitting behind. The other players told Bloch to get lost. Bloch went into the back room. A slide lecture was going on there. Bloch watched for a while. It was a lecture on missionary hospitals in Southeast Asia. Bloch, who was interrupting loudly, started to argue with people again. He turned around and walked out.

He thought about going back inside, but he could not think of anything to say if he did. He went to the second café. There he asked to have the fan turned off. What's more, the lights were much too dim, he said. When the waitress sat down with him, he soon pretended that he wanted to put his arm around her; she realized that he was only pretending and leaned back even before he could make it clear to her that he was just pretending. Bloch wanted to justify himself by really putting his arm around the waitress, but she had already stood up. When Bloch started to get up, the waitress walked away. Now Bloch should have pretended that he wanted to follow her. But he had had enough, and he left the café.

In his room at the inn he woke up just before dawn. All at once, everything around him was unbearable. He wondered whether he had wakened just because at a certain moment, shortly before dawn, everything all at once became unbearable. The mattress he was lying on had caved in, the wardrobes and bureaus stood far away against the walls, the ceiling overhead was unbearably high. It was so quiet in the half-dark room, out in the hall and especially out on the street, that Bloch could not stand it any longer. A fierce nausea gripped him. He immediately vomited into the sink. He vomited for a while, with no relief. He lay back down on the bed. He was not dizzy; on the contrary, he saw everything with excruciating stability. It did not help to lean out the window and look along the street. A tarpaulin lay motionless over a parked car. Inside the room he noticed the two water pipes along the wall; they ran parallel to each other, cut off above by the ceiling and below by the floor. Everything he saw was cut off in the most unbearable way. The nausea did not so much elate him as depress him even more. It seemed as though a crowbar had pried him away from what he saw—or, rather, as though the things around him had all been pulled away from him. The wardrobe, the sink, the suitcase, the door: only now did he realize that he, as if compelled, was thinking of the word for each thing. Each glimpse of a thing was immediately followed by its word. The chair, the clothes hangers, the key. It had become so quiet earlier that no noises could distract him now; and because it had grown, on the one hand, so light that he could see the things all around him and, on the other hand, so quiet that no sound could distract him from them, he had seen the things as though they were, at the same time, advertisements for themselves. In fact, his nausea was the same kind of nausea that had sometimes been brought on by certain jingles, pop songs, or national anthems that he felt compelled to repeat word for word or hum to himself until he fell asleep. He held his breath as though he had hiccups. When he took another breath, it came back. He held his breath again. After a while this began to help, and he fell asleep.

The next morning he could not imagine any of that anymore. The dining room had been straightened up, and a tax official walked around while the innkeeper told him the prices of everything. The innkeeper showed the official the receipt for a coffeemaker and the freezer; the fact that the two men were discussing prices made his state during the night seem all the more ridiculous to Bloch. He had put the newspapers aside after quickly leafing through them and was now listening only to the tax official, who was arguing with the innkeeper about an ice-cream freezer. The innkeeper's mother and the girl joined them; all of them talked at once. Bloch broke in to ask what the furnishings for one room in the inn might cost. The innkeeper answered that he had bought the furniture quite cheap from nearby farmers who had either moved away or left the country altogether. He told Bloch a price.

Bloch wanted that price broken down item by item. The innkeeper asked the girl for the inventory list for a room and gave the price he had paid for each item as well as the price he thought he could get for a chest or a wardrobe. The tax official, who had been taking notes up to that point, stopped writing and asked the girl for a glass of wine. Bloch, satisfied, was ready to leave. The tax official explained that whenever he saw an item, say a washing machine, he always asked the price immediately, and then when he saw the item again, say a washing machine of the same make, he would recognize it not by its external features, that is, a washing machine by the knobs that regulated the wash cycle, but by what the item, say a washing machine, had cost when he first saw it, that is, by its price. The price, of course, he remembered precisely, and that way he could recognize almost any item. And what if the item was worthless, asked Bloch. He had nothing to do with items that had no market value, the tax official replied, at least not in his work.

The mute schoolboy still had not been found. Though the bicycle had been impounded and the surrounding area was being searched, the shot that might have been the signal that one of the policemen had come across something had not been fired. Anyway, in the barbershop where Bloch had gone, the noise of the hair dryer behind the screen was so loud that he could not hear anything from outside. He asked to have the hair at the back of his neck clipped. While the barber was washing his hands, the girl brushed off Bloch's collar. Now the hair dryer was turned off, and he heard paper rustling behind the screen. There was a bang. But it was only a curler that had fallen into a metal pan behind the screen.

Bloch asked the girl if she went home for lunch. The girl answered that she didn't live in town, she came every morning by train; for lunch she went to a café or stayed with the other girl here in the shop. Bloch asked whether she bought a round-trip ticket every day. The girl told him that she was commuting on a weekly ticket. "How much is a weekly ticket?" Bloch asked immediately. But before the girl could answer, he said that it was none of his business. Nevertheless, the girl told him the price. From behind the screen the other girl said, "Why are you asking, if it's none of your business?" Bloch, who was already standing up waiting for his change, read the price list next to the mirror, and went out.

He noticed that he had an odd compulsion to find out the price of everything. He was actually relieved, to see the prices of newly arrived goods marked with whitewash on the window of a grocery store. On a fruit display in front of the store a price sign had fallen over. He set it right. The movement was enough to bring somebody out to ask if he wanted to buy something. At another store a rocking chair had been covered by a long dress. A price tag with a pin stuck through it lay on the chair next to the dress. Bloch was long undecided whether the price was for the chair or for the dress; one or the other must not be for sale. He stood so long in front of them that, again, somebody came out and questioned him. He questioned back. He was told that the price tag with the pin must have fallen off the dress: it was clear, wasn't it, that the tag couldn't have anything to do with the chair: naturally, that was private property. He had just wanted to ask, said Bloch, moving on. The other person called after him to tell him where he could buy that kind of rocking chair. In the café Bloch asked the price of the juke box. It didn't belong to him, said the owner, he just leased it. That's not what he meant, Bloch answered, he just wanted to know the price. Not until the owner had told him the price was Bloch satisfied. But he wasn't sure, the owner said. Bloch now began to ask about other things in the café that the owner had to know the prices of because they were his. The owner then talked about the public swimming pool, which had cost much more than the original estimate. "How much more?" Bloch asked. The owner didn't know. Bloch became impatient. "And what was the estimate?" asked Bloch. Again the owner didn't have the answer. Anyway, last spring a corpse had been found in one of the changing booths; it must have been lying there all winter. The head was stuck in a plastic shopping bag. The dead man had been a Gypsy. Some Gypsies had settled in this region; they'd built themselves little huts at the edge of the woods with the reparation money they'd received for being confined in the concentration camps. "It's supposed to be very clean inside," the owner said. The policemen who had questioned the inhabitants during their search for the missing boy had been surprised by the freshly scrubbed floors and the general neatness of the rooms everywhere. But it was just that neatness, the owner went on, that actually fed their suspicions, for the Gypsies certainly wouldn't have scrubbed the floors without good reason. Bloch didn't let up and asked whether the reparations had been enough to cover the costs of building the huts. The owner couldn't say what the reparations had amounted to. "Building materials and labor were still cheap in those days," the owner said. Curiously, Bloch turned over the sales slip that was stuck to the bottom of the beer glass. "Is this worth anything?" he asked, reaching into his pocket and setting a stone on the table. Without picking up the stone, the owner answered that you could find stones like that at every step around here. Bloch said nothing. Then the owner picked up the stone, let it roll around the hollow of his hand, and put it back on the table. Finished! Bloch promptly put the stone away.

In the doorway he met the two girls from the barbershop. He invited them to go with him to the other café. The second girl said that the juke box there didn't have any records. Bloch asked what she meant. She told him that the records in the juke box were no good. Bloch went ahead and they followed after him. They ordered something to drink and unwrapped their sandwiches. Bloch leaned forward and talked with them. They showed him their I.D. cards. When he touched the plastic covers, his hands immediately began to sweat. They asked him if he was a soldier. The second one had a date that night with a traveling salesman: but they'd make it a foursome because there was nothing to talk about when there were only two of you. "When there are four of you, somebody will say something, then somebody else. You can tell each other jokes." Bloch did not know what to answer. In the next room a baby was crawling on the floor. A dog was bounding around the child and licking its face. The telephone on the counter rang; as long as it was ringing, Bloch stopped listening to the conversation. Soldiers mostly didn't have any money, one of the girls said. Bloch did not answer. When he looked at their hands, they explained that their fingernails were so black because of the hair-setting lotion. "It doesn't help to polish them, the rims always stay black." Bloch looked up. "We buy all our dresses ready-made." "We do each other's hair." "In the summer it's usually getting light by the time we finally get home." "I prefer the slow dances." "On the trip home we don't joke around as much anymore, then we forget about talking." She took everything too seriously, the first girl said. Yesterday on the way to the train station she had even looked in the orchard for the missing schoolboy. Instead of handing back their I.D. cards, Bloch just put them down on the table, as if it hadn't been right for him to look at them. He watched the dampness of his fingerprints evaporate from the plastic. When they asked him what he did, he told them that he had been a soccer goalie. He explained that goalkeepers could keep on playing longer than fielders. "Zamora was already quite old," said Bloch. In reply, they talked about the soccer players they had known personally. When there was a game in their town, they stood behind the visiting team's goal and heckled the goalie to make him nervous. Most goalies were bowlegged.

Bloch noticed that each time he mentioned something and talked about it, the two of them countered with a story about their own experiences with the same or a similar thing or with a story they had heard about it. For instance, if Bloch talked about the ribs he had broken while playing, they told him that a few days ago one of the workers at the sawmill had fallen off a lumber pile and broken his ribs; and if Bloch then mentioned that his lips had had to have stitches more than once, they answered by talking about a fight on TV in which a boxer's eyebrows had been split open; and when Bloch told how once he had slammed into a goal post during a lunge and split his tongue, they immediately replied that the schoolboy also had a cleft tongue.

Besides, they talked about things and especially about people he couldn't possibly know, as though he did know them, and was one of their group. Maria had hit Otto over the head with her alligator bag. Uncle had come down in the cellar, chased Alfred into the yard, and beaten the Italian kitchen maid with a birch rod. Edward had let her out at the intersection, so that she had to walk the rest of the way in the middle of the night; she had to go through the Child Murderer's Forest, so that Walter and Karl wouldn't see her on the Foreigners' Path, and she'd finally taken off the dancing slippers Herr Friedrich had given her. Bloch, on the other hand, explained, whenever he mentioned a name, whom he was talking about. Even when he mentioned an object, he used a description to identify it.

When the name Victor came up, Bloch added, "a friend of mine," and when he talked about a lateral free kick, he not only described what a lateral free kick was but explained, while the girls waited for the story to go on, the general rules about free kicks. When he mentioned a corner kick that had been awarded by a referee, he even felt he owed them the explanation that he was not talking about the corner of a room. The longer he talked, the less natural what he said seemed to Bloch. Gradually it began to seem that every word needed an explanation. He had to watch himself so that he didn't get stuck in the middle of a sentence. A couple of times, when he thought out a sentence even while he said it, he made a slip of the tongue; when what the girls were saying ended exactly as he thought it would, he couldn't answer at first. As long as they had gone on with this familiar talk, he had also forgotten the surroundings more and more; he had even stopped noticing the child and the dog in the next room; but when he began to hesitate and did not know how to go on and finally searched for sentences he might still say, the surroundings became conspicuous again, and he noticed details everywhere. Finally he asked whether Alfred was her boyfriend; whether a birch rod was always kept on top of the wardrobe; whether Herr Friedrich was a traveling salesman; and whether perhaps the Foreigners' Path was called that because it led past a settlement of foreigners. They answered readily; and gradually, instead of bleached hair with dark roots, instead of the single pin at the neck, instead of a black-rimmed fingernail, instead of the single pimple on the shaved eyebrow, instead of the split lining of the empty café chair, Bloch once again became aware of contours, movements. voices, exclamations, and figures all together. And with a single sure rapid movement he also caught the purse that had suddenly slipped off the table. The first girl offered him a bite of her sandwich, and when she held it toward him, he bit into it as though this was the most natural thing in the world.

Outside, he heard that the schoolchildren had been given the day off so that they could all look for the boy. But all they found were a couple of things that, except for a broken pocket mirror, had nothing to do with the missing boy. The plastic cover of the mirror had identified it as the property of the mute. Even though the area where the mirror was discovered had been carefully searched, no other clues were found. The policeman who was telling Bloch all this added that the whereabouts of one of the Gypsies had remained unknown since the day of the disappearance. Bloch was surprised that the policeman bothered to stop across the street to shout all this information over to him. He called back to ask if the public pool had been searched yet. The policeman answered that the pool was locked; nobody could get in there, not even a Gypsy.

Outside town, Bloch noticed that the cornfields had been almost completely trampled down, so that yellow pumpkin blossoms were

visible between the bent stalks; in the middle of the cornfield, always in the shade, the pumpkins had only now begun to blossom.
Broken corncobs, partially peeled and gnawed by the schoolchildren, were scattered all over the street; the black silk that had
been torn off the cobs lay next to them. Even in town Bloch had
watched the children throwing balls of the black fibers at each
other while they waited for the bus. The cornsilk was so wet that
every time Bloch stepped on it, it squished as though he were
walking across marshy ground. He almost fell over a weasel that
had been run over; its tongue had been driven quite far out of its
mouth. Bloch stopped and touched the long slim tongue, black
with blood, with the tip of his shoe, it was hard and rigid. He
shoved the weasel to the road edge with his foot and walked on.

At the bridge he left the road and walked along the brook in the
direction of the border. Gradually, the brook seemed to become
deeper; anyway, the water flowed more and more slowly. The hazelnut bushes on both sides hung so far over the brook that the
surface was barely visible. Quite far away, a scythe was swishing
as it moved. The slower the water flowed, the muddier it seemed
to become. Approaching a bend the brook stopped flowing altogether, and the water became completely opaque. From far away
there was the sound of a tractor clattering as though it had nothing
to do with any of this. Black bunches of overripe blackberries
hung in the thicket. Tiny oil flecks floated on the still surface of
the water.

Bubbles could be seen rising from the bottom of the water every
so often. The tips of the hazelnut bushes hung into the brook. Now
there was no outside sound to distract attention. The bubbles had
scarcely reached the surface when they disappeared again. Something leaped out so quickly that you couldn't tell if it had been
a fish.

When after a while Bloch moved suddenly, a gurgling sound ran
through the water. He stepped onto a footbridge that led across
the brook and, motionless, looked down at the water. The water
was so still that the tops of the leaves floating on it stayed completely dry.

Water bugs were dashing back and forth, and above them one
could see, without lifting one's head, a swarm of gnats. At one
spot the water rippled ever so slightly. There was another splash
as a fish leaped out of the water. At the edge, you could see one

toad sitting on top of another. A clump of earth came loose from the bank, and there was another bubbling under the water. The minute events on the water's surface seemed so important that when they recurred they could be seen and remembered simultaneously. And the leaves moved so slowly on the water that you felt like watching them without blinking, until your eyes hurt, for fear that you might mistake the movement of your eyelids for the movement of the leaves. Not even the branches almost dipping into the muddy water were reflected in it.

Outside his field of vision something began to bother Bloch, who was staring fixedly at the water. He blinked as if it was his eyes' fault but did not look around. Gradually it came into his field of vision. For a while he saw it without really taking it in; his whole consciousness seemed to be a blind spot. Then, as when in a movie comedy somebody casually opens a crate and goes right on talking, then does a double take and rushes back to the crate, he saw below him in the water the corpse of a child.

He had then gone back to the road. Along the curve with the last houses before the border a policeman on a motorbike came toward him. Bloch had already seen him in the mirror that stood beside the curve. Then he really appeared, sitting up straight on his bike, wearing white gloves, one hand on the handlebars the other on his stomach, the tires were spattered with mud. A turnip leaf fluttered in the spokes. The policeman's face revealed nothing. The longer Bloch looked after the figure of the policeman on the bike, the more it seemed to him that he was slowly looking up from a newspaper and through a window out into the open: the policeman moved farther and farther away and mattered less and less to him. At the same time. it struck Bloch that what he saw while looking after the policeman looked for a moment like a simile for something else. The policeman disappeared from the picture, and Bloch's attention grew completely superficial. In the tavern by the border, where he went next, he found no one at first, though the door to the barroom was open.

He stood there for a while, then opened the door again and closed it carefully from the inside. He sat down at a table in the corner and passed the time by pushing the little balls used for keeping score in card games back and forth. Finally he shuffled the deck of cards that had been stuck between the rows of balls and played by himself. He became obsessed with playing; a card fell under the table. He bent down and saw the landlady's little girl squatting under another table, between the chairs that had been set all around it. Bloch straightened up and went on playing; the cards were so worn that each single card seemed swollen to him. He looked into the room of the neighbor's house, where the trestle table was now empty; the casement windows stood wide open. Children were shouting on the street outside, and the girl under the table quickly pushed away the chairs and ran out.

The waitress came in from the yard. As if she were answering his sitting there, she said the landlady had gone to the castle to have the lease renewed. The waitress had been followed by a young man dragging two crates of beer bottles, one in each hand; even so, his mouth was not closed. Bloch spoke to him, but the waitress said he shouldn't, the guy couldn't talk when he was pulling such heavy loads. The young man, who, it seemed, was slightly feeble-minded had stacked the crates behind the bar. The waitress said to him: "Did you pour the ashes on the bed again instead of into the brook? Have you stopped jumping the goats? Have you started cutting open pumpkins again and smearing the stuff all over your face?" She stood next to the door, holding a beer bottle, but he did not answer. When she showed him the bottle, he came toward her. She gave him the bottle and let him out. A cat dashed in, leaped at a fly in the air and gulped the fly right down. The waitress had closed the door. While the door had been open, Bloch had heard the phone ringing in the customs shed next door.

Following close behind the young man, Bloch then went up to the castle. He walked slowly because he did not want to catch up with him; he watched him as he pointed excitedly up into a pear tree and heard him say, "Swarm of bees," and at first believed that he really did see a swarm of bees hanging there, until he realized, after looking at the other trees, that it was just that the trunks had thickened at some points. He saw the young man hurl the beer bottle up into the tree, as if to prove that it was bees that he saw. The dregs of the beer sprayed against the trunk, the bottle fell onto a heap of rotting peas in the grass; flies and wasps immediately swarmed up out of the pears. While Bloch walked alongside the young man, he heard him talking about the "bathing nut" he'd seen swimming in the brook yesterday; his fingers had been all shriveled up, and there was a big bubble of foam in front of his mouth. Bloch asked him if he himself knew how to swim. He saw the young man force his mouth open wide and nod emphatically, but then he heard him say, "No." Bloch walked ahead and could hear that he was still talking but did not look back again.

Outside the castle, he knocked on the window of the gatekeeper's cottage. He went up so close to the pane that he could see inside. There was a tub full of plums on the table. The gatekeeper, who was lying on the sofa, had just wakened; he made signs that Bloch did not know how to answer. He nodded. The gatekeeper came out with a key and opened the gate but immediately turned around again and walked ahead. "A gatekeeper with a key!" thought Bloch; again it seemed as if he should be seeing all this only in a figurative sense. He realized that the gatekeeper planned to show him through the building. He decided to clear up the confusion but, even though the gatekeeper did not say much, he never had the chance. There were fish heads nailed all over the entrance door. Bloch had started to explain, but he must have missed the right moment again. They were inside already.

In the library the gatekeeper read to him from the estate books how many shares of the harvest the peasants used to have to turn over to the lord of the manor as rent. Bloch had no chance to interrupt him then, because the gatekeeper was just translating a Latin entry dealing with an insubordinate peasant. "'He had to depart from the estate,' the gatekeeper read, 'and some time later he was discovered in the forest, hanging by his feet from a branch, his head in an anthill.'" The estate book was so thick that the gatekeeper had to use both hands to shut it. Bloch asked if the house was inhabited. The gatekeeper answered that visitors were not allowed into the private quarters. Bloch heard a clicking sound, but it was just the gatekeeper locking the estate book back up. "'The darkness in the fir forests,'" the gatekeeper recited from memory, "'had caused him to take leave of his senses.'" Outside the window there was a sound like a heavy apple coming loose from a branch. But nothing hit the ground. Bloch looked out the window and saw the estate owner's son in the garden carrying a long pole; at the tip of the pole hung a sack with metal prongs that he used to yank apples off the tree and into the sack, while the landlady stood on the grass below with her apron spread out.

In the next room, panels of butterflies were hanging. The gatekeeper showed him how splotchy his hands had become from preparing them. Even so, many butterflies had fallen off the pins that had held them in place: underneath the cases Bloch saw the dust on the floor. He stepped closer and inspected those butterflies that were still held in place by the pins. When the gatekeeper closed the door behind him, something fell to the floor outside his field of vision and pulverized even while it fell. Bloch saw an emperor moth that seemed almost completely overgrown with a woolly green film. He did not bend forward or step back. He read the labels under the empty pins. Some of the butterflies had changed so much that they could be recognized only by the descriptions. "'A corpse in the living room,'" recited the gatekeeper, standing in the doorway to the next room. Outside, someone screamed, and an apple hit the ground. Bloch, looking out the window, saw that an empty branch had snapped back. The landlady put the apple that had fallen to the ground on the pile of other damaged apples.

Later on, a school class from outside the town joined them. and the gatekeeper interrupted his tour to begin it all over again. Bloch took this chance to leave.

Out on the street, at the stop for the mail bus, he sat on a bench that, as a brass plate on it attested, had been donated by the local savings bank. The houses were so far away that they could hardly be distinguished from each other; when bells began to toll, they could not be seen in the belfry. A plane flew overhead, so high that he could not see it; only once did it glint. Next to him on the bench there was a dried-up snail spoor. The grass under the bench was wet with last night's dew; the cellophane wrapper of a cigarette box was fogged with mist. To his left he saw . . . To his right there was . . . Behind him he saw . . . He got hungry and walked away.

Back at the tavern, Bloch ordered the cold plate. The waitress, using an automatic bread-cutter, sliced bread and sausage and brought him the sausage slices on a plate; she had squeezed some mustard on top. Bloch ate; it was getting dark already. Outside, a child had hidden himself so well while playing that he had not been found. Only after the game was over did Bloch see him walk along the deserted street. He pushed the plate aside, pushed the coaster aside as well, pushed the salt shaker away .

The waitress put the little girl to bed. Later the child came back into the barroom in her nightgown and ran around among the customers. Every so often, moths fluttered up from the floor. After she came back, the landlady carried the child back into the bedroom.

The curtains were pulled shut, and the barroom filled up. Several young men could be seen standing at the bar; every time they laughed, they took one step backward. Next to them stood girls in nylon coats, as if they were about to leave again immediately. When one of the young men told a story, the others could be seen to stiffen up just before they all screamed with laughter. The people who sat preferred to sit against the wall. The mechanical hand in the jukebox could be seen grabbing a record and the tone arm coming down on it, and some people who were waiting for their records could be heard quieting down; it was no use, it didn't change anything. And it didn't change anything that you could see the wristwatch slip out from under the sleeve and down to the wrist when the waitress let her arm drop, that the lever on the coffee machine rose slowly, and that you could hear somebody hold a match box to his ear and shake it before opening it. You saw how completely empty glasses were repeatedly brought to the lips, how the waitress lifted a glass to check whether she could take it away, how the young men pummeled each other's faces in fun. Nothing helped. Only when somebody shouted for his check did things become real again.

Bloch was quite drunk. Everything seemed to be out of his reach. He was so far away from what was happening around him that he himself no longer appeared in what he saw and heard. "Like aerial photographs," he thought while looking at the antlers and horns on the wall. The noises seemed to him like static, like the coughing and clearing of throats during radio broadcasts of church services.

Later the estate owner's son came in. He was wearing knickers and hung his coat so close to Bloch that Bloch had to lean to one side.

The landlady sat down with the estate owner's son, and she could be heard asking him, after she had sat down, what he wanted to drink and then shouting the order to the waitress. For a while Bloch saw them both drinking from the same glass; whenever the young man said something, the landlady nudged him in the ribs; and when she wiped the flat of her hand across his face, he could be seen snapping and licking at it Then the landlady had sat down at another table, where she went on with her routine motions by fingering another young man's hair. The estate owner's son had stood up again and reached for his cigarettes in the coat behind Bloch. When Bloch shook his head in answer to a question about whether the coat bothered him, he realized that he had not lifted his eyes from one and the same spot for quite a while. Bloch shouted, "My check!" and everybody seemed to become serious again for a moment. The landlady, whose head was bent backward because she was just opening a bottle of wine, made a sign to the waitress, who was standing behind the bar washing glasses, which she put on the foam-rubber mat that soaked up the water, and the waitress walked toward him, between the young men standing at the bar, and gave him his change, with fingers that were cold, and as he stood up, he put the wet coins in his pocket immediately; a joke, thought Bloch; perhaps the sequence of events seemed so laborious to him because he was drunk

He got up and walked to the door; he opened the door and went outside—everything was all right.

Just to make sure, he stood there for a while. Every once in a while somebody came out to relieve himself. Others, who were just arriving, started to sing along as soon as they heard the juke box, even when they were still outside. Bloch moved off.

Back in town; back at the inn; back in his room. "Eleven words altogether," thought Bloch with relief. He heard bath water draining out overhead anyway, he heard gurgling and then, finally, a snuffling and smacking.

He must have just dropped off, when he woke up again. For a moment it seemed as if he had fallen out of himself. He realized that he lay in bed. "Not fit to be moved," thought Bloch. A cancer. He became aware of himself, as if he had suddenly degenerated. He did not matter anymore. No matter how still he lay, he was one big wriggling and retching; his lying there was so sharply distinct and glaring that he could not escape into even one picture that he might have compared himself with. The way he lay there, he was something lewd, obscene, inappropriate, thoroughly obnoxious. "Bury it!" thought Bloch. "Prohibit it, remove it!" He thought he was touching himself unpleasantly but realized that his awareness of himself was so intense that he felt it like a sense of touch all over his body; as though his consciousness, as though his thoughts, had become palpable, aggressive, abusive toward himself. Defenseless, incapable of defending himself, he lay there. Nauseatingly his insides turned out; not alien, only repulsively different. It had been a jolt, and with one jolt he had become unnatural, had been torn out of context. He lay there, as impossible as he was

real; no comparisons now. His awareness of himself was so strong
that he was scared to death. He was sweating. A coin fell on the
floor and rolled under the bed; He listened attentively: a comparison? Then he had fallen asleep.

Waking up again. "Two, three, four." Bloch started to count.
His situation had not changed, but he must have grown used to it
in his sleep. He pocketed the coin that had fallen under the bed
and went downstairs. When he put on an act, one word still nicely
yielded the next. A rainy October day; early morning; a dusty
windowpane; it worked. He greeted the innkeeper; the innkeeper
was just putting the newspapers into their racks; the girl was pushing a tray through the service hatch between the kitchen and dining
room: it was still working. If he kept up his guard, it could go on
like this, one thing at a time; he sat at the table he always sat at;
he opened the newspaper he opened every day; he read the paragraph in the paper that said an important lead in the Gerda T.
case was being followed into the southern part of the country; the
doodles in the margin of the newspaper that had been found in the
dead girl's apartment had furthered the investigation. One sentence
yielded the next sentence. And then, and then, and then. . . . For a
little while it was possible to look ahead without worrying.

After a while, although he was still sitting in the dining room
listing the things that went on out on the street, Bloch caught
himself becoming aware of a sentence: "For he had been idle too
long." Since that sentence looked like a final sentence to Bloch he
thought back to how he had come to it. What had come before it?
Oh, yes. earlier he had thought, "Surprised by the shot, he'd let
the ball roll right through his legs." And before this sentence he
had thought about the photographers who annoyed him behind
the cage. And before that, "Somebody had stopped behind him but
had only whistled for his dog." And before that sentence? Before
that sentence he had thought about a woman who had stopped in
a park, had turned around, and had looked at something behind
him the way one looks at an unruly child. And before that? Before
that, the innkeeper had talked about the mute schoolboy, who'd
been found dead right near the border. And before the schoolboy
he had thought of the ball that had bounced up just in front of the
goal line. And before the thought of the ball, he had seen the
market woman jump up from her stool on the street and run after
a schoolboy. And the market woman had been preceded by a sen-

tence in the paper: "The carpenter was hindered in his pursuit of the thief by the fact that he was still wearing his apron." But he had read the sentence in the paper just when he thought of how his jacket had been pulled down over his arms during a mugging,. And he had come to the mugging when he had bumped his shin painfully against the table. And before that? He could not remember anymore what had made him bump his shin against the table. He searched the sequence for a clue about what might have come before: did it have to do with the movement? Or with the pain? Or with the sound of table and shin? But it did not go any farther back. Then he noticed, in the paper in front of him, a picture of an apartment door that, because there was a corpse behind it, had had to be broken open. So, he thought, it all started with this apartment door, until he had brought himself back to the sentence, "He had been idle too long."

Everything had gone well for a while after that: the lip movements of the people he talked to coincided with what he heard them say; the houses were not just façades; heavy sacks of meal were being dragged from the loading ramp of the dairy into the storage room; when somebody shouted something far down the street, it sounded as though it actually came from down there. The people walking past on the sidewalk across the street did not appear to have been paid to walk past in the background; the fellow with the adhesive tape under his eye had a genuine scab; and the rain seemed to fall not just in the foreground of the picture but everywhere. Bloch then found himself under the projecting roof of a church. He must have got there through a side alley and stopped under the roof when it started to rain.

Inside the church he noticed that it was brighter than he had expected. So, after quickly sitting down in a pew, he could look up at the painted ceiling. After a while he recognized it: it was reproduced in the brochure that was placed in every room at the inn. Bloch, who had brought a copy because it also contained a sketchy map of the town and its vicinity with all its streets and paths, pulled out the brochure and read that different painters had worked on the background and foreground of the picture; the figures in the foreground had been finished long before the other painter had finished filling in the background. Bloch looked from the page up into the vault; because he did not know them, the figures—they probably represented people from the Bible—bored him; still, it was pleasant to look up at the vault while it rained harder and harder outside. The painting stretched all the way across the ceiling of the church. The background represented the sky, almost cloudless and an almost even blue; here and there a few fluffy clouds could be seen; at one spot, quite far above the figures, a bird had been painted. Bloch guessed the exact area the painter had had to fill with paint. Had it been hard to paint such an even blue? It was a blue that was so light that white had probably been mixed into the paint. And in mixing them didn't you have to be careful that the shade of blue didn't change from day to day ? On the other hand, the blue was not absolutely even but changed within a single brush stroke. So you couldn't just paint the ceiling an even blue but actually had to paint a picture. The background did not become a sky because the paint was blindly slapped on the plaster base—which, moreover, had to be wet— with as big a brush as possible, maybe even with a broom, but, Bloch reflected, the painter had to paint an actual sky with small variations in the blue which, nevertheless, had to be so indistinct that nobody would think they were a mistake in the mixing. In fact, the background did not look like a sky because you were used to imagining a sky in the background but because the sky had been painted there, stroke by stroke. It had been painted with such precision, thought Bloch, that it almost looked drawn; it was much more precise, anyway, than the figures in the foreground. Had he added the bird out of sheer rage? And had he painted the bird right at the start or had he only added it when he was finished? Might the background painter have been in some kind of despair? Nothing indicated this, and such an interpretation immediately seemed ridiculous to Bloch. Altogether it seemed to him as if his preoccupation with the painting, as if his walking back and forth, his sitting here and there, his going out, his coming in, were nothing but excuses. He stood up. "No distractions," he muttered to himself. As if to contradict himself, he went outside, walked straight across the street into an entryway, and stood there defiantly among the empty milk bottles—not that anyone came to ask him to account for his presence there—until it stopped raining. Then he went to a café and sat there for a while with his legs stretched out—not that anyone did him the favor of stumbling over them and starting a fight.

When he looked out, he saw a segment of the marketplace with the school bus; in the café he saw, to the left and to the right, segments of the walls, one with an unlighted stove with a bunch of flowers on it, the one on the other side with a coat rack with an umbrella hanging from it. He noticed another segment with the jukebox with a point of light slowly wandering through it before it stopped at the selected number, and next to it a cigarette machine with another bunch of flowers on top; then still another segment with the café owner behind the bar and next to him the waitress for whom he was opening a bottle, which the waitress put on the tray; and, finally, a segment of himself with his legs stretched out, the dirty tips of his wet shoes, and also the huge ashtray on the table and next to it a vase, which was smaller, and the filled wine glass on the next table where nobody was sitting right now. His angle of vision onto the square corresponded, as he realized now that the school bus had left, almost exactly with the angle on picture postcards; here a segment of the memorial column by the fountain; there, at the edge of the picture, a segment of the bicycle stand.

Bloch was irritated. Within the segments themselves he saw the details with grating distinctness: as if the parts he saw stood for the whole. Again the details seemed to him like nameplates. "Neon signs," he thought. So he saw the waitress's ear with one earring as a sign of the entire person; and a purse on a nearby table, slightly open so that he could recognize a polka-dotted scarf in it, stood for the woman holding the coffee cup who sat behind it and, with her other hand, pausing only now and then at a picture, rapidly leafed through a magazine. A tower of ice-cream dishes dovetailed into each other on the bar seemed a simile for the café owner, and the puddle on the floor by the coat rack represented the umbrella hanging above it. Instead of the heads of the customers, Bloch saw the dirty spots on the wall at the level of their heads. He was so irritated that he looked at the grimy cord that the waitress was just pulling to turn off the wall lights—it had grown brighter outside again—as if the entire lighting arrangement was designed especially to tax his strength. Also, his head ached because he had been caught in the rain.

The grating details seemed to stain and completely distort the figures and the surroundings they fitted into. The only defense was to name the things one by one and use those names as insults against the people themselves. The owner behind the bar might be called an ice-cream dish, and you could tell the waitress that she was a hole through the ear lobe. And you also felt like saying to the woman with the magazine, "You Purse, you," and to the man at the next table, who had finally come out of the back room and, standing up, finished his wine while he paid, "You Spot on Your Pants," or to shout after him as he set the empty glass on the table and walked out that he was a fingerprint, a doorknob, the slit in the back of his coat, a rain puddle, a bicycle clip, a fender, and so on, until the figure outside had disappeared on his bicycle. . . . Even the conversation and especially the exclamations—"What?" and "I see"—seemed so grating that one wanted to repeat the words out loud, scornfully.

Bloch went into a butcher shop and bought two salami sandwiches. He did not want to eat at the tavern because his money was running low. He looked over the sausages dangling together from a pole and pointed at the one he wanted the girl to slice. A boy came in with a note in his hand. At first the customs guard thought the schoolboy's corpse was a mattress that had been washed up, the girl had just said. She took two rolls out of a carton and sliced them in half without separating them completely. The bread was so stale that Bloch heard it crunch as the knife cut into it. The girl pulled the rolls apart and put the sliced meat inside. Bloch said that he had time and she should wait on the child first. He saw the boy silently holding the note out. The girl leaned forward and read it. Then the chunk she was hacking off the meat slipped off the board and fell on the stone floor. "Plop," said the child. The chunk had stayed where it had fallen. The girl picked it up, scraped it off with the edge of her knife, and wrapped it up. Outside, Bloch saw the schoolchildren walking by with their umbrellas open, even though it had stopped raining. He opened the door for the boy and watched the girl tear the skin off the sausage end and put the slices inside the second roll.

Business was bad, the girl said. "There aren't any houses except on this side of the street where the shop is, so that, first of all, nobody lives across the street who could see from there that there is a shop here and, second of all, the people going by never walk on the other side of the street, so they pass by so close that they don't see that there is a store here, especially since the shop window isn't much bigger than the livingroom windows of the houses next door."

Bloch was surprised that the people didn't walk on the other side of the street as well, where there was more room and where it was sunnier. Probably everybody feels some need to walk right next to the houses, he said. The girl, who had not understood him because he had become disgusted with talking in the middle of the sentence and had only mumbled the rest, laughed as though all she had expected for an answer was a joke. In fact, when a few people passed by the shop window, it got so dark in the shop that it did seem like a joke.

"First of all . . . second of all . . ." Bloch repeated to himself what the girl had said; it seemed uncanny to him how someone could begin to speak and at the same time know how the sentence would end. Outside, he ate the sandwiches while he walked along. He wadded up the waxed paper they were wrapped in and was ready to throw it away. There was no trash basket nearby. For a while he walked along with the balled-up paper, first in one direction and then in another. He put the paper in his coat pocket, took it out again, and finally threw it through a fence into an orchard. Chickens came running from all directions at once but turned back before they had pecked the paper ball open.

In front of him Bloch saw three men walk diagonally across the street, two in uniform and the one in the middle in a black Sunday suit with a tie hanging over his shoulder, where it had been blown either by the wind or by fast running. He watched as the policemen led the Gypsy into the police station. They walked next to each other as far as the door, and the Gypsy, it seemed, moved easily and willingly between the two policemen and talked with them; when one of the policemen pushed open the door, the other did not grab the Gypsy but just touched his elbow lightly from behind. The Gypsy looked over his shoulder at the policeman and gave a friendly smile; the collar under the knot of the Gypsy's tie was open. It seemed to Bloch as if the Gypsy was so deeply trapped that all he could do when he was touched on the arm was look at the policemen with helpless friendliness.

Bloch followed them into the building, which also housed the post office; for just a moment he believed that if anybody saw him eating a sandwich out in public, they could not possibly think that he was involved in anything. "Involved"? He could not even let himself think that he had to justify his presence here, while they were bringing in the Gypsy, by any action such as, say, eating salami sandwiches. He could justify himself only when he was questioned and accused of something, and because he had to avoid even thinking that he might be questioned, he also could not let himself think about how to prepare justifications in advance for this possibility—this possibility did not even exist. So if he was asked, whether he had watched while the Gypsy was being brought in, he would not have to deny it and pretend that he had been distracted because he was eating a sandwich but could admit that he had witnessed the event. "Witnessed"? Bloch interrupted himself while he was waiting in the post office for his phone connection; "admit"? What did these words have to do with this event, which for him was of no significance. Didn't they give it a significance he was making every effort to deny? "Deny"? Bloch interrupted himself again. There was nothing to deny. He had to keep his guard up against words that transformed what he wanted to say into some kind of statement.

His call had gone through. Absorbed in avoiding the impression that he was prepared to make a statement, he caught himself wrapping a handkerchief over the receiver. Slightly disconcerted, he put the handkerchief back in his pocket. How had he come from the thought of unguarded talk to the handkerchief? He was told that the friend he was calling had to stay quartered with his team in a training camp until the important match on Sunday and could not be reached by phone. Bloch gave the postmistress another number. She asked him to pay for the first call first. Bloch paid and sat on a bench to wait for the second call. The phone rang and he stood up. But it was only a birthday telegram arriving. The postmistress wrote it down and confirmed it word by word. Bloch walked back and forth. One of the mailmen had returned from his route and was now loudly reporting to the girl. Bloch sat down. Outside on the street, now that it was early afternoon, there was no distraction. Bloch had become impatient but did not shown it. He heard the mailman say that the Gypsy had been hiding all this time near the border in one of those lean-to shelters the customs guards used. "Anyone can say that," said Bloch. The mailman turned toward him and stopped talking. What he claimed to be the latest news, Bloch went on, anybody could have read yesterday, the day before yesterday, even the day before the day before yesterday, in the papers. What he said didn't mean anything, nothing at all, nothing whatsoever. The mailman had turned his back to Bloch even while Bloch was still talking and was now speaking quietly with the postmistress, in a murmur that sounded to Bloch like those passages in foreign films that are left untranslated because they are supposed to be incomprehensible anyway. Bloch couldn't reach them anymore with his remark. All at once the fact that it was in a post office where he "couldn't reach anybody anymore" seemed to him not like a fact at all but like a bad joke, like one of those word games that, say, sportswriters play, which he had always loathed. Even the mailman's story about the Gypsy had seemed to him crudely suggestive, a clumsy insinuation, like the birthday telegram, whose words were so commonplace that they simply could not mean what they said. And it wasn't only the conversation that was insinuating; everything around him was also meant to suggest something to him. "As though they wink and make signs at me," thought Bloch. For what was it supposed to mean that the lid of the inkwell lay right next to the well on the blotter and that the blotter on the desk had obviously been replaced just today, so only a few impressions were legible on it? And wouldn't it be more proper to say "so that" instead of "so"? *So that* the impressions would therefore be legible. And now the postmistress picked up the phone and spelled out the birthday telegram letter by letter. What was she hinting at by that? What was behind her dictating "All the best," "With kind regards": what was that supposed to mean? What did those phrases stand for? Who was behind the cover name "your loving grandparents"? Even that morning Bloch had instantly recognized the short slogan "Why not phone?" as a trap.

It seemed to him as if the mailman and the postmistress were in the know. "The postmistress and the mailman," he corrected himself. Now the loathsome word-game sickness had struck even him, and in broad daylight. "Broad daylight"? He must have hit on that phrase somehow. That expression seemed witty to him, in an unpleasant way. But were the other words in the sentence any better? If you said the word "sickness" to yourself, after a few repetitions you couldn't help laughing at it. "A sickness strikes me": silly. "I am stricken by a sickness": just as silly. "The postmistress and the mailman"; "the mailman and the postmistress"; "the postmistress and the mailman": one big joke. Have you heard the one about the mailman and the postmistress? "Everything seems like a heading," thought Bloch: THE BIRTHDAY TELEGRAM, THE INKWELL LID, THE SCRAPS OF BLOTTER ON THE FLOOR. The rack where the various rubber stamps hung looked as if it had been sketched. He looked at it for a long time but did not figure out what was supposed to be funny about the stand. On the other hand, there had to be a joke in it: otherwise, why should it look sketched to him? Or was it another trap? Was the thing there so that he would make a slip of the tongue? Bloch looked somewhere else, looked at another place, and looked somewhere else again. Does this ink pad mean anything to you? What do you think of when you see this filled-out check? What do you associate with that drawer being open? It seemed to Bloch that he should take inventory of the room, so that the objects he paused at or that he left out during his count could serve as evidence. The mailman slapped the flat of his hand against the big bag that was still hanging from his shoulder. "The mailman slaps the bag and takes it off," thought Bloch, word for word. "Now he puts it on the table and walks into the package room." He described the events to himself like a radio announcer to the public, as if this was the only way he could see them for himself. After a while it helped.

He stopped pacing because the phone rang. As always when the phone rang, he felt he had known it would a moment before it did. The postmistress picked up the phone and then pointed to the booth. Already inside the booth, he wondered whether perhaps he had misunderstood her gesture, if perhaps it had been meant for no one in particular. He picked up the receiver and asked his ex-wife, who had started by giving only her first name, as though she knew it was him, to send some money to general delivery. A peculiar silence followed. Bloch heard some whispering that wasn't meant for him. "Where are you?" the woman asked. He'd got cold feet and now he was high and dry, Bloch said and laughed as though he had said something extremely witty. The woman didn't answer. Bloch heard more whispering. It was very difficult, said the woman. Why? asked Bloch. She hadn't been talking to him, answered the woman. "Where should I send the money?" His pockets would be empty soon if she didn't give him a hand, Bloch said. The woman remained silent. Then the phone was hung up at her end.

"The snows of yesteryear," Bloch thought, unexpectedly, as he came out of the booth. What was that supposed to mean? In fact, he had heard that the underbrush was so tangled and thick at the border that patches of snow could be found at certain spots even during the early summer. But that was not what he had meant. Besides, people had no business in the underbrush. "No business"? How did he mean that? "The way I say it," thought Bloch.

At the savings bank he traded in the American dollar bill he had carried with him for a long time. He also tried to exchange a Brazilian bill, but the bank did not trade that currency; besides, they didn't know the exchange rate.

When Bloch came in, the bank teller was counting out coins, wrapping them up in rolls, and stretching rubber bands around the rolls. Bloch put the dollar bill on the counter. Next to it there was a music box; only when he gave it a second look did Bloch recognize it as a contribution box for some charity. The teller looked up but went on counting. Before he had been asked to, Bloch slid the bill under the partition through to the other side. The teller was lining up the rolls in a single row next to him. Bloch bent down and blew the bill in front of the teller, and the teller unfolded the bill, smoothed it with the edge of his hand, and ran his fingertips over it. Bloch saw that his fingertips were quite black. Another teller came out of the back room; to witness something, thought Bloch. He asked to have the change—in which there was not even one bill—put in an envelope and shoved the coins back under the partition. The official, in the same way he had lined up the piles earlier, stuffed the coins into an envelope and pushed the envelope back to Bloch. Bloch thought that if everybody asked to have their money put in envelopes, the savings bank would eventually go broke. They could do the same thing with everything they bought: maybe the heavy demand for packaging would slowly but surely drive businesses bankrupt? Anyway, it was fun to think about.

In a stationery store Bloch bought a tourist map of the region and had it well wrapped. He also bought a pencil: the pencil he asked to have put in a paper bag . With the rolled-up map in his hand, he walked on; he felt more harmless now than before, when his hands had been empty.

Outside the town, at a spot where he had a full view of the area, he sat down on a bench and, using the pencil, compared the details on the map with the items in the landscape in front of him. Key to the symbols: these circles meant a deciduous forest, those triangles a coniferous one, and when you looked up from the map, you were astonished that it was true. Over there, the terrain had to be swampy; over there, there had to be a wayside shrine; over there, there had to be a railroad crossing. If you walked along this dirt road, you had to cross a bridge here, then had to come across a wagon trail, then had to walk up a steep incline, where, since somebody might be waiting on top, you had to turn off the path and run across this field, had to run toward this forest—luckily, a coniferous forest—but someone might possibly come at you out of the forest, so that you had to double back and then run down this slope toward this farmhouse, had to run past this shed, then run along this brook, had to leap over it at this spot because a jeep might come at you here, then zigzag across this field, slip through this hedge onto the street where a truck was just going by, which you could stop and then you were safe. Bloch stopped short. "If it's a question of murder, your mind jumps from one thing to another," he had heard somebody say in a movie.

He was relieved to discover a square on the map that he could not find in the landscape: the house that had to be there wasn't there, and the road that curved at this spot was in reality straight. It seemed to Bloch that this discrepancy might be helpful to him.

He watched a dog running toward a man in a field; then he realized that he was not watching the dog anymore but the man, who was moving like somebody trying to block somebody else's way. Now he saw a little boy standing behind the man, and he realized that he was not watching the man and the dog, as would have been expected, but the boy, who, from this distance, seemed to be fidgeting; but then he realized that it was the boy's screaming that seemed like fidgeting to him. In the meantime, the man had grabbed the dog by the collar and all three, dog, man, and boy, had walked off in the same direction. "Who was that meant for?" thought Bloch.

On the ground in front of him a different picture: ants approaching a crumb of bread. He realized once again that he wasn't watching the ants but, on the contrary, the fly sitting on the bread crumb.

Everything he saw was conspicuous. The pictures did not seem natural but looked as if they had been made specifically for the occasion. They served some purpose. As you looked at them, they jumped out at you. "Like call letters," thought Bloch. Like commands. When he closed his eyes and looked again afterwards, everything seemed to be different. The segments that could be seen seemed to glimmer and tremble at their edges.

From a sitting position, Bloch, without really getting up, had immediately walked away. After a while he stopped, then immediately broke into a run from a standing position. He got off to a quick start, suddenly stopped short, changed direction, ran at a steady pace, then changed his step, changed his step again, stopped short, then ran backward. turned around while running backward, ran forward again, again turned around to run backward, went backward, turned around to run forward, after a few steps changed to a sprint, stopped short, sat down on a curbstone, and immediately went back to running from a sitting position.

When he stopped and then walked on, the pictures seemed to dim from the edges; finally they had turned completely black except for a circle in the middle. "Like when somebody in a movie looks through a telescope," he thought. He wiped the sweat off his legs with his trousers. He walked past a cellar where, because the cellar door was half open, tea leaves shimmered in a peculiar way. "Like potatoes," Bloch thought.

Of course, the building in front of him had only one story, the shutters were fastened, the roof tiles were covered with moss (another one of those words!), the door was closed. PUBLIC SCHOOL was written above it, behind in the garden somebody was chopping wood, it had to be the school janitor, of course, and in front of the school naturally there was a hedge; yes, everything was in order, nothing was missing, not even the sponge underneath the blackboard in the dusky classroom and the chalk box next to it, not even the semicircles on the outside walls underneath the windows and the other marks that, in explanation, confirmed that these scratches were made by window hooks; in every respect it was as though everything you saw or heard confirmed to you that it was true to its word.

In the classroom the lid of the coal bucket was open, and in the bucket itself the handle of the coal shovel could he seen (an April fool's joke), and the floor with the wide boards, the cracks still wet from mopping, not forgetting the map on the wall, the sink next to the blackboard, and the corn husks on the windowsill: one single, cheap imitation. No, he would not let himself be tricked by April fool's jokes like these.

It was as if he were drawing wider and wider circles. He had forgotten the lightning rod next to the door, and now it seemed to him like a cue. He was supposed to start. He helped himself out by walking around the school back to the yard and talking with the janitor in the woodshed. Woodshed, janitor, yard: cues. He watched while the janitor put a log on the chopping block and lifted up the ax. He said a couple of words from the yard, the janitor stopped, answered, and as he struck at the log, it fell to one side before he had hit it, and the ax hit the chopping block so that the pile of unchopped logs in the background collapsed. Another one of those cues. But the only thing that happened was that he called to the janitor in the dim woodshed, asking whether this was the only classroom for the whole school, and the janitor answered that for the whole school there was only this one classroom.

No wonder the children hadn't even learned to speak by the time they left school, the janitor said suddenly, slamming the ax into the chopping block and coming out of the shed: they couldn't manage even to finish a single sentence of their own, they talked to each other almost entirely in single words. and they wouldn't talk at all unless you asked them to, and what they learned was only memorized stuff that they rattled off by rote; except for that, they couldn't make whole sentences. "Actually, all of them, more or less, have a speech defect," said the janitor.

What was that supposed to mean? What reason did the janitor have for that? What did it have to do with him? Nothing? Yes, but why did the janitor act as if it had something to do with him?

Bloch should have answered, but he did not let himself get involved. Once he got started, he would have to go on talking. So he walked around the yard awhile longer, helped the janitor pick up the logs that had been flung out of the shed during the chopping, and then, little by little, wandered unobtrusively back out onto the street and was able to make his getaway with no trouble.

He walked past the athletic field. It was after work, and the soccer team was practicing. The ground was so wet that drops sprayed out from the grass when a player kicked the ball. Bloch watched for a while, but it was getting dark, and he left.

In the restaurant at the railroad station he ate a croquette and drank a couple of glasses of beer. On the platform outside, he sat down on a bench. A girl in spike heels walked back and forth on the gravel. A phone rang in the traffic supervisor's office. A railroad official stood in the door, smoking. Somebody came out of the waiting room and stopped again immediately. There was more rattling in the office, and loud talking, like somebody talking into a telephone, could be heard. It had grown dark by now.

It was fairly quiet. Here and there someone could be seen drawing on a cigarette. A faucet was turned on hard and was turned off again at once—as though somebody had been startled. Farther away people were talking in the dark; sonorous sounds could be heard, as in a half-sleep: ah ee. Somebody yelled: "Ow!" There was no way to tell whether a man or a woman had yelled. Very far away someone could be heard saying, very distinctly, "You look worn out." Between the railroad tracks, just as distinctly, a railroad worker could be seen standing and scratching his head. Bloch thought he was asleep.

An incoming train could be seen. You could watch a few passengers getting off, looking as if they were undecided whether to get off or not. A drunk got off last of all and slammed the door shut. The official on the platform could be seen as he gave a signal with his flashlight, and then the train was leaving.

In the waiting room Bloch looked at the schedule. No more trains stopped at the station today. Anyway, it was late enough now to go to the movies.

Some people were already in the lobby of the movie house. Bloch sat down with them, his ticket in his hand. More and more people came. It was pleasant to hear so many sounds. Bloch went out in front of the theater, stood out there with some other people, then went back into the movie house.

In the movie somebody shot a rifle at a man who was sitting far away at a campfire with his back turned. Nothing happened; the man did not fall over, just sat there, did not even look to see who had fired. Some time passed. Then the man slowly sank to one side and lay there without moving. That's the trouble with these old guns, the gunman said to his partner: No impact. But the man had actually been dead all the time he was sitting there at the campfire.

After the movie he rode out to the border with two guys in a car. A stone slammed against the bottom of the car. Bloch, who was in the back seat, became alert again.

Since this had been pay day, he could not find a single empty table at the tavern. He sat down with some other people. The landlady came and put her hand on his shoulder. He understood and ordered drinks for the whole table.

To pay, he put a folded bill on the table. Somebody next to him unfolded the bill and said that another one might be tucked inside it. Bloch said. "So what?" and refolded the bill. The guy unfolded the bill again and pushed an ashtray on top of it. Bloch reached into the ashtray and, underhand, threw the butts into the guy's face. Somebody pulled his chair out from under him, so that he slid under the table.

Bloch jumped up and in a flash slammed his forearm against the chest of the guy, who had pulled away his chair. The guy fell against the wall and groaned loudly because he couldn't catch his breath. A couple of men twisted Bloch's arms behind his back and shoved him out the door. He did not fall, just staggered around and ran right back in.

He swung at the guy who had unfolded the bill. A kick hit him from behind, and he fell against the table with the guy. Even while they were falling, Bloch slugged away at him.

Somebody grabbed him by the legs and hauled him away. Bloch kicked him in the ribs, and he let go. A few others got hold of Bloch and dragged him out. On the street they put a headlock on him and marched him back and forth like that. They stopped in front of the customs shed with him, pushed his head against the doorbell, and went away.

A guard came out, saw Bloch standing there, and went back inside. Bloch ran after the guys and tackled one of them from behind. The others rushed him. Bloch stepped to one side and butted his head into somebody's stomach. A few more people came out of the tavern. Somebody threw a coat over his head. He kicked him in the shins, but somebody else was tying the arms of the coat together. Then they swiftly beat him down and went back into the tavern.

Bloch got loose from the coat and ran after them. One of them stopped but did not turn around. Bloch charged him; the guy just walked away, and Bloch sprawled on the ground.

After a while he got up and went into the tavern. He started to say something, but when he moved his tongue, the blood in his mouth bubbled. He sat down at one of the tables and indicated with his finger to show that he wanted a drink. The others at the table paid him no attention. The waitress brought him a bottle of beer without the glass. He thought he saw tiny flies running back and forth on the table, but it was just cigarette smoke.

He was too weak to lift the beer bottle with one hand, so he clutched it with both hands and bent over so that it didn't have to be lifted too high. His ears were so sensitive that at times the cards didn't fall but were slammed on the next table, and at the bar the sponge didn't fall but slapped into the sink; and the landlady's daughter, with clogs on her bare feet, didn't walk through the barroom but clattered through the barroom; the wine didn't flow but gurgled into the glasses; and the music didn't play but boomed from the juke box.

He heard a woman cry out in fright, but in a tavern a woman's cry didn't mean anything; therefore, the woman could not have cried out in fright. Nevertheless, he had been jolted by the cry; it was only because of the noise, because the cry had been so shrill.

Little by little the other details lost their significance: the foam in the empty beer bottle meant no more to him than the cigarette box that the guy next to him tore open just enough so that he managed to extract a single cigarette with his fingernails. Nor did the used matches lying loose everywhere in the cracks between the floorboards occupy his attention anymore, and the fingernail impressions in the putty along the window frame no longer seemed to have anything to do with him. Everything left him cold now, stood once more in its place; like peacetime, thought Bloch. The stuffed grouse above the juke box no longer forced one to draw conclusions; and the flies sleeping on the ceiling did not suggest anything anymore.

You could see a fellow combing his hair with his fingers, you could see girls walking backward as they danced, you could see guys standing up and buttoning their coats, you could hear cards flicking as they were shuffled, but you didn't have to dwell on it anymore.

Bloch got tired. The tireder he got, the more clearly he took in everything, distinguished one thing from another. He saw how the door invariably stayed open when somebody went out, and how somebody else always got up and shut the door again. He was so tired that he saw each thing by itself, especially the contours, as though there was nothing to the things but their contours. He saw and heard everything with total immediacy, without first having to translate it into words, as before, or comprehending it only in terms of words or word games. He was in a state where everything seemed natural to him.

Later the landlady sat down with him, and he put his arm around her so naturally that she did not even seem to notice. He dropped a couple of coins into the juke box as though it were nothing and danced effortlessly with the landlady. He noticed that every time she said something she added his name to it.

It wasn't important anymore that he could see the waitress clasping one hand with the other, nor was there anything special about the thick curtains, and it was only natural that more and more people left. They could be heard as they relieved themselves out on the street and then walked away.

It got quieter in the barroom, so that the records in the juke box played very distinctly. In the pause between records people talked more softly or almost held their breath; it was a relief when the next record came on. It seemed to Bloch that you could talk about these occurrences as things that recurred forever; the course of a single day, he thought; things that you wrote about on picture postcards. "At night we sit in the tavern and listen to records." He got tireder and tireder, and outside the apples were dropping off the trees.

When nobody but him was left, the landlady went into the kitchen. Bloch sat there and waited until the record was over. He turned off the juke box, so that now there was light only in the kitchen. The landlady sat at the table and did her accounts. Bloch approached her, a coaster in his hand. She looked up when he came out of the barroom and looked at him while he approached her. It was too late when he remembered the coaster; he started to hide it quickly, before she saw it, but the landlady looked away from him and at the coaster in his hand and asked him what he was doing with it, if perhaps she had written a bill on it that hadn't been paid. Bloch dropped the coaster and sat down next to the landlady, not doing one thing smoothly after the other but hesitating at each move. She went on counting, talked with him while she did, then cleared away the money. Bloch said he'd just forgotten about the coaster in his hand; it hadn't meant anything.

She asked him to have a bite with her. She set a wooden board in front of him. There was no knife, he said, though she had laid the knife next to the board. She had to bring the laundry in from the garden, she said, it was just starting to rain. It wasn't raining, he corrected her, it was only dripping from the trees because there was a little wind. But she had gone out already, and since she left the door open, he could see that it actually was raining. He saw her come back and shouted that she had dropped a shirt, but it turned out that it was only a rag for the floor, which had been lying in the entryway all along. When she lit the candle on the table, he saw the wax dripping on a plate because she had tilted the candle slightly in her hand. She should watch out, he said, wax was dripping onto the clean plate. But she was already setting the candle in the spilled wax, which was still liquid, and she pressed it down until it stood by itself. "I didn't know that you were going to put the candle on the plate," Bloch said. She started to sit down where there was no chair, and Bloch shouted, "Watch out!" though she had just squatted to pick up a coin that had fallen under the table while she was counting. When she went into the bedroom to take care of the girl, he immediately asked for her; once when she left the table he even called after her to ask where she was going.

She turned on the radio on the kitchen cabinet; it was nice to watch her walking back and forth while the music came out of the radio. When somebody in a movie turned on the radio, the program was instantly interrupted for a bulletin about a wanted man.

While they sat at the table, they talked to each other. It seemed to Bloch that he could not say anything serious. He cracked jokes, but the landlady took everything he said literally. He said that her blouse was striped like a soccer jersey and was about to go on, but she asked him whether he didn't like her blouse, what bothered him about it. It did no good to assure her that he was only joking and that the blouse went very nicely with her pale skin; she went on to ask if her skin was too pale for him. He said, jokingly, that the kitchen was furnished almost like a city kitchen, and she asked why he said "almost." Did people there keep their things cleaner? Even when Bloch joked about the estate owner's son (he'd proposed to her, hadn't he?), she took him literally and said the estate owner's son wasn't available. He tried to explain, using a comparison, that he had not meant it seriously, but she took the comparison literally as well. "I didn't mean anything by it," Bloch said. "You must have had a reason for saying it," the landlady answered. Bloch laughed. The landlady asked why he was laughing at her.

The little girl called from the bedroom. She went in and calmed her down. When she came back, Bloch had stood up. She stood in front of him and looked at him for a while. But then she talked about herself. Because she was standing so close to him, he could not answer and took a step backward. She did not follow him, but hesitated. Bloch wanted to touch her. When he finally moved his hand, she looked to one side. Bloch let his hand drop and pretended that he had made a joke. The landlady sat on the other side of the table and went on talking.

He started to say something, but then he could not think of what it was he wanted to say. He tried to remember: he could not remember what it was about, but it had something to do with disgust. Then a movement of the landlady's hand reminded him of something else. He could not think of what it was this time either, but it had something to do with shame. His perceptions of movements and things did not remind him of other movements and things but of sensations and feelings, and he did not remember the feelings as if they were from the past but re-lived them as happening in the present: he did not remember shame, and disgust but only felt ashamed and disgusted now that he remembered without being able to think of the things that had brought on shame and disgust. The mixture of disgust and shame was so strong that his whole body started to itch.

A piece of metal knocked against the windowpane outside. The landlady answered his question by saying that it was the wire from the lightning rod that had come loose. Bloch, who had seen a lightning rod at the school, immediately concluded that this repetition was intentional; it could be no accident that he ran across a lightning rod twice in a row. Altogether he found everything alike; all things reminded him of each other. What was the meaning of the repeated appearances of lightning rods? How should he interpret the lightning rod? "Lightning rod"? Surely that was just another word game? Did it mean that he was safe from harm? Or did it indicate that he should tell the landlady everything? And why were the cookies on the wooden plate fish shaped? What did they suggest? Should he be "mute as a fish"? Was he not permitted to go on talking? Was that what the cookies on the wooden plate were trying to tell him? It was as if he did not see any of this but read it off a posted list of regulations.

Yes, they were regulations. The dishrag hanging over the faucet told him to do something. Even the cap of the beer bottle left on the table, which by now had been cleared, summoned him to do something. Everything fell into place: everywhere he saw a summons: to do one thing, not to do another. Everything was spelled out for him, the shelf where the spice boxes were, a shelf with jars of freshly made jam . . . things repeated themselves. Bloch noticed that for quite a while he had stopped talking to himself: the landlady was at the sink gathering bits of bread out of the saucers. You had to clean up after him all the time, she said, he didn't even shut the table drawer when he took out the silverware; he just left books he had looked through open, he took off his coat and just let it drop.

Bloch answered that he really felt that he had to let everything drop. It wouldn't take much for him to let go of this ashtray in his hand, it even surprised him to see that the ashtray was still in his hand. He had stood up, still holding the ashtray in front of him. The landlady looked at him. He stared at the ashtray awhile, then he put it down. As if in anticipation of the insinuations all around him, which repeated themselves. Bloch repeated what he had said. He was so awkward that he repeated it once more. He saw the landlady shake her arm over the sink. She said that a piece of apple had slipped up her sleeve and now it didn't want to come out. Didn't want to come out? Bloch imitated her by shaking his own sleeve. It seemed to him that if he imitated everything he would stay on the safe side, so to speak. But she noticed it immediately and mimicked his imitation of her.

As she did that, she came near the refrigerator, on top of which there was a bakery carton. Bloch watched her as she, still mimicking him, touched the carton behind her. Since he was watching her so intently, she shoved her elbow back once more. The carton began to slip and slowly tipped over the rounded edges of the refrigerator. Bloch could still have caught it, but he watched until it hit the floor.

While the landlady bent down to pick up the carton, he walked one way and then another; wherever he stopped he shoved things into the corner—a chair, a lighter on the stove, an egg cup on the kitchen table. "Is everything all right?" he asked. He asked her what he wanted her to ask him. But before she could answer, something knocked on the window in a way the wire from a lightning rod would never knock against a pane. Bloch had known it a moment beforehand.

The landlady opened the window. A customs guard was outside asking to borrow an umbrella for the walk back to town. Bloch said that he might as well go along with him, and the landlady handed him the umbrella, which hung under the work pants on the door frame. He promised to bring it back the next day. As long as he hadn't brought it back, nothing could go wrong.

On the street he opened the umbrella; the rain immediately rattled so loudly that he did not hear whether she had answered him. The guard came running along the wall of the house to get under the umbrella, and they started off.

They were only a few steps away when the light in the tavern was turned off and it became completely dark. It was so dark that Bloch put his hand over his eyes. Behind the wall that they were just passing he heard the snorting of cows. Something ran past him. "I almost stepped on a hedgehog just then!" the guard exclaimed.

Bloch asked how he could have seen a hedgehog in the dark. The guard answered, "That's part of my profession. Even if all you see is one movement or hear just one noise, you must be able to identify the thing that made that movement or sound. Even when something moves at the very edge of your vision, you must be able to recognize it, in fact even be able to determine what color it is, though actually you can recognize colors only at the center of your retina." They had passed the houses by the border by now and were walking along a shortcut beside the brook. The path was covered with sand of some kind, which became brighter as Bloch grew more accustomed to the dark.

"Of course, we're not kept very busy here," the guard said. "Since the border has been mined, there's no smuggling going on here anymore. So your alertness slips, you get tired and can't concentrate anymore. And then when something does happen, you don't even react."

Bloch saw something running toward him and stepped behind the guard. A dog brushed him as it ran past.

"And then if somebody suddenly steps in front of you, you don't even know how to grab hold of him. You're in the wrong position from the start and when you finally get yourself right, you depend on your partner, who is standing next to you, to catch him, and all along your partner is depending on you to catch him yourself—

and the guy you're after gives you the slip." The slip? Bloch heard the customs guard next to him under the umbrella take a deep breath.

Behind him the sand crunched. He turned around and saw that the dog had come back. They walked on, the dog running alongside sniffing at the backs of his knees. Bloch stopped, broke off a hazelnut twig by the brook, and chased the dog away.

"If you're facing each other," the guard went on, "it's important to look the other guy in the eye. Before he starts to run, his eyes show which direction he'll take. But you've also got to watch his legs at the same time. Which leg is he putting his weight on? The direction that leg is pointing is the direction he'll want to take. But if the other guy wants to fool you and not run in that direction, he'll have to shift his weight just before he takes off, and that takes so long that you can rush him in the meantime." Bloch looked down at the brook, whose roaring could be heard but which could not be seen. A heavy bird flew up out of a thicket. Chickens in a coop could be heard scratching and pecking their beaks against the boards.

"Actually, there aren't any hard-and-fast rules," said the guard. "You're always at a disadvantage because the other guy also watches to see how you're reacting to him. All you can ever do is react. And when he starts to run, he'll change his direction after the first step, and you're the one whose weight is on the wrong foot."

Meanwhile, they had come back to the paved road and were approaching the edge of town. Here and there they stepped on wet sawdust which the rain had swept out to the street. Bloch asked himself whether the guard went into so much detail about something that could be said in one sentence because he was really trying to say something else by it. "He spoke *from memory*," thought Bloch. As a test, he himself started to talk at great length about something that usually required only one sentence, but the guard seemed to think that this was completely natural and didn't ask him what he was driving at. So the guard seemed to have meant what he said before quite literally.

In the center of town some people who had been taking a dancing lesson came toward them. "Dancing lesson"? What did that phrase suggest? One girl had been searching for something in her "purse" as she passed, and another had been wearing boots with "high tops." Were these abbreviations for something? He heard the purse snapping shut behind him; he almost closed up his umbrella in reply.

He held the umbrella over the customs guard as far as the municipal housing project. "So far I have only a rented apartment, but I'm saving up to buy one for myself," said the guard, standing on the staircase. Bloch had come in, too. Would he like to come up for a drink? Bloch refused but remained standing. The lights went off again while the guard was going up the stairs. Bloch leaned against the mailboxes downstairs. Outside, quite high up, a plane flew past. "The mail plane," the guard shouted down into the dark, and pushed the light switch. It echoed in the stairwell. Bloch had quickly gone out.

At the inn he learned that a large tourist group had arrived and had been put up on cots in the bowling alley; that's why it was so quiet down there tonight. Bloch asked the girl who told him about this whether she wanted to come upstairs with him. She answered, gravely, that that was impossible tonight. Later, in his room, he heard her walk down the hall and go past his door. The rain had made the room so cold that it seemed to him as if damp sawdust had been spread all over. He set the umbrella tip-down in the sink and lay down on the bed fully dressed.

Bloch got sleepy. He made a few tired gestures to make light of his sleepiness, but that made him even sleepier. Various things he had said during the day came back to him; he tried to get rid of them by breathing out. Then he felt himself falling asleep; as before the end of a paragraph, he thought.

Pheasants were flying through fire, and drovers were walking along a cornfield, and the bellboy was writing the room number with chalk on his briefcase, and a leafless briar was full of swallows and snails.

He woke up gradually and realized that somebody was breathing loudly in the next room and that the rhythm of the breathing was forming itself into sentences in his half-sleep; he heard the exhalation as a long-drawn-out "and," and the extended sound of the inhalation then transformed itself inside him into sentences that—after the dash that corresponded to the pause between the inhalation and the exhalation—invariably attached themselves to the "and." Soldiers with pointed dress shoes stood in front of the movie house, and the match box was put down on the cigarette pack, and a vase was on the TV set, and a truck filled with sand whizzed past the bus, and a hitchhiker had a bunch of grapes in his other hand, and outside the door somebody said, "Open up. please."

"Open up, please." Those last three words did not fit at all into the breathing from next door, which became more and more distinct while the sentences were slowly beginning to fade out. He was wide awake now. Somebody knocked on the door again and said, "Open up, please." He must have been awakened by that, since the rain had stopped.

He sat up quickly, a bedspring snapped back into place, the chambermaid was outside the door with the breakfast tray. He hadn't ordered breakfast, he could barely manage to say before she had excused herself and knocked on the door across the hall.

Alone in the room, he found every thing re-arranged. He turned on the faucet. A fly immediately fell off the mirror into the sink and was washed down at once. He sat down on the bed: just now that chair had been to his right, and now it was to his left. Was the picture reversed? He looked at it from left to right, then from right to left. He repeated the look from left to right; this look seemed to him like reading. He saw a "wardrobe," "then" "a" "small" "table," "then" "a" "wastebasket," "then" "a" "drape"; while looking from right to left, however, he saw ⊣, next to it the ⊓, under it the ⊖, next to it the ⊡, on top of it his ⊸, and when he looked around, he saw the ⊟, next to it the ⊙ and the ⊙. He sat on the ⌣, under it there was a ⊷, next to it a ⊏. He walked to the ⊞ : ⊞ :

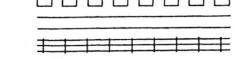

Bloch closed the curtains and went out.

The dining room downstairs was filled with the tourists. The innkeeper led Bloch into the other room, where the innkeeper's mother was sitting in front of the TV set with the curtains closed. The innkeeper opened the curtains and took a position next to Bloch; first, Bloch saw him standing to his left; then, when he looked up again, it was the other way around. Bloch ordered breakfast and asked for the newspaper. The innkeeper said that the tourists were reading it just now. Bloch ran his fingers over his face; his cheeks seemed to be numb. He was cold. The flies on the floor were crawling so slowly that at first he mistook them for beetles. A bee rose from the windowsill but fell back immediately. The people outside were leaping over the puddles; they were carrying heavy shopping bags. Bloch ran his fingers all over his face.

The innkeeper came in with the tray and said that the newspaper still wasn't free. He spoke so softly that Bloch also spoke softly when he answered. "There's no hurry," he whispered. The screen of the TV set was dusty here in the daylight, and the window that the schoolchildren looked through as they walked past was reflected in it. Bloch ate and listened to the show. The innkeeper's mother moaned from time to time.

Outside he noticed a stand with a bag full of newspapers. He went outside, dropped a coin into the slot next to the bag, and then took out a paper. He had so much practice in opening papers that he read the description of himself even as he was going inside. He had attracted a woman's attention on the bus because some change had fallen out of his pocket; she had bent down for it, and had noticed that it was American money. Subsequently, she had heard that similar coins had been found beside the dead cashier. No one took her story seriously at first, but then it turned out that her description matched the description given by one of the cashier's friends who, when he called for the cashier in his car the night before the murder, had seen a man standing near the movie house.

Bloch sat back down in the other room and looked at the picture they had drawn of him according to the woman's description. Did that mean that they did not know his name yet? When had the paper been printed? He saw that it was the first edition, which usually came out the evening before. The headline and the picture looked to him as if they had been pasted onto the paper; like newspapers in movies, he thought: there the real headlines were also replaced by headlines that fitted the film; or like those headlines you could have made up about yourself in penny arcades.

The doodles in the margin had been deciphered as the word "Dumm" and, moreover, with a capital at the beginning; so it was probably a proper name. Was a person named Dumm involved in the matter? Bloch remembered telling the cashier about his friend Dumm, the soccer player.

When the girl cleared the table, Bloch did not close the paper. He learned that the Gypsy had been released, that the mute schoolboy's death had been an accident. The paper carried only a school picture of the boy because he had never been photographed alone. A cushion that the innkeeper's mother was using as a backrest fell from the armchair onto the floor. Bloch picked it up and went out with the paper. He saw the inn's copy lying on the card table; the tourists had left by now. The paper—it was the weekend edition—was so thick that it did not fit into the rack.

When a car drove past him, he stupidly—for it was quite bright out—wondered why its headlights were turned off. Nothing in particular happened. He saw the boxes of apples being poured into sacks in the orchards. A bicycle that passed him slid back and forth in the mud. He saw two farmers shaking hands in a store doorway; their hands were so dry that he heard them rustling. Tractors had left muddy tracks from the dirt paths on the asphalt. He saw an old woman bent over in front of a display window, a finger to her lips. The parking spaces in front of the stores were emptying; the customers who were still arriving came in through the back doors. "Suds" "poured" "over" "the doorsteps." Featherbeds "were lying" "behind" "the windowpanes." The blackboards listing prices were being carried back into the stores. "The chickens" "pecked at" "grapes that had been dropped." The turkeys squatted heavily in the wire cages in the orchards. The salesgirls stood outside the doors and put their hands on their hips. The owner stood inside the dark store, absolutely still behind the scale. "Lumps of yeast" "lay" "on the counter."

Bloch stood against the wall of a house. There was an odd sound when a casement window that was ajar next to him opened all the way. He had walked on immediately.

He stopped in front of a brand-new building that was still unoccupied but already had glass in its windows. The rooms were so empty that the landscape on the other side could be seen through the windows. Bloch felt as though he had built the house himself. He himself had installed the wall outlets and even set in the windowpanes. The crowbar, the sandwich wrapping, and the plastic food container had also been put on the windowsill by him.

He took a second look: no, the light switches stayed light switches, and the lawn chairs in the landscape behind the house stayed lawn chairs.

He walked on because—

Did he have to give a reason for walking, so that—?

What did he have in mind when—? Did he have to justify the "when" by—? Did this go on until—? Had he reached the point where—?

Why did anything have to be inferred from the fact that he was walking here? Did he have to give a reason for stopping, here? Why did he have to have something in mind when he walked past a swimming pool?

These "so thats," "becauses," and "whens" were like regulations; he decided to avoid them in order not to—

It was as if a window that was slightly ajar was gently opened beside him. Everything thinkable, everything visible, was occupied. It was not a scream that startled him but a sentence upside down at the end of a series of normal sentences. Everything seemed to have been newly named.

The stores were already closed. The window displays, now that nobody was walking back and forth in front of them anymore, looked too full. Not a single spot was without at least a stack of cans on it. A half-torn receipt hung out of the cash register. The stores were so stuffed that. . . .

"The stores were so stuffed that you couldn't point to anything anymore because. . . ." The stores were so stuffed that you couldn't point to anything anymore because the individual items hid each other. The parking spaces were now completely empty except for the bicycles of the salesgirls.

After lunch Bloch went to the athletic field. Even from far away he heard the spectators yelling. When he got there, the reserves were still playing a pre-game match. He sat down on a bench at the sidelines and read the paper as far as the supplements. He heard a sound as if a chunk of meat had fallen on a stone floor; he looked up and saw that the wet heavy ball had smacked off a player's head.

He got up and walked away. When he came back, the main match had already started. The benches were filled, and he walked beside the playing field to the space behind the goal. He did not want to stand too close behind the goal, and he climbed up the bank to the street. He walked along the street as far as the corner flag. It seemed to him that a button was coming off his jacket and popping on the street; he picked up the button and put it in his pocket.

He started talking to some man who was standing next to him. He asked which teams were playing and about their standings in the league. They shouldn't play the ball so high in a strong wind like this, he said.

He noticed that the man next to him had buckles on his shoes. I don't know either, the man answered. "I'm a salesman, and I'm here for only a few days."

"The men are yelling much too much," Bloch said. "A good game goes very quietly."

"There's no coach to tell them what to do from the sidelines," answered the salesman. It seemed to Bloch as though they were talking to each other for the benefit of some third party.

"On a small field like this you have to decide very quickly when to pass," he said.

He heard a slap as if the ball had hit a goal post. Bloch told about how he had once played against a team whose players were all barefoot; every time they kicked the ball, the slapping sound had gone right through him.

"In the stadium I once saw a player break his leg," the salesman said. "You could hear the cracking sound all the way up in the top rows."

Bloch saw the other spectators around him talking to each other. He did not watch the one who happened to be speaking but always watched the one who was listening. He asked the salesman whether he had ever tried to look away from the forward at the beginning of a rush and, instead, to look at the goalie the forwards were rushing toward.

"It's very difficult to take your eyes off the forwards and the ball and watch the goalie," Bloch said. "You have to tear yourself away from the ball; it's a completely unnatural thing to do." Instead of seeing the ball, you saw how the goalkeeper ran back and forth with his hands on his thighs, how he bent to the left and right and screamed at his defense. "Usually you don't notice him until the ball has been shot at the goal."

They walked along the sideline together. Bloch heard panting as though a linesman were running past them. "It's a strange sight to watch the goalie running back and forth like that, without the ball but expecting it," he said.

He couldn't watch that way for very long, answered the salesman; you couldn't help but look back at the forwards. If you looked at the goalkeeper, it seemed as if you had to look cross-eyed. It was like seeing somebody walk toward the door and instead of looking at the man, you looked at the doorknob. It made your head hurt, and you couldn't breathe properly anymore.

"You get used to it.," said Bloch, "but it's ridiculous."

A penalty kick was called. All the spectators rushed behind the goal.

"The goalkeeper is trying to figure out which corner the kicker will send the ball into," Bloch said. "If he knows the kicker, he knows which corner he usually goes for. But maybe the kicker is also counting on the goalie's figuring this out. So the goalie goes on figuring that just today the ball might go into the other corner. But what if the kicker follows the goalkeeper's thinking and plans to shoot into the usual corner after all? And so on. and so on."

Bloch saw how all the players gradually cleared the penalty area. The penalty kicker adjusted the ball. Then he too backed out of the penalty area.

"When the kicker starts his run, the goalkeeper unconsciously shows with his body which way he'll throw himself even before the ball is kicked, and the kicker can simply kick in the other direction," Bloch said. "The goalie might just as well try to pry open a door with a piece of straw."

The kicker suddenly started his run. The goalkeeper, who was wearing a bright yellow jersey, stood absolutely still, and the penalty kicker shot the ball into his hands.

Translated by Michael Roloff

Herbert Heckmann

UBUville—The City of the Grand Egg

My hometown is UBUville. It is located in a nameless country, because our government still can't decide upon a name. They do not like to commit themselves when confronted with so many alternatives. Our neighbors think we are backward; perhaps, if I may say so, because we deplore the wearing of clothes. Even tourists must comply at the border with our regulation on nudity. The Great UBU, whose works we study most carefully and exactly in order to enrich our lives, states at one point, "He who clothes himself has something to conceal."

In our country we drill for oil, but with little success. However, we do have peanuts here, and graves from the Stone Age. UBUville is a rapidly growing town of 50,000 inhabitants, most of whom live in egg-shaped houses. From a distance the town looks like the egg depot of a gigantic bird. The Great UBU considers the egg archetypical of life itself. In our language it is called "uch." "Uch" is also the word for thought or idea, when you pronounce it somewhat more gutturally.

The seat of the government, which we call the Council of the Great Egg, is in UBUville. Every year the Great Egg is elected, generally a small child just learning to talk and think, and an old man who also can barely think and talk. These two then brood over the future of our country. The Little Egg is the parliament, which determines whether or not the decisions of the Big Egg are to be taken seriously. On the other hand, everyone is free to do as he pleases. Every year on the fourth of April we celebrate our one and only state holiday with a huge egg dance.

The Great UBU, whose monument, by the way, can be seen in UBUville—a ten-foot-high egg with human features radiating deep understanding—shapes our lives with his teachings. His first axiom is, "Truth through Error; Error through Truth." Once a week everyone must laugh at himself; the rest of the time one may laugh at others. There is, in fact, a lot of laughing here, an observation I made only after visiting other lands. Our language requires the use of muscles with which one laughs much more than those for frowning, so that the mastery of it is well-nigh impossible for persons of a melancholy disposition.

Our main dish is the soft-boiled egg. We have approximately seven hundred egg recipes, from the raw state to its highest refinement through fire. The presence of egg-laying hens in our society is thus quite comprehensible. Sometimes, though, it gets to the point where we can't hear ourselves think for all the cackling. The Great UBU is probably exaggerating when he boldly states that cackling is a kind of hymn to life. On this one point, at least, I disagree with him,

In contrast to our neighbors, we have a three-day week—relaxation comes right after exertion. The Great UBU says, "Work should be recuperation from recuperation—and recuperation, recuperation from work." Moreover, he who wishes to display affection and love in any manner may stop working. Such intermissions are even encouraged.

I place these indiscriminate comments at the beginning of my travelogue so as to render my mode of behavior in Germany more comprehensible. I am especially indebted to Herbert Heckmann, who was quite helpful with the review of my notes. Of course, I must admit—and I do not wish to wear my heart upon my sleeve, as the Germans say—that he helped a great deal with the editing, because the Germans prefer only the essentials. We, on the other hand, love details. As the Great UBU says, "Truth is the juiciest part of the whole thing." (By the way, I intend to use the language which is customary in Germany, the one which the great DUDEN requires of his subjects.)

March 14

About ten o'clock our time the boss called me in and disclosed that I was to fly to Germany on business, in order to ascertain whether there was any interest there in our oil. I was alarmed, for I had only a very vague conception of Germany, The Great UBU had been through Germany once and had shouted from the Rhine, "Oh, you Germans, you are always looking through binoculars, so that everything becomes extraordinarily large." On another occasion, he deplored their obsession for titles. Even he himself felt compelled to make his appearance with a title. He called himself "Omahu-UBU," which means, roughly, "Joyful Event UBU."

March 15

Great difficulties mastering the German language. For one thing, because the German teacher whom I requested fainted at the border, when she learned about our custom of living without clothing. Only after unnerving arts of persuasion did she agree "to decode the secret of the German language," as she described it.

"If I were naked," she screamed hysterically, "you'd just start getting ideas."

"If it suits you," I replied soothingly, "I'd just like to learn German."

On another occasion it turned out that Fräulein Grabert had very little command of our language. There is a big difference between UBURU, as our language is called, and German. We have almost no abstractions whatsoever, and our vocabulary for sense perceptions is at least three times larger than the equivalent in German, Three years ago an Englishman attempted to compile a grammar of UBURU. Our students Of UBUology still consider it a masterpiece of involuntary humor. When the Englishman found out about it, he departed this life. Our language is not spoken, but sung, in which respect Fräulein Grabert wasn't altogether talented. The nakedness also confused her. She was ashamed of inadmissible thoughts. Finally, I could say some polite phrases, after a fashion, count to one hundred, ask the time of day, comment on the weather, and sing "Am Brunnen vor dem Tore."

But these were not the only preparations I was to undertake: I also had to adjust to the awkward business of wearing clothes. I wired my measurements to a tailor in London and, draped with fine woolens, for the first time in my life I felt ashamed as I strolled back and forth in my room. I couldn't imagine how I was to distinguish one clothed person from another. Suddenly, I was one among many.

September 25

Departed UBUville for Cairo by plane. My friends brought me a case of eggs. They were afraid I might starve in Germany. They also mistrusted German hens. I felt quite silly, standing there in my suit, and began to perspire. From a bird's-eye-view, my homeland really looks very ordinary.

During the flight I attempted to read several German newspapers that I had brought along in order to facilitate the transition to a new language. As the Great UBU is my witness! I understood not one single word.

Boarded a German plane in Cairo. The stewardesses fed me all the way to Frankfurt. They had the curious notion that one can overcome fear by consuming incredible quantities of food. My stomach was upset several times. I also got to rehearse my first courtesies and learned how to listen intently without understanding a word. One particular stewardess caught my eye, and I casually attempted to communicate this attraction to her. Somehow I must have used a wrong word, for she turned red even to the roots of her hair and replied, "I am on duty." The word "duty" seems to bestow strength, when one says it.

It was raining in Frankfurt. The clouds over Germany are somewhat grayer than at home. Herr Ocker, whom I had informed of my arrival, ran toward me with an umbrella, said he was Herr Ocker, and shook my hand vigorously. Fräulein Grabert hadn't told me about this duel one must endure in Germany upon meeting a person. When at last Herr Ocker lay flat on the ground, several men in elegant suits grabbed me by the arms and demanded my passport. Herr Ocker soon calmed down, beat the dust from his coat, and would have offered me his hand a second time, had he not noticed my horror. My case of eggs elicited great mistrust at customs.

"What's in the crate?" they asked me.

"Eggs," I replied, in conformity with the truth.

"Anyone can say that," said a customs official who, in addition to his elegant suit, was wearing a hatlike headgear on which he placed his hand at particular intervals. Why, I do not know. He took an egg, cracked it on the side of the crate, and behold—it was an egg.

"You could have told me that in the first place," he growled and permitted me to pass. I was in Germany and I took a deep breath. It smelled like damp clothing. The people were in a hurry and they seemed to be very proud of the little suitcases they were carrying around with them. They behaved as though they had nothing to do with one another.

Herr Ocker carried the egg crate along behind me. I had put him into a good humor with the golden egg, which we present to persons whose merit we anticipate. I was driven in a taxi to the hotel in which a room with a private bath and a view of a construction site had been reserved for me. Herr Ocker said good-bye at some distance and suggested that I rest up a bit from the trip. He would pick me up the next morning in time for a conference, he said, and made a bow this time, which I attempted to imitate as best I could. In this country courtesy consists of conveying for a moment the impression that one is meeting his fellow man on the same level.

Mostly out of curiosity I pressed a button on the wall, and a man dressed in white appeared. He reminded me of a dove.

"I'm hungry," I said, in order to say something to which I could in turn respond, and pointed to the case of eggs. "Would you kindly cook some eggs for me?"

"Sir," he replied, smiling discreetly, "that will not be necessary. We have plenty of eggs."

"Well, then, may I offer them to you as a gift? They're eggs from my country." He hesitated, said something I did not understand, lifted the crate to his shoulder, and departed.

I just had time to undress, when he reappeared with a tray upon which there stood the three egg cups.

"Excuse me," he stammered, upon seeing me naked. He stared where I wasn't, namely at the ceiling, and tripped over a chair. The eggs rolled across the rug and disappeared under the bed.

"I'll take care of it," he stuttered. To come right to the point (Herbert Heckmann thought this incident unimportant): He brought me three new eggs which, as I was eating them, brought forth a feeling of nostalgia.

"No one egg is like any other," said the Great UBU.

September 26

Slept quite restlessly. Depressed. The sound of running water next door. Gargling. Then, in the restaurant, kidney-shaped ornaments and pictures of amoebae. People reading newspapers with disinterested expressions. Shuffling of papers and yawning. Well-groomed heads. Self-assured obesity. Weary faces, surly hands that beheaded the eggs with a table knife. Women in dresses who sit up straight. Their lips color the cup's rim with lipstick. Some stare crossly at their husbands, who appear to have enjoyed a good night's sleep. The waiters dance in ill-humor. The look of importance that is not destroyed even by a smile is remarkable. When someone laughs, then and only then, because he can think of nothing better. They laugh during the pauses. I forgot to eat my egg for watching. I should have forgotten it altogether. It tasted like an exhausted rooster.

Read in the Great UBU. Underlined the sentence, "When confronting the question as to whether the hen or the egg came first, the rooster crowed." Precisely. (Here Herbert Heckmann deleted something. I mention it only because it annoys me.) Herr Ocker arrived at ten o'clock on the dot and paid me his compliments. I asked him, "Did you sleep well?"

"Right now I'm a grass-widower," he replied. Suddenly the expression on his face changed. He cleared his throat, in order to outline in serious terms our plan for the day. (Clearing the throat has several different meanings in Germany, at which, unfortunately, I can only guess.)

"How can you be so sure that all of this is going to happen?" I asked, noticing that I had insulted him with the question. Where I come from, we believe in the self-determination of things. Decisions have to mellow for some time. "One should not meddle clumsily with the future through hasty planning," said the Great UBU.

"One has to proceed systematically," replied Herr Ocker, almost defensively, as he straightened his tie. "Otherwise, how would we ever get anything done?"

"You mean there is a plan for everything?" I insisted.

"In all modesty, I assure you there is," he replied. I didn't know exactly what Herr Ocker was up to, though I suspected that what he called "plan" was nothing more than the best opportunity to cheat me. I restrained myself completely and quietly studied his broad face, which was confined to practiced gravity. The fleshy parts were flabby and tired, nose sagging, and the mouth sullen from having spoken so many important words. It would take an onion to make Herr Ocker cry. Then he began to explain lots of things to me. He made use of his hand, which had been strengthened by pounding on the table, and glanced occasionally at his watch, as though it were his beloved. I reveled in sweet incomprehension, laughed when it seemed appropriate, and, finally, I said, "We shall see." (That, by the way, is the figure of speech which we often employ in UBURU, especially after we have commented on things we know absolutely nothing about.)

My first conversations with German businessmen were during a luncheon in front of toothpicks and flowers. I suffered from the absence of eggs. I spoke memorized sentences about my homeland and from sheer enthusiasm I broke into song, as is customary in my mother tongue.

"How do you like Germany?" inquired a Herr Doktor, a name that one hears frequently in Germany.

"I can't really say much yet," I replied to disappointed faces.

"We're getting ahead of things again. We're meddling again."

"Do you know UBU?" I asked across the table, in search of a topic I knew more about, as I played with the toothpicks.

"UBU! Of course, completely out of date. Now we have the pill."

"I mean another UBU," I replied.

"Of course, how could I forget. You mean UBU, the president of your country."

"We don't have a president."

"Then I was misinformed."

"UBU is our great teacher."

"But not one of these pocket-sized Marxists."

Herr Doktor always knew just what I didn't want to say, so he could talk about what he knew. He asked me questions that he was only too happy to answer himself. When he took issue with something, it always seemed like sublimated murder.

My head was buzzing, and in desperation I said "Please!" in hopes that they would leave me in peace. I also began to mix up my hosts in their well-pressed suits, and with golden rings on their fingers they looked so similar that I proceeded to address them all as Herr Doktor, which they received with pricked-up ears (a pricked-up ear is our designation for enthusiasm).

After the meal, jokes were told, apparently a form of entertainment in which one elicits laughter from the listeners with little stories, by being the first one to laugh. I laughed the way we do back home, with stomach in and head thrown back, but not at the jokes, which I didn't understand. Instead, I laughed at the laughing of the story-tellers, which apparently had nothing to do with the humor of the joke. If one of them momentarily left the table, those remaining moved closer together and talked about the absentee, which amused them even more than the jokes. I recalled a comment from the Great UBU: "The value of one's fellow man depends upon how much one can talk about him."

When they all had exhausted themselves, they shook hands and said they had to hurry along. I stayed on with several gentlemen in order to talk business. Herr Ocker sat next to me, fishing papers out of his briefcase, shoving them under my nose, and saying: "I've already drawn everything up."

The briefcase must be invaluable to Germans. One could almost consider it the national costume. Wherever you see a briefcase, there is also a German who appears to be carrying his life's work around in it. Herr Ocker led the discussion. Every time he spoke of logic, I paid very close attention, for I had discovered that he employed the word "logic" only when he was unable to convince me in any other way.

In the Great UBU, it is said that with strangers one should pay attention not so much to what they say as to what they do not say. I remained silent and finally said, "We shall see."

Herr Ocker shut his briefcase disapprovingly. Evening in the theater. Herr Ocker smelled like peppermint. The women in expensive gowns, the men with sharp creases in their trousers. A piece was performed which, as well as I could judge, attacked German society fiercely but very clumsily. Strangely enough, the critique was enthusiastically received by the audience. Were they blind? Or do they consider the dramatist a paid, and therefore innocuous, fool, about whose criticism one laughs but does not reflect? In this country, knowledge of oneself seems to be a social game in which one appears in one's best suit and sucks peppermint.

The actors strained every nerve and screamed as though harpooned. But the best actors were the spectators themselves. They behaved as though they were thoroughly enjoying the critique aimed at them, and hid their eyes behind opera glasses. The applause at the end strained me a great deal. I tried to outdo Herr Ocker, who was working at it like a madman. The whole affair resembled a military maneuver, and I could almost see gunpowder smoke above their flushed reddened heads.

In the lamentations of the Great UBU one finds the thesis: "Woe unto the country that hushes her writers with applause."

As we were leaving, Herr Ocker told me, "Above all, there must be culture. It elevates us to the pinnacles of humanity." (Herbert Heckmann, whom I consulted about the meaning of the statement, unfortunately was not able to interpret it for me.) Though I was very tired, I accompanied Herr Ocker, who wanted to teach me even more about German life, to an after-hours bar.

When does it all cease to be theater and begin to be life? Or at what point does it become theater and cease to be life?

The Great UBU writes: "In the beginning there was sublime boredom; then mankind invented entertainment, and it wasn't long before sublime boredom prevailed once more." Herr Ocker ordered a bottle of champagne, nevertheless. I watched him watch girls, who were watching him. Some other girls were stripping to very loud music on the stage. In this country, for reasons unknown to me, nudity must be something so rare that one needs music with it. Apparently, the play that I saw in the dimly lighted room was by an inexperienced dramatist, for the scenes recurred too often.

After the third bottle of champagne, Herr Ocker began to talk about his past. At first it was not at all clear to me what had led him to these confessions. "No one who has not been through it knows how it really was. My very existence was at stake."

I clapped my hands with fear. Still not sure what he was leading up to, I thought of a family tragedy and cleared my throat sympathetically. Soon, however, I knew what Herr Ocker meant: Herr Ocker wanted to vindicate himself, but, as is customary with Germans—I permit myself this generalization—they love generalities. Herr Ocker was no longer Herr Ocker, Herr Ocker was a case study. Herr Ocker had been deceived.

"After all, we're only human, and every man must see to it that the home fires keep burning."

Did I really know what Herr Ocker was talking about? I took heart and asked, "About what do I have the honor of hearing you speak?" (I love to formulate questions in German. They are the next best thing to singing.)

"I am speaking of the Hitler era," replied Herr Ocker, ashamed to have been so frank. A dark-haired girl on the stage was doing a hand-stand. Herr Ocker observed her in a state of melancholy. I remained silent.

I have engaged in similar conversations with other Germans: that is, I have listened to them. Germans live with a past that was really quite different. Cloak-and-dagger stories are among the most beloved children's books. Only on the rarest occasions can you find them living in the present, and then only in the presence of grand stories about their history. But let us return to Herr Ocker. I shall never forget how he paid the check.

"Charge it," he said proudly. (Charging, as Herbert Heckmann explained, is an opportunity to deduct personal entertainment expenses for the benefit of the community.)

September 28

I requested a day off in order to look around some by myself. I was completely exhausted and suffered from gas pains. German cuisine is torturing me. I regretted having given away the eggs from home. Read in the Great UBU, "A sound stomach makes a strong mind."

At the hotel I rented a bicycle, the chief means of transportation at home, because the noise from automobiles encroaches upon the hens' egg-laying and poisons one's mind. I am revived once I am on a bicycle seat. The upper part of my body stretched over the handlebars, feet pressed against the pedals, with trembling calves I rush over the streets. The wind whistles in my ears and the tires sing.

"Only he who kicks about can liberate himself from diapers," says the Great UBU.

In anticipation of the pedaling, unfortunately, I forgot to get dressed and left my room in customary nudity. I walked about fifteen paces, when a woman caught sight of me, screamed, and fainted. For the Great UBU's sake! The hotel was transformed into a mob scene, and the German language into a thunderous rumbling. They threw a raincoat over me and led me away. At headquarters, which in Germany is always nearer than you think, I was required to state my name and, as briefly as possible, explain why I had approached the woman.

"I was going to ride my bicycle," I replied quite truthfully.

"You must be drunk."

"Why no, not at all," I countered emphatically.

"Let's start over from the beginning." The elegantly dressed policeman rubbed his forehead in hopes that in this manner he could illustrate his approach to the problem. "You approached the lady at 10:11 A.M."

"I had to approach her, because she was standing right in the middle of the hallway I was hurrying down. As I just mentioned, I wanted to go for a ride on my bike."

"In the nude?"

"Where I come from, we detest the wearing of clothes."

"Must be *some* place. May I see your passport?"

I couldn't help laughing, and replied: "Let's see you search the pockets of a naked man."

"Do you realize to whom you are speaking?" he asked abruptly.

"A human being, if I'm not mistaken."

"An officer of the law, to be quite specific. And I will not tolerate your attitude. Now, let's start from the beginning."

I hate repetition. So this time I told a different tale, and when I noticed the degree of malicious pleasure with which the policeman was listening to me, I decided to tell yet another version of the event.

"What then is the real truth?" he shrieked.

I almost quoted the Great UBU, who said, "Truth is a lie's stroke of luck," but I preferred to remain silent, and watched the second-hand on the wall clock. I had discovered that Germans love to look at clocks, and now I hoped that imitation would begin to alter my miserable situation. It didn't help much. Without a passport I was a clean slate, upon which any well-dressed policeman could write whatever he wished. In spite of my heated protest, I was led to a room that had a single window with bars. Not bad, I thought, at least I'll be safe from disagreeable callers. Suddenly the door for which I had received no key was flung open. With a very serious expression on his face Herr Ocker appeared and handed me some clothes, with which I departed from the police, a free man. He was quite upset, and insisted that I extend an apology to the woman. I attended to the matter by bringing the customary golden egg to her room. I stayed so long, that I never did get back to the bicycle ride. (Herbert Heckmann advised me to omit this most comical passage, as such scenes are already all-too-common and graphically portrayed in contemporary literature. So anyone who isn't sufficiently familiar with these things can simply look them up.)

As usual, on this day I saw nothing more of Germany than a hotel room.

This event had stirred up considerable dust. A reporter came up to my room and began to pump me.

"What do you intend to accomplish with your nudity?"

"Immediacy."

"Have you no shame?"

"Sure, but only when I have done something stupid."

"What do you think of Germany?"

"It is a very industrious and serious-minded country."

"Wherein do you see the future of your own country?"

"In bicycling."

The reporter looked at me helplessly and left. I read in the Great UBU.

October 1

Finally on the bicycle. Herr Ocker had definitely advised against it and added that in the first place it was too dangerous; secondly, it did not become a person of status. He wanted to drive me around a bit in the area. But when he saw that I was determined to ride the bike, he wished me well and regretted that he could not kick around with me. When he was a boy, he too had ridden a bicycle and had once pedaled through the countryside.

"We Germans have an intimate relationship with Nature," he said sadly. I attempted to envision Herr Ocker as a child of Nature, with a dirty nose and red cheeks. Instead I saw only a well-groomed gentleman tugging away at his briefcase. Herr Ocker waved to me, and as I turned the next corner I knew exactly what he would say about me: "That man is really out of his mind."

Unfortunately, my ride ended very soon, because I had forgotten to acquaint myself with the street signs in Germany, which lead you where you don't want to go.

An impressively dressed policeman halted me and inquired, "Apparently you can't read."

I contradicted him in all modesty, but it didn't help things. I really should have known that policemen are always right. Paid a fine and, intimidated, I pushed my bicycle back to the hotel.

My attempt to reach the Rhine by train was more successful. Everyone had recommended this trip to me. The Rhine, they said, is the very heart of Germany and is sung about in many a song.

In my compartment there sat a very fat man, who was wearing suspenders in addition to a belt, and he was breathing very heavily while reading a newspaper primarily composed of headlines. When he noted that I too was reading his paper, he grumbled, "This is my newspaper."

"Of course, whatever you say," I replied, and glanced out of the window.

"It's my newspaper and mine alone, and if you want to read one, then you can buy one for yourself. These foreigners are always so nosy." He stared at me hostilely. I didn't know where else I was supposed to look. The newspaper crackled seductively under my nose, and again I began to read the headlines. Enraged, the fat man jumped up, folded the newspaper, and left the compartment, cursing foreigners from whom there was no escape.

"They'll take over the government next. Things were definitely better back then."

This was not the first time I had heard the expression "back then." In German it has a very solemn ring to it.

Mountainous vineyards swept by, small train stations and station signs. I saw many construction sites. The Great UBU phrased it accurately: "Whosoever builds much, leaves many rocks behind." The Germans must abhor vacuums. Any time a speck of Nature becomes visible, they quickly cover it up with houses.

Finally on the Rhine. I rode a steamer and watched the dirty water flow by. A teacher was explaining rock formations of the bordering hills to his pupils. I listened with one ear. A young man in a corduroy sport jacket was kneading a girl's hand. The teacher proceeded to history. The young man said, "Am I glad I'm not in school anymore. We had to know the tributaries of the Rhine and the dates of the emperors and kings."

The girl stood on tiptoes.

"But you don't know when I was born."

The teacher was talking about some authors. One little boy asked softly, "Is Loreley spelled with or without an h?"

"With two *l*'s," whispered his neighbor. The young man pretended to throw the girl's purse into the Rhine. The girl was clinging to his arm. In this manner they got closer. The teacher said, "I want a report on our excursion from each of you, but no copying." A woman in a colorful peasant costume was selling souvenirs and peanuts. The castles to the right and left were almost all ruins. They were also to be seen on the postcards he was selling.

I mustered the courage to ask my neighbor, a thin, disgruntled-looking man who was looking on and feeding paper to the fish, "Excuse me, but why don't they restore the demolished castles?"

He stared at me almost enraged. "I won't take offense at this question, as you are obviously a foreigner. They are ruins and ruins are part of the grandiose trappings of the Rhine. They are symbols of the grandeur of the past."

I glanced to the right and the left. There was that troublesome word *symbol* again. The Germans appear to be living on symbols. That's probably why they are so well-nourished. When they eat an apple, they aren't just eating an apple, but also that which the apple signifies.

I went ashore at Rüdesheim. The school class left the ship two-by-two. Since it was raining heavily, I fled to a tavern, where a frolicsome crowd greeted me loudly. I had to sit next to a young man who was so loud that I was able to understand only the echo of his words. They were singing songs—and their songs never seemed to end. They were about love, parting, wine, about youth, and once again about love and Father Rhine and the hazelnut and the Westerwald—and once a song finally ended, they raised their glasses, looked at each other very earnestly, as though they were about to come to blows, drank, raised their glasses again, clicked their tongues, and began a new song.

One-two-three! They sang, squalling with fat cheeks and trembling Adam's apple, and slapped themselves and those next to them on the thigh, laughed, snorted, groaned, and panted. I feared the worst and started to leave.

"Hold on!" screamed one of them. "No party poopers around here."

And once again I was sitting there, drinking to the health of unknown personages while destroying my own. With a wild lunge I jumped up and ran out of the place. I can't say for sure whether the wine drinkers then killed each other off. I never saw them again.

Too tired tonight for the Great UBU.

October 2–5

Spent some time with Herr Ocker, who showed me the sights around Frankfurt. I learned the song, "Ach du lieber Augustine." Herr Ocker was very exuberant and told me all about his first love affair. Whenever he sang, he closed his eyes.

Wearisome attendance at cultural events. Observed Germans listening to music. They love to wag their heads, each a conductor in his own right. Under the influence of culture, great severity steals into their faces and resides there for some time. The Great UBU says, "Culture is the ability of mankind to look down upon itself." The Germans look up to themselves through culture.

Herr Ocker pressed for the signed contract. He was still carrying the briefcase along behind me.

October 6

In Germany there are lots of dogs. Their owners walk them in the mornings and at night. When one steps in dog's dung, they say, it's a sign of good luck. I must be the luckiest person on earth. During my walks through the city I was occasionally approached by women who asked me, "Got some time for me?" I didn't know exactly how to respond. At the next opportunity I asked Herr Ocker, who did know. Now I understand the expression I hear so often, "I don't have time."

First ride on the streetcar. I'm still surprised that I ever got in and out again alive. The Germans always want to be first: in science, on the street, and in the streetcar. They have rather well-developed elbows and knees. The thesis of the Great UBU suits them: "The straightest path goes up the wall."

Spent the evening with Herr Ocker at a lecture by a German professor of philosophy, whose name I have heard time and again. The lecture room was packed. Students were standing in the aisles. The highbrows sat there wearing glasses. Women were putting on rouge. When the professor mounted the podium, a small birdlike man who, it was apparent, thought about life rather than living it, a paralyzing silence descended. A young girl was sharpening her pencil.

Then there resounded a sublime sing-song, which is widespread in Germany in the name of philosophy. I heard the word EXISTENCE and the word ESSENCE and the word VOID whirl about in confusion, as far as German grammar would allow. I heard the word BASIS and everything was underscored by self-conscious coughing and clearing of the throat. There was hissing and rumbling, an aria consisting of dissonant consonants and lengthened vowels. His voice hopped from word to word, slurred in the lows and screeched in the highs, and the audience nodded approving heads. The singsong became more and more hortatory and, with flapping gestures, the birdlike little man seemed to be taking off from the earth— into a realm in which existence, not life, prevailed, freedom with no one free, love and no lovers, a realm in which concepts alone flew around and were captured by bloodless creatures with butterfly nets. Once the professor had concluded his singsong, he gave us his profile, whereupon an almost enchanted silence grew loud. I applauded first, in order to get my feet back on the ground.

The Great UBU once noted, "Contemplation is supposed to remain in one's head, not dissipate like bubbles in the sky. Compose thyself, many have been lost before."

Herr Ocker was quite impressed by my applause. "I see," he said, weighing each word, "you have peered into the heart of Germany."

"Yes," I replied calmly, longing for the cheerful clucking of the hens back home, for soft-boiled eggs, and a bicycle.

October 9

Nothing special. Walked aimlessly in the streets. The creases in my suit lost their sharpness. I bought myself a hat, so that I could remove it for pretty ladies. I aroused the mistrust of elegantly dressed policemen because I was talking to myself in my mother tongue.

Spent the evening at Herr Ocker's home. His wife received me with many apologies. I met their son, who was suffering from being so much like his father. Tense atmosphere. We ate for want of something to talk about. After dinner I drank some liqueur. Herr Ocker casually asked me whether I had decided to sign the trade agreement. I promised to do so the following day. Then Herr Ocker became very relaxed and related part of his life's story.

"You're exaggerating, Carl," his wife cried out.

"It's all a big lie," said the son contemptuously, leaving Herr Ocker all alone with his boasting.

I mentioned the thesis of the Great UBU, "Sometimes it would be better, if the sons would beget the fathers."

"Some father you'd bring forth," gloated Herr Ocker to his son.

As I was taking my leave, I resolved to translate the Great UBU into German, but immediately thereafter abandoned the resolution. The Germans would only write thick books about UBU. They can't contain themselves. They are compelled to classify everything. They would make an anthology out of the Great UBU. I shuddered at the thought and didn't sleep at all well.

October 12

A large dinner, after business was concluded. Several speeches were about me and the negotiation that joins two peoples. I received a barometer and a calendar for the next century. For the last time in Germany I mentioned the Great UBU. They laughed, when I accidentally sat down between two chairs.

October 14

In the air again. I could hardly wait to get home again. Below me lay Germany.

Most of all I would like to have shed my second skin, which they call clothing. I would like to have sung, but I know how difficult it is to be onself in the temperate zones. They have a law against your every wish.

More later from UBUville.

Translated by Thomas I. Bacon

Helmut Heißenbüttel

Texts

SCHEMATIC DEVELOPMENT OF TRADITION

those who were not there were more numerous than those who
were there always those who are not there are more numerous than
those who are there

so those who were there thought of those who were not there
and so always those who are there think of those who are not there
and all that those who are there do and resolve to do occurs in
memory of those who are not there

did those who were not there also think of those who were there

those who were there did not know those who are there do not
know and those who will be there will not know those who are
there do not know whether one can speak of memory with regard
to those who are not there those who were not there were there at
one time

even when they had been there too those who had not been there
had been more numerous than those who had been there those
who had been there had been fewer than those who had not been
there as long as those who had been there could remember

but if those who were not there have always been more numerous than those who were there and if always fewer have been there
than were not there and if all that those who have been there
are there and will be there do and resolve to do occurs in memory
of those who are not there then those who are there are always
only there in the name of those who are not there only in the name
of those who were not there those who were there were really there

to be really there means to be there in the name of those who
are not there means to be there in the name of those who are more
numerous and always would be more numerous immeasurably
more to be there no longer and be more numerous means the crite-
rion for being there to have been there is that which determines
always has determined and always will determine being there

and those who had been there became those who were no longer
there and those who are there will become those who will no longer
be there and of that which they did or resolved to do in memory
of those who were not there they took something with them and
of that which they now do or resolve to do in memory of those
who are no longer there they will have taken something with them
when they will no longer be there and so those who are no longer
there have already taken with them an immeasurable amount of
that which those who were there did and resolved to do in memory
of those who were not there an immeasurable amount is in the
possession of those who are not there and it will continue to be
more the fact that they have it in their possession and that this
possession continues to grow is that which in regard to those who
are not there one could call the memory of those who are there

because those who are no longer there have once been there

not to be there is something of which one thinks in being there
and to be there is consumption of the possession still being accumulated by those who are not there

in the name of those who are no longer there and are more
numerous because those who are no longer there and are more
numerous have a name and we are there in that name

SOCIAL CONTRACT

one is with another and assuming they are the only ones that exist
the one is like this and the other is not like this either the one
becomes half not like this and the other becomes half like this or
they try to separate or the one kills the other or the other kills the
one and the matter is settled

but now there are three and still assuming they are the only ones
that exist the one is like this the second also the third is not like
this or the one is like this the second and third are not like this etc.
then either one becomes half like this and the other two half not

like this or vice versa or all of them become neither like this nor not like this etc. or they try to separate or two kills the third or one kills the other two and at once the matter is settled

but now there are four or five or fifty or a thousand or a hundred thousand or a million or two billion and a half and each is different from the other many of them not very different but all a bit many too are a bit alike of course and because again and again there are a few a bit alike they get on all right and there isn't violence and murder all the time till there is no one left but those who get on because of one bit of likeness between them are now a bit more different from those who get on because of another bit of likeness between them

and if now they don't find something a bit alike in those others things go wrong and there are violence and murder attack and defense blitzkrieg chain bombing invasion and capitulation and still the matter is not settled

but now at last many more who are a bit alike and get on find a bit of likeness in the many others who are a bit alike and many others again find many others again and now on the one hand there are those first many more who are a bit alike and then a bit of a bit more and finally still a bit of a bit more and get on and on the other hand there are those other many more who are a bit alike in another way and then another bit of a bit more and finally still another bit of a bit more and get on and assuming they are the only ones that exist two billion and a half at a rough estimate they now form two blocks and cannot get on even if all of them

It is completely light now in the shop. The light fills the room all the way to the back door. Where Moses leans against the wall, it is completely white, so that one thinks that he becomes more and more a part of the wall. Including every word that he speaks. "I know," Moses says, "you are quite right. I'm going to feel the wrath of my God."

FINAL SOLUTION

they just happened to think that up one day
who happened to think that up one day
that just happened to occur to them
to whom did that just happen to occur

to one of them that just happened to occur
one of them just happened to think that up one day
one of them just happened to just think that up one day
or perhaps more than one of them thought it up at the same time
perhaps that occurred to more than one of them together
and how did they carry out the thing that occurred to them

if one wants to get anything done one has to be for something and
not just something one happens to think up but something for
which one can be or at least something for which a lot of people
would like to be or at least something one imagines a lot of people
would like to be for
    and they just happened to think that up one day
    they thought that up and then they hit on the idea when they
wanted to start doing something but what they hit on was not
something one can be for but something one can be against or
better something one can bring most people around to being
against for when one can bring most people around to being
against something one needn't be so precise anymore about the
thing one can be for and the fact that one needn't be so precise
about it anymore has its advantages for if most people can just let
themselves go they usually don't care what it is they are for
    and so they hit on that idea when they'd started to just think up
something of the kind
    so they hit on the idea that what one is against must be some-
thing one can see touch revile humiliate spit at lock up strike down
annihilate because what one can't see touch revile humiliate spit
at lock up strike down annihilate one can only speak of and what
one can only speak of can change and one never quite knows what
it will turn into whatever one may say against it
    and so they hit on that idea and did that
    so they hit on that idea and did that and when they had done
that they tried to bring most people around and when they had
brought most people around to joining in they hit on the idea that
what one is against so long as it's still there remains changeable
and that only what's gone becomes unchangeable and so they
forced those they had brought around to joining in to annihilate
that which they had been brought around to being against to regard
it like malaria mosquitoes or chickweed or wireworm that have to
be exterminated and when they had managed that they called those

they had brought around to doing that murderers and turned them too into malaria mosquitoes and chickweed and wireworm and kept them down as they had wanted to keep them down without being for anything but just to keep them down forever

and that just happened to occur to them they hit on the idea that one can do all those things

that just happened to occur to them when they wanted to do something and then they hit on the idea that all one needs is to bring some people around to being for something at first and to being against something and so on until they can't get out of it anymore and run around in circles for all eternity or rather till there is no one left for that won't take them till all eternity

but why did they think that up or didn't they think anything of it except that they wanted to do something perhaps because it was too boring for them as it was before that occurred to them and they hit on the idea

yes of course they carried it so far only so that in the end they themselves could plunge into it and put an end to themselves and to everything for people like that are always people who want to put an end to it but they don't want to go by themselves but everyone must go with them

so that's the kind of people to whom something like that just happens to occur

CATALOGUE OF THE INCORRIGIBLE

there are incorrigible people who think that everything will be the same again

there are incorrigible people who know that nothing will be the same again but who behave as though it will be

there are incorrigible people who know that nothing will be the same again they behave as though it will be and try to pass on the tale

there are incorrigible people who know that nothing will be the same again and they don't behave as though it will be but they haven't understood how things are

there are incorrigible people who have understood how things are but they believe that everything will be the same again and that they'll bring it off again one day

there are incorrigible people who have understood how things
are and think they have understood that it will be the same again
if not quite as it was the first time
　　there are incorrigible people who have understood how things
are but they don't believe in what they have understood and think
that things are always changing
　　there are incorrigible people who know that nothing will be the
same again and have understood how things are and still can't give
up and try once more
　　there are incorrigible people who know that nothing will be the
same again and have understood how things are and still can't give
up and theorize about it
　　there are incorrigible people who act as though nothing happened and live in splendor and joy
　　there are incorrigible people who act as though nothing happened and have understood how things are and do again what
they please
　　there are incorrigible people who act as though nothing happened and have understood how things are and know that it will
never be the same again and do again what they please
　　incorrigible survivors

SHORT STORY

she had something going with her she had something going with
him
　　what did he have going with her what did she have going with
him
　　he also had something going with him there she also had something going with her there
　　what did he also have going with him there what did she also
have going with her there
　　he had something going with her and also with him there
　　what did he have going with her and also with him there
　　she had something going with him and also with her there
　　what did she have going with him and also with her there

he had something going with himself she had something going
with herself

what did he have going with himself what did she have going with herself

he had it did he have it she had it did she have it

he had something going with her and also with him there and with himself she had something going with him and also with her there and with herself he had something going with her and also with him there and with himself and even with her there she had something going with him and also with her there and with herself and even with him there he there had something going with him and her and her there she there had something going with her and him and him there did he there also have something going with himself did she there also have something going with herself

Translated by Michael Hamburger

Michael Krüger

The Pet

I am, if I may begin frankly, a best-selling author. For twenty years—unnoticed or misunderstood by literary critics and envied by every other author who cannot subsist on royalties—I have been writing a family chronicle that up to now, if I have calculated correctly, has appeared in fourteen volumes that, further, have been translated into all the living languages of the world, so that in my archive, with all the special book club and paperback editions, around five hundred different editions of my diligence are found. I do not mention these details out of vanity—although the world-wide acceptance of my writing, in spite of literary critics, could certainly have made me conceited—rather to indicate in what dimensions my work and, closely associated with it, my responsibility to my reading public can be viewed.

The considerable income from the sales of my books is distributed among the members of my family. If a living person plays a leading role, he receives up to two percent of the income per book from domestic sales; living secondary persons receive half of that. If a family member is portrayed in a particularly unfavorable light, a special compensation is agreed upon that can be up to four percent of the accrued book club fees (domestic). My father's sister, Aunt Hilda, who has to play the silly in all the novels, for many years received all her fees in hard currency, which makes it possible for her now, after the collapse of socialist ideology, to reside in Bohemia in a renovated baroque palace. Meanwhile she manages the entire former East bloc and Asia. The film and television rights are managed by my brothers, who maintain offices in Los Angeles and Munich and facilitate cost-favorable TV company productions by way of Hungary.

Merchandising is taken care of by my mother's family. Most in demand are teacups with pictures of the main characters and a worldwide production of T-shirts printed with pithy sentences from my novels. Altogether at this time about four hundred persons live from my books or from firms that were founded by the money earned by my books.

So the entire utilization and management of my rights remain in the family, whose head—my father—is not only the chairman of the supervisory council of our worldwide operations but at the same time also looks after the numerous honorary obligations, receives international and ultimately local prizes still attainable, as my representative accepts honorary doctorates, checks the dissertations, and supervises the archives. I myself am active in our empire exclusively as a writer. Since I discovered my style rather early— earlier than the unhappy Kafka and earlier, too, than Thomas Mann, for example, who was exemplary in regard to economy of style—there were no serious artistic crises in my life. And since in the case of normal families a conscientious composition and stylistic embellishment of a family chronicle would be sure to produce ca. thirty medium-sized volumes, with my enormous proportion of relatives I could have produced my annual three hundred pages for twenty years at least, if not longer, without ever having to invent an incident or even a gesture. Indeed, I would have remained a modest, happy author, a man living alone without great needs, a man enjoying the small things in life, who respects the printed word, if one day an event had not taken place in my life that literally changed everything and that, in the final analysis, is the reason that for the first time in my career as a writer I am not bent over a new series for my family chronicle but am writing the report presented here.

After the publication of my eighth or ninth novel, which like all its predecessors was an international success as a book, as a movie, and as a TV series, my German publisher at the time, with thoroughly good intentions, gave me an animal because he was mistakenly of the opinion that my family kept too tight a rein on me and would not even permit me a life companion or anything of that sort. In his sweet naiveté he could not believe that writing novels single-handedly on the typewriter could replace just about any living creature for me. He couldn't get it into his head that I pursued the by no means enervating, rather invigorating labor of the composition of my stories so stubbornly only because I could keep my family away with this work, if not humankind as a whole. Anyone who has pledged himself to art is lost for humankind.

Still, I accepted the gift that he gave me for reaching a million copies (within ten months), although the family council would rather have seen a book bound in gold or an increase of royalties. To be brief, it was a black, tousled, furry animal the size of a squirrel, with charcoal-colored button eyes, that seemed to feel at home immediately in my study.

I was just about to describe in a long flashback the wedding of my maternal grandmother and my raving grandfather, the beginning of a union doomed in every respect, and I was happy to have the unpretentious, poised little animal nearby. It could effortlessly climb up the walls and then, a black spot, dangle in a corner of the room. Or the animal made itself comfortable in the lamp and darkened the room. Sometimes it wasn't seen for days and could not be lured out of its hiding place by any word of endearment. Then again, at night, when I had written my three pages and typed them up, it was lying in my bed and, when I threw back the covers, scurried away, leaving behind a repulsive black wreath of hair.

I would have taken a certain pleasure in this droll little guy, which now as a cat and now as a guinea pig was of use in my book, if it had not had one terrible feature. It grew. It grew even when you simply looked at it. Now it lay light as a feather on my shoulder, nibbling at the hair on the back of my neck, then a sack-shaped creature came down onto my knees, and when another chapter was finished, there stared at me a formless creature with no similarity at all to the animal given me.

At first the family council was interested in what the sex of the animal might be. Experts were called in, the director of the zoo was supposed to make a certification available, libraries were queried, but all efforts to unravel the animal's secret came to naught. I called the animal when I wanted to see it, and occasionally the animal gave me the increasingly dubious pleasure of visiting me while I worked.

For in the meanwhile the animal had reached the size of a sheep, and when my mother was finally born and the marriage of my grandparents had fallen apart as was to be expected—the main event in the fifteenth volume—a hairy monster the size of a yak lay in my apartment, a heavy-breathing, living creature that had become insidious, that withdrew gasping into a corner or moved to the door and uttered piteous sounds.

I was forced to move into new quarters on the edge of town, into an old school with a gymnasium, because downtown became too uncomfortable for me. The postman began to make innuendoes in the neighborhood, the publisher—whom I had meanwhile quit— could not resist telling other authors in his publishing house about the animal. The municipal garbage collector became distrustful because I had to request more and more garbage cans to dispose of the unimaginable amount of dung. My neighbors, otherwise inclined to the artistic, pointed out the stench that settled in their son's clothing and jeopardized his going to school, which only the son seemed to take lightly. Finally I received a visit by a young woman from the health department, together with whom I had to push the animal away from the doorway in order to let her in at all. A change of apartments had become unavoidable.

Now I live in the old schoolhouse, the animal in the gymnasium, but there is no more thought of regular work. At the decisive scenes that require the highest degree of concentration, the animal began to roar and gave me no peace until I had brought it a bucket of water or twenty pounds of meat. Since you could no longer tell where it's head was located, I threw the meat through the handiest window and had to wait until the roaring colossus had gotten itself into position to pick up its food.

Altogether the animal offered an image of such repulsive malevolence and unavailing, unhappy surliness that occasionally I was overcome by the notion of doing away with it. But always when I was about to carry out the disgraceful plan and armed with a rifle approached the gymnasium, the ill-smelling animal lay there sleeping, curled up, like a gigantic heap of decaying leaves, so that I abandoned my murderous plans and proceeded to my desk again quickly to scribble onto paper a sketch for my new book.

Meantime I was completing only half a page per day, which for an author of my renown can only be really bad. The first rumors of my decreasing creative powers leaked out; fundamental doubts about the construction of my novelistic work made the rounds; more recent doctoral works from every imaginable country claimed to notice that my sure style, which remained the same from book to book, was revealing certain inadvertent slips; and when finally the firm had a profit of not twenty per cent as usual but of two per cent less, the family council had an emergency meeting. A hotel near me was rented, in which the family alone resided for a weekend in order to keep away unwanted witnesses. My father presided in the conference room, my brothers and cousins of both sexes sat around the table, their families behind them in the second row, my Aunt Hilda, who meanwhile had married a stateless Lebanese and then insisted that she have a book to herself about this episode, was sitting opposite my father and as usual interfered with the fixed agenda. It consisted of four points. First point: business report and exoneration of the board of directors. Point two: establishment of the themes of the next three books and a discussion about their marketing. Point three: the animal. Point four: miscellaneous.

Point one ended with the regrettable conclusion that the firm had succeeded in avoiding collapse only through clever purchases of real estate on the one hand, through financial manipulations in America on the other. The books—this was the really alarming news—formed only sixty percent of the returns, the remainder being produced through real estate and financial dealings: Not a solid basis for business in our time, as my father remarked in my direction.

Point two ended as usual in a horrible argument because the maternal side, which had taken possession of the left side of the conference table with the sun to their backs, was of the opinion that they, measured by the disadvantageous depiction in the most recent books, should receive a higher fee than up to now or would have to be featured centrally in the next book, which led to strong exchanges of words with the paternal side, which presented the well-founded opinion that, in the name of the unconditional realism of the general project, a more advantageous depiction would be downright impossible or would amount to a falsification.

Then finally lunch came, which offered a lot of time for the formation of factions, which I could not take part in, however, because I was driven by my father's chauffeur to feed the animal, which was waiting for us already with its frightful cries.

At three o'clock sharp we began the establishment of the character line-up for the upcoming novels. Each of the aunts present received their big entrances and several precisely fixed supporting appearances. My mother's cousins and their horrible wives, altogether no-goods and parasites and besides that ugly and pretentious, had center stage in novel number sixteen, which was supposed to describe through what deceitful machinations they intended to get hold of a large part of our firm's money. I wanted to give special prominence to an old uncle because his nouveau riche allure was a particular challenge for a writer, but I found no majority for a real exposé because that very Uncle Richard was successful in real estate in Eastern-bloc countries. Immediately after the collapse of Communism he had bought up old residences around the Eastern capitals, gotten rid of the tenants, had a bit of plaster applied to the façades, and was selling them again for a price tenfold higher, in Prague for even more. If he was indeed to be depicted as a rascal—and in support of that was his Nazi past and a deceitful bankruptcy in Herne in the 70s that had to be ironed out from the international success of my first book, and so was an appealing subject that also screamed for filming—but please, only after his death. Until then, as he said hypocritically, he wanted to perform many good services for the firm—and for himself as well, of course, for he had a steady monthly income of 20,000 marks, to which premiums and dividends were added so that it came to an annual salary of 350,000 marks.

When novels seventeen and eighteen were so arranged that their connections to the TV series were also accurate, point three could finally be discussed: the animal. The nettled mood in the conference room was further heated up by the fact that the press secretary, a thoroughly long-winded journalist who had sneaked into our family by marriage, held up an article about me and the animal from an Italian magazine and sent it around the table, an article that bristled with malevolent, unappetizing aspersions. It went so far as to impute a relationship between me and the hairy colossus, which for its part was depicted on a double page in color: a black heap in a gymnasium, framed by bars and rings, in one corner a flayed calf, in another a bathtub that served as a water trough. A repulsive sight. THE FRIEND OF THE BEST-SELLING AUTHOR was in capital letters underneath, and in a box in the upper-right corner I was pictured as, wrapped in a leather apron, I shoved the bloody half of a calf through a window. On the following page I was to be seen again, at my desk, my head propped in my hands, this time with the subtitle: A WRITER IN CRISIS? When the press secretary reported that the rights to the illegal, surreptitiously taken pictures had been sold to twelve newspapers all around the world, such a clear wave of solidarity of the voting members rose up against me that my father could do nothing more than call upon the person responsible for this adversity. I had to stand up and reply to ever-more-aggressive questions, which often could not be distinguished from insults. But how to respond? The animal was there, and it continued to grow. Indeed, I brought the mood of the conference to its apex when I requested the finance committee to make available a capital investment in the amount of several million marks in case the gymnasium were no longer sufficient as the environment and living space for the animal.

Although it was the first time that I demanded something from the firm that exceeded my monthly salary—I had paid for my present residence and the gymnasium out of my own funds, and the daily supply of meat was paid for from my private account—my request was denied straightout, with two abstentions. The unanimous opinion was: We are responsible for the marketing of your depiction of our family, not for your private upkeep of animals. Uncle Richard even went a step further. It's either us or the animal, he said to applause, and I had to watch even my father rub his hands together. Either you return to your normal production of three pages per day and consequently have the animal put down on the spot—yes, he used that repulsive phrase—or we will retract our family history from you immediately.

I requested time to consider. Coffee was ordered. Aunt Hilda and her Lebanese demanded champagne. Uncle Richard, proud of having reduced the affair to a functioning friend-enemy scheme, ordered a large double whiskey. For those present under eighteen years of age not yet entitled to vote, whom I did not even know by sight for the most part, there were soft drinks and cookies. I had my father's chauffeur drive me to the schoolhouse and went to the animal. Like the photograph in the illustrated magazine it lay as a slightly agitated, hairy mass in the gymnasium and occasionally emitted plaintive sighs as though it were aware of the decisions of the family council. The chauffeur helped me lift the corners of the animal to be able to sweep out the offal more easily, then I filled the tub with fresh water, and in less than half an hour we were back in the hotel again.

The president requested quiet; the family—which knew for the most part about what was going on only from hearsay, since they had not seen the animal in recent years—took their seats; the conversation hushed: It was my turn to speak.

To be brief, I decided against the family and for the animal. How I came to this decision, which was of profound consequence for my life to come, I cannot describe exactly. I see myself standing next to my father in front of the group, inwardly perturbed, outwardly calm, casting a long look at my silent family. There they all sat, my aunts and uncles, male and female cousins, my in-laws, the whole bunch sat there expectantly, staring at me, a slightly agitated heap of family history, a pile of offal. I had to laugh. An immense surge of laughter rose up in me and broke out suddenly, a slobbering tempest, so that laughing loudly, bursting out as though not in my right mind, and finally struggling for breath and for control of myself, I announced my decision. The result had been foreseeable, considering the state of affairs, but was still unique in its effect. There was a tumult. Some screamed; others struck the table so hard that the cups rattled; one uncle advanced on me with raised fists, fell over a child who began to cry, and was floored by its father, a cousin. One great aunt surrendered to a faint. A wonderful scene to which one could easily have devoted twelve to fifteen pages. I was cursed; my uncle was accused of having forced me to take this alternative; my father, as the chairman of the supervisory council, was reproached for not having stopped the misfortune in time. A heap of shards.

At the first available opportunity I got away and went home and threw the novel I had started into the stove. The lawyers would take care of the rest. I can confirm here that the royalties of the original editions were given me for the length of the copyright, which will suffice anyway to keep the voracious animal and me above water for some time. For the rest of the family a welfare plan was developed that is to be financed from the sale of the firm. The younger members were given the prospect that an apprenticeship would be financed. Aunts and uncles too old for retraining received free lodging and board in a hotel in Altötting that remained in the family. By the way, the family council still attempted to offer our story to a ghostwriter, but his stylistic talents were insufficient to put a suspenseful and generally interesting story onto paper. The concoction that resulted didn't even find a publisher.

For myself, I can for the time being continue to live in the school because the animal, contrary to expectations, has not continued to grow. With the help of a shepherd who lives nearby I sheared off the animal's fur almost to its hide, whereby it admittedly does not look less unattractive, but certainly no longer looks so intimidating. But above all I can now look into its eyes again, which makes our association easier. I broke off discussions with a circus. Since the animal cannot metamorphose itself, there was no demand. It would have had to be carried like a carpet into the menagerie, where it would have lain flat on the floor without moving. A flat stunt after the high-wire act—that's not enough for an audience in love with illusion. They didn't want to use it even as a filler for intermission, and I refused to let it be trained.

I cannot say that I have loved the animal since, but I do believe that I understand it. It has become a part of my life, and perhaps not the worst part. I have begun to make drawings for a book about the animal that is to appear one day with the publisher who gave it to me. A contract has been signed.

This report will be filed with my lawyer. It has been written in the event that a part of the family puts into action what has come to my ears as a rumor.

Translated by A. Leslie Willson

Ulrike Längle

The Devil Is the Friend of Man

You just have to be sly, and as dead as possible, then life becomes somehow bearable. Felix, though, never succeeded in this. Was it that he was not sly enough, was it that he was still too much alive? In any case, life as such was a burden to him. Until he received a surprising offer. A cigarette manufacturer decided to invest some of his profits in culture. The manufacturer wanted to found a magazine that would resurrect a genre that had been widespread in the early eighteenth century but had now completely died out: the Dialogue of the Dead. Every fourteen days, Felix, who had the honor of editing the magazine, was to compose such a dialogue, which was to form, along with other articles, the content of the *Hades Correspondent*, as the product was called.

Before Felix began work on his first dialogue, he spent weeks of intensive research studying the genre. He read through volumes of dialogues from the early eighteenth century. He entitled his premier dialogue: "The Devil is the Friend of Man." Well, if I'm going to do this, I'm going to do it right, he thought to himself. So he chose the Devil as interlocutor in the first dialogue of the nascent *Hades Correspondent*, although this certainly was not consistent with generic norms. To be precise, the Devil never comes up in dialogues of the dead because he is not technically dead, just as he is not really alive either: He operates outside of such categories. However, Felix wanted the Devil as a conversation partner, so he threw himself into his work whole-heartedly.

In the first paragraph, he has the Devil engage in conversation with a recently deceased head of state who had argued vehemently for a united Europe, and whom all of the potential readers should still remember well. Apparently in his mid-fifties, jovial, and wearing an elegant double-breasted suit, the Devil received his guest like a visiting statesman in a cave on Charon's Shore that had been remodeled as a conference room. Dead souls from the four corners of the earth traversed the river, and not just prospective Europeans who would now never experience that future of unity and who could at best say: "Had we lived longer, we could have been Europeans, but now, unfortunately, we are only Englishmen, Frenchmen, Greeks, or Austrians, some at least semi-Europeans, some just neighbors standing at the fence, full of longing or shaking with fear, when the bony hand of death simply ripped us all away from the feast of a future common market.

"You see all those guests on the ferry?" said the statesman as he broadly swept his hand indicating all of Charon's customers. "How much trouble with customs and passport controls one could have spared these simple people, who now are all equals, if they could all have entered Hades as European citizens! What do you think?"

The Devil could not resist a diabolic smile and said: "You know, we here in the Underworld are not so picky. On the contrary. Our ferryman would get bored if he couldn't leaf through all the passports with their different forms and different stamps. And the people themselves feel better in the afterlife if they had strong roots before. Pardon me, but Europe as the sole root is a bit meager. Botanically speaking, you would be dealing with the kind of tap root that, for example, a pine tree has. We prefer for various reasons diversely formed roots, if only to supply adequate raw material for those here who passionately carve the roots of family trees as a hobby."

The statesman was taken aback; he had considered the Devil to be the product of the Enlightenment, and thus of the French Revolution, and had therefore reckoned with the Devil's approval.

"Humans are just different, even when dead," the Devil concluded.

The statesman persevered: "But consider, if you will, Europeans in Hell can be kept in line much easier. They are standardized, especially as far as their souls are concerned, which has to be the most important aspect for you. The European Standardized Dead, Quality Group H, these are your candidates for Hell," he added somewhat colloquially. "Surely this would be a labor-saving measure even for you, and it would free your personnel to do tasks that better suit their qualifications," he declared enthusiastically.

"Do you really think that I am overqualified for this job?" asked the Devil with a sardonic smile. "For my part, I can think of nothing I'd rather do than spend my time with different candidates for Hell. Consider for a moment my imagination: There is nothing better for it than to think up diverse tortures." The sardonic smile changed to a satanic one.

"But," exclaimed the European statesman, "but the chaos that these dead will certainly cause here too! Just before I left for this diplomatic conference with you, I read in the papers that traffic chaos had erupted in the Philippines. Around a thousand cooks and volunteers had made a giant sausage, so they could get into the *Guinness Book of World Records*, and they paraded that sausage through the capital city. No one can cause traffic chaos with a European Standardized Sausage; you can be sure of that."

The Devil still was not convinced. The statesman resorted to his final argument: "But think of the invaluable advantages that you could accrue from our statistics! We in Europe are not far enough along yet, but I could imagine a cooperative effort. In Alabama, the Southern Baptists decided that 46.1 percent of the population of Alabama could end up in Hell. They published a map of the state and a statistical analysis in which they show the geographical distribution of the 1.86 million people who will be damned eternally. Something like that for Europe, a Pan-European register of the Hell-bound, wouldn't you like that?"

For the first time, the Devil appeared to hesitate a moment, but then he came to a decision: "No. That would take all the suspense out of death. After all, we here in the Underworld make bets about whether this one or that one lands in Heaven or Hell, or how ever you wish to call our different departments. All the suspense would just be ruined."

The hands of the European statesman sank despondently into his lap. The Devil jovially offered him a cigarette, brand name Lucky Styx, made locally down there. The statesman took a couple of draws, and his face lit up a little. "This is really quite a good blend you folks smoke," he remarked admiringly.

"Small wonder," laughed the Devil. "We have specialists down here with experience from all over the world. Too bad we can't reveal the recipe to mankind. Why, there would be a run on Hell that no one could stop."

With these words, Felix ended his first dialogue of the dead, though not without promising the readers that, in the next issue, he would tell them which earthly cigarette brand came closest to the Devil's own.

Translated by Scott G. Williams
(with Ulrike Längle, Grit Liebscher, Hiram Maxim, Ann Reitz)

Friederike Mayröcker

In a Rundown Neighborhood

A storm of images, he said, like a wind, he said, they come.

and it's all so limited by time, he said, and I would have thought, he said, one day I could have won him to our side, he said.

back then, he said, when we all drove together to the fish restaurant and I helped her out, she had answered while she placed her right foot down and immediately thereafter her left and at the same time ducked her head so she wouldn't bump it, had answered, why not, why not, who knows, maybe one of these days you can win him for your people, he said, but then it became clear that the time was all too limited, he said.

coming from a rough world, he said, from a rough world, returning from a rough world into a smooth world, he said, it's all limited.

her letter, he said, was written in an old-fashioned way, adorned with flourishes but the tone was sincere and the space between the lines like the breath of a person much moved and then, he said, we drove to new orleans, he said, all of us together, he said, and I believe he loved the old city where once the french ruled and later in a rundown neighborhood, he said, the jazz negroes.

I look forward very much to your being here, he said, it will be spring.

I have a rose, he said, on my windowsill, I have a rose today.

I also do not have much more time, he said.

on my windowsill I have a rose today, he said, picked for me by my wife this morning, he said, roses bloom here like that even in december, he said. I hope, he said, you will be able to meet your translator, he said, a young banker.

I know exactly, he said, what he will then say, he said, don't draw those damn symbols all over, he will say, reality is really damned attractive, he will say, reality, he said.

as we were leaving the hotel in cologne, he said, there stood beuys, somewhat elevated, in the gateway, he said, with outspread arms, thin whitish eagle-nosed face, surrounded by young people, spoke, was questioned, answered, and the rain poured, and because of the strong gusty wind some had lowered their umbrellas, he said, because of the wind.

and as beuys moved his arms up and down, he said, I thought all he lacks is a monk's cowl, he said.

in a rundown neighborhood, he said, it really rained, he said, and she called us at night though she lived directly below us and could just as easily have come up those few steps to knock at our door, and when she suddenly called us up, he said, we shouldn't make such a racket, he said, because they couldn't go to sleep downstairs, he said, we have to put up with that, he said, and it is also only this short moment, he said, snuffing out, he said, or maybe to be snuffed out, he said, this dionysian stupor, he said, this dirty mutation, he said, that awaits us all.

when the green sides of the leaves, he said, are interspersed with white dots, spots, and stripes, he said, it will be a beautiful season, and I am very happy about your being here, it will be spring, a beautiful season.

the alpine republic, he said, where once the french ruled and later, in a rundown neighborhood, the jazz negroes.

that with just half a gesture, he said, in order to evoke calmness in the other guy, he said, the freezing over of friendly waters, he said, on the telephone, he said, she had told me that she was as fond of me as before, but that she does not believe she could stand my presence at this time, let a couple of weeks pass, we might let weeks pass, he said, we have to resign ourselves, he said, to this and that, so that it will all be limited, he said.

the effort, he said, that we spend to maintain our existence, he said, how in vain, he said, she wore a pink bathing cap, he said, stood in the annex of a shoe accessory store and asked to go along.

yes, he said, better to receive injustice than to do it, and in the end one is marked by what one has done, he said, human vipers, wolf people, he said, sirenes.

she wore a pink bathing cap, he said, a misunderstanding on his part, he said, that's the way it's got to be.

and basically, he said, one could divide people into two groups, into groups of those who are important and those who aren't important, he said, and beuys stood again with raised arms while it stormed, and prophesied something, it poured and blew through the gateway and the people had lowered their umbrellas because of the storm, despite the rain, he said.

out of the hand of a pastry baker, he said, who actually drives a caterpillar tractor, he said, the tin shears, he said, places, he said, the placelessness, he said, and still always better, he said, to receive injustice than to do it, he said. tin shears, he said, places, he said, the placelessness, grasping, he said, one winter morning almost without twilight, he said.

what torments us, he said, what strikes us, he said, what touches us, on my windowsill today, he said, even in december the roses bloom here, he said, on my windowsill, in a rundown neighborhood, on my windowsill I have a rose today, that my wife picked for me this morning, he said, even in december the roses bloom, he said, in a rundown neighborhood, he said, I don't have much more time either, he said.

Translated by Michael P. Elzay

Hans Erich Nossack

The Pocketknife

My room is on the first floor. I sleep with a window open—because of the oxygen, you know. This is not the main thing, however. The reason I mention it: It's not at all difficult to climb into my place. One need only place one's hands on the windowsill and then pull oneself up. I'm not an athlete, but I'm sure I could demonstrate it for you—without much noise. One would have to watch out for the metal strip on the sill.

There are many soldiers in our area, white, brown, and black. They train in the woods at night for the next war. No doubt one of them could see the open window and say to himself: Why shouldn't I have a nice snooze there while the others are training? The thought comes easily. Besides, it's warmer in the room. Yes, and then he finds me in here. That would be very unpleasant. It would be unpleasant for both of us.

One takes risks. Up to now, however, I haven't been murdered, as you see. I sleep very lightly. There is gravel on the paths outside. It crunches when somebody walks on it, and I'm wide awake at once. He would have to sneak up in stocking feet, but that hurts. Of course, a cat could also jump in; cats are curious, after all. Imagine that you're lying peacefully in bed and all of a sudden a big tomcat is standing on the windowsill. That would startle you, too.

Speaking of startlement. One day—yes, it happened in broad daylight at that—I'm sitting at the table thinking. All at once a head looks in through the window and asks: "Do you want to give something for the Kingdom of God?" I scream at him: "No, not interested!" I was startled. You would have been startled, too, if a head appeared in your window and asked such a thing. It was someone from Jehovah's Witnesses. Afterward I was sorry about it.

But that's not the main thing. Of course, there is also all kinds of night life out there, even a very active night life, I imagine. One can see the traces of it in the morning in the garden. Someone has let his droppings fall here and there, or left a yellow spot in the grass; stained by urine, forgive me. Sometimes someone has merely milled around in a pile of leaves and not put it back in order afterward. Nevertheless, they are usually very considerate, one must admit. Once or twice it's happened that the lid to someone's garbage can has fallen down the cellar stairs. This naturally causes a murderous ruckus—very annoying when someone is doing his best to be quiet. But as I say, these are exceptions. I can't complain.

Besides, one can be mistaken sometimes. One thinks: Uh-oh! somebody's sneaking up, but then it's really only the large leaves of the vine on the house slapping together with a metallic sound. I'm merely trying to prove to you with all of this that I sleep very lightly. It's not that easy to surprise me.

But never mind that and let's get to the apple trees. That is to say, it's not really a question of the apple trees, either. They are just a pretext, so to speak. The apple trees are just incidental. You can rightly ask: Why apple trees, of all things? Why not plum trees? But the apple trees are already there, and one has to hold on to something. Sorry I didn't plant them, I love them very much, actually.

Not because of the apples, no. The apples don't interest me; one can buy them at the store, if one is determined to eat some. Moreover, they usually fall off before they're ripe. We frequently have sudden high winds—the mountains are not far, you see—and in the morning, then, the apples are lying in the grass. Fine, if they want to. After all, I'm not a fruit dealer. If you want to, you can make applesauce out of them.

I love the apples trees in the winter, too. The branches, the way they reach out with their limbs and feel about, I like that. I believe that's called structure nowadays, but that's all the same. And please don't take offense when I say: I love. A vague concept, to be sure. It sounds even silly when one says: I love the apple trees. Nevertheless, they force me to think about them; that's the point. There

they stand outside in the cold—and it gets damned cold here sometimes. Not that I feel sorry for them, that would be too simple,
but I ask myself: How do they stand it? What can they be thinking,
for surely they are thinking something, it's not possible otherwise.
There must be a way of finding out. Especially when they are bare,
the writing ought to be easier to decipher, you would think. The
blue shadows in the snow have also been sketched in very distinctly,
without superfluous embellishments. That's all expressed very
clearly and soberly. What do they want to communicate to us then?
Or if not to us—one shouldn't overestimate oneself—to whom do
they want to communicate?

Pity that you can't find out. The apple trees are standing there,
and here I sit, and both of us are thinking something, there's no
doubt about that, and in between us. . . . Yes, this very In-between.
Too bad! It bothers me. Please don't laugh.

But let's get to the point. One day they begin to bloom, in spite
of everything. And how they bloom! You're struck dumb with
wonder. If you don't keep control of yourself, tears even come to
your eyes. This doesn't happen with any of the other lavishly
praised blossoms. With roses, for example, you can always say:
Look, how beautiful! and that's that. But not with apple blossoms.
Try it. You can't get it out. A similar thing occurs at most with the
bluebells you sometimes see growing in forest meadows. You give
a start and don't dare open your mouth. It would break the spell.
But I'm straying from the point. With the bluebells it's different,
too: tears don't come to your eyes. And please, don't think I'm
sentimental because of this. It has nothing to do with me. It concerns the apple trees. By this I only mean to say: Whoever doesn't
give a start and interrupt his conversation when faced with a blossoming apple tree or even a blossoming apple twig is . . . is . . . not
to be trusted. Give it a try sometime. I advise you to be careful.

In short, you're at a loss for words, or you don't have the ear
for it. Yes, that seems to me to be more exact: You lack the ear for
it. You see, at night it's very quiet, and I lie there or sit there, it
makes no difference, and the window is open. I'm alone, I'm wide
awake. You'd think that I could hear what's being said about the
apple trees, or near them, or what they are saying among themselves, but no. If it were only a matter of a foreign language that
I don't yet understand, that wouldn't be so bad. In time it could
be learned by comparative studies. But no! Although I know there's

talking going on, I can't hear anything. My ear, as I've said, that's what's lacking. And if your ear is not worth anything, that, sir— if you don't mind my saying so—is really very distressing. I'm intentionally avoiding any stronger language for my concern. We do want to remain objective, realistic.

As a result I've even gotten up at night and gone outside. I said to myself hopefully, if you walk back and forth out there under the apple trees, maybe you'll hear it. Maybe somebody's just whispering out there so as not to disturb the night. But nothing doing. I got the sniffles in the process. I'm deaf. What, you're supposed to resign yourself to that? And those who are talking outside don't suspect that I'm deaf. They are talking to me and believe I can hear them. They think I'm indifferent because I don't answer. It can't go on, you must realize that. It really can't go on. I'm not saying this out of soft-heartedness. If I were soft-hearted, I would have stayed in bed.

That wouldn't suffice for me. My curiosity, if you will, wouldn't permit it. I could simply have closed the window. Oxygen or no oxygen. Some people maintain that it's better for the nerves to sleep in a closed room. But I'm not interested in nerves; I live alone anyway. I had to find out what was going on with the apple trees. I wanted to take part a little in the activity that was going on out there—not only at blossom time, no, winters and summers. In the fall, for example, one is in the habit of picking up one or the other apple, inspecting it well, and letting it fall back into the grass again because it's not ripe. That is audible, naturally. My ears are good enough to hear such things. At blossom time, however, activity picks up considerably. One can feel it. Some nights it became downright oppressive. Here you have proof that the blossoming is more important than the apples. It wasn't a frivolous expression of taste on my part. It's a fact, a totally unromantic fact.

Fine! Fine! Let's stick to the facts. So, a few nights ago I can't bear it any longer. The press out there is too great. (The space by the apple trees is probably no longer adequate for them.) It swells up to the window and nestles up and even into the room so that I, too, am crowded by it. In short, it is no longer bearable. You suffocate from it.

So, I lean out of the window and call: "Please, a little louder! I can't hear you. You can see, I'm ready for anything." What else should I have said, anyway?

I ask out loud. After all, it's night. Everyone is asleep, and I'm alone. No danger of someone hearing me talking. But please, keep that to yourself. That would be embarrassing to me.

I can't say how loud, but loud enough in any case, for someone did hear me, sir, of that you can rest assured. Those out there have better ears than I. They hear me speaking. They not only hear me, they also understand my language, while I . . .

Because they definitely did speak out there and wave and call and wanted to make themselves understood and were surprised that I didn't react. They were definitely discussing the matter and trying to decide how they could communicate with me. Not just one, or a couple of them, but many, many. There were more and more of them. They came either of their own accord as if they were being attracted, or they were fetched so they could help. Yes, they were looking for those who had more experience and could give a clue as to what was to be done in such a situation.

Oh you should have seen the crowd. They streamed by from all directions. Seen? Did I say "seen"? Yes, you're right: How come "seen"? For naturally. . . . But, nevertheless, it was seen. The night billowed toward me—the night, the apple trees, everything. So violent was the thronging, like a picture, a canvas that's just barely fastened to its frame, like a backdrop on which the night and the apple trees are painted, or like a heavy curtain—or whatever—and there's a throng behind it. I could have touched it, and it was touching me also. Especially toward the window where I stood there was a large bulge. They were thronging there the strongest and were about to tear the picture.

A stretchable material, but unbelievably tough. And, what's more, not transparent. That is, not transparent to me, for those on the other side *could* see me. Some kind of modern synthetic material. There are such sunglasses with mirror lenses. Whoever has them on his nose can see anything he wants, but the likes of us see only the empty mirror, and no eyes. Very unpleasant, yes.

And over and above this, soundproof; for, as I said, not the slightest sound to be heard. What can you do when faced with such material? What would you have done? Put yourself in my place. I was holding my breath; I leaned farther forward in order to hear something. I held my ear against the material, so to speak, or whatever it was. Please, a little louder! Could be that I repeated it. Who can remember such things?

Finally they must have realized that I couldn't hear them. The bulge in the picture remained; they leaned against it with all their might, so very close, in order to be able to see me better, and stared at me. And those who were standing farther away rose to their tiptoes and braced themselves against those who were standing in front. Probably for their part they were holding their breaths. It was like a pause, very quiet. More than quiet because it was already quiet before. They must have given each other a sign. Psst! Psst! Be still now.

Then I realized what they had thought up. There must have been a very clever one among them, who was advising them, one who had more experience. They'd been waiting for him. All at once I saw it.

At first only a somewhat brighter spot. Right in front of the window where the picture was bulging in the most—or already in the window frame. Like an illusion. And I squeezed my eyes shut, too. I didn't want to be deceived. Yet, when I open them again, I see it more clearly. The spot has already become clearer and gets more and more clear. And whiter. They are carrying something to me, very slowly and carefully. In order to keep from scaring me away, most likely. They are carrying it up to the material that separates us, up to my eyes, and holding it there pressed flatly against the material so that I can see it, and they give me some time, and wait.

It was a sheet of paper, a square sheet of paper, a white sheet of notepaper. And across the top they'd written something, in large, clear letters. In our handwriting. In my handwriting. They'd copied my handwriting in order to make it easier for me, and so that I can understand them, too. And now they were all anxiously waiting.

On it they'd written in large letters. . . . Please, brace yourself. Because you won't have expected this. They hadn't even forgotten to draw the question mark on the paper, even though you and I would have understood it, too, even without the question mark. They'd written—one hardly dares say it: *"Is that Paradise there?"* Only the four words and the question mark.

I ask you, Paradise! Childish! Really ridiculous! You stay awake night after night, wide awake, as I said, in order to find out what they want of you, you're prepared for anything, you're ready to do them any favor, and they . . . they think of nothing, but to ask

you about Paradise. Why about Paradise? About which paradise?
Really, it's too ridiculous for words.

I don't know how you would have reacted. I don't know how I
reacted. Presumably I shrugged my shoulders and made a motion
of helplessness with my hands, like now. How is one supposed
to act? Such gestures happen all by themselves. They don't mean
anything, they're not intended to be malicious, you don't intend
to be insulting, but. . . . All right, the ones with the question saw
my gesture. I'm sorry.

How could I suspect, either, that they were so impatient. They
should have waited only a second longer, and I would have played
along. I would have tried to attune myself to them. Really! You
can't answer such a question on the spur of the moment without
speaking nonsense and doing damage. Anyway, Paradise. Such
matters are very remote. How many of us have time to occupy
ourselves with such things? I know, apparently to some it seems
very important. Fine, that's their business. I have nothing against
it. But if you're going to ask me for advice, you've at least got to
give me a second's time to think about it.

They, however, didn't give me any time. They took my gesture
for the answer. What a pitiful misunderstanding. They drew back
the paper at once, and they themselves also withdrew. All of them.
They didn't even leave a sentry there. The material or the curtain
flowed back. The picture pulled itself out flat again. Only the apple
trees were there. And the night. On the neighboring property a
dog was barking.

And how I was freezing! I had only my pajamas on. At apple
blossom time it usually becomes quite cool at night in our area.
One must always take night freezes into account.

That damned dog next door! Since we're already talking about
it, let's consider once more very soberly what could have been
done. And, of course, without fudging. Not much could have been
accomplished with words, that much is clear. They would have
noticed at once that words are only feeble excuses. They might
have listened out of politeness, but in their hearts they would have
thought: He doesn't really understand what it's all about. It's all a
swindle! And afterward you feel ashamed.

But what if I had taken the pocketknife, just imagine that, if you
will. You see, I keep a small pocketknife, for cutting open books.
It's always lying within reach on my desk. I see to it that it's always

very sharp. I sharpen it on the whetstone in the kitchen. I also use it to cut the cuticles on my fingernails, forgive me. Just imagine—for the idea comes easily—I had reached for the pocketknife in order to try to slit the picture or material. Right at the place where everything was bulging in through the window at me and was very taut. Of course, we don't know for sure whether the pocketknife would have been strong enough for the material or not, but let's just assume that it was. Naturally, I would only have made a very small slit, just as a test, so to speak. Just to find out if one could get a better understanding of what those on the other side want. Not "want," no, because they've already written what they want on the paper—only in order to take part a bit in their conversation.

No, the risk is too great. I threw the pocketknife down again. Understand me correctly: I'm not a coward. If you're used to being alone at night and wide awake to boot, you must be ready to take a few risks. But it's not a question of me at all; I didn't think of my risks, but of theirs on the other side.

Look, even if you take it upon yourself to cut a very tiny slit, who is going to guarantee that the pocketknife won't go right through and tear everything to pieces? Everything! Because the bulge in the picture was already much too taut. Taut enough to rip. Dangerously taut.

And that wouldn't even have been the most hazardous part of it. There is something much worse. The ones on the other side are pressing with all their might in order to be as close as possible to me. That has to be taken into consideration. What if I were to injure one of them with the pocketknife? And blood were to flow through the slit? At first only a few drops and then more and more. And I couldn't tie off the wound and tape it.

No. I have no right to do that. Don't hold it against me.

Translated by Marc Tangner

Helga Novak

Journey of a Woman Nihilist to Verona in Late Autumn

The train is packed full. Countless suitcases, parcels, boxes—the racks filled to overflowing. Not to mention the panting, steaming travelers.

Allegedly, Mara has to perform some job in Verona.

She says, so many people here in the fall and in the middle of the night?

I say, they are going home to vote.

Mara says, casting a vote is the first step towards the slaughterhouse.

I say, you have ten hours to persuade them to accept your theory.

Mara says, let's just get out of here, for God's sake! Out! I'm getting claustrophobia.

Whether she has something up her sleeve or takes to her heels—I go along with her regularly, like a faithful dog.

We move over into the car with couchettes. It, too, is packed.

Mara is tall, and looks like a cross-country runner. Her nose, her cheekbones, and her chin—the individual parts of her face stick out, as if sniffing. Particularly characteristic is her thick growth of hair. She had Lucie snip off her dark-brown and curled hair down to a length of less than an inch so that she could wear a wig, as she does now. Her eyebrows, on the other hand, keep on growing and they join each other above her nose. Even her legs are dark with hair. Mara seldom wears skirts.

The engineer in the upper right-hand bunk can't sleep. Whenever he opens his mouth, there is a hailstorm of words.

. . . Organization, of course, is guided division of labor, the engineer is in charge of the conventional plant, while the director of projects bears the overall responsibility, already you have the report from the construction office, bang bang bang bang, this is the crane, for reasons of safety, the assemblage, of course, takes place on a Sunday, at first we can't get past the scaffolding, pull yourselves together, more, more, that's it, off, off with the main traction, all right, bang bang bang bang bang, now we'll send out the survey crew, meanwhile we are told to set up the weather tower, boom, boom, boom, the cost ceiling has been determined and of course by means of . . .

Mara leaves the compartment. I follow her and say, well, I really like those voters we just left much better.

Mara turns away from me and says, your show of your love for the people is beginning to get on my nerves.

Mara is dogmatic.

She, who despises any kind of authority, constantly interrupts me.

Or is she the domineering type?

Verona received us with an impenetrable fog. The city walls and gates were dripping with wetness. Everything was dark if not black. Mara seemed to enjoy the mist, which made people's faces unrecognizable. I couldn't figure out how she was going to meet anybody in a place like this. The wet cold made me feel uncomfortable, and I directed my steps toward a hotel, which was new, ugly, and built of concrete. Mara said, for shame! I said, well, at least they're heated; besides, you've emphasized often enough that there's no such thing as beauty, or if there is, it's a fraud. The hotel was expensive but warm. The arena opposite looked slippery, as though it had been given a coat of diluted tar.

Mara hired me as a private tutor for her two children. Moreover, she takes me along on long trips because of my decent appearance. Since I carry out her orders and keep my mouth shut, I do fairly well. She and her friends seem to trust me, even though they know that I have a habit of taking notes. Since they treat my writing with disdain, I am slowly beginning to wonder why they let me do it without interfering. Do they perhaps intend to employ me as a ghostwriter eventually? Nonsense, their trust is based solely on my sense of discretion, or indeed on my adaptability. Whatever risks they take in my case, our connection is profitable to them—this they know.

Mara appears to be quite familiar with the feeling of dread. The Scaliger Bridge has been smeared all over. A swastika here, a circle around the capital A (for anarchists) there. I say, now I'm going to stand in front of the capital A, and you take a picture of me. Mara tugs at my sleeve, saying, for God's sake, let's get away from here fast. I say, perhaps this is how we'll lure your contact man out of his hiding place. Mara casts hasty glances in all directions and says, I can't afford such pranks.

At times Mara is foolhardy, at other times she is scared.

My patience is being tried. I bombard Mara with questions: Now what? Where's the fellow you're supposed to meet? What does he look like? When will he show up? That's none of your goddamn business, she retorts, I'll take care of everything, while you crawl around in old churches.

Why shouldn't I go to San Zeno, I say, since I happen to be here anyway?

Mara: That's all junk that ought to be blown up.

I: You can't smoke out everything that's old. Old people don't let themselves be sent to the barricades any more, either.

Mara: Old people can be made to change their minds more easily than can stone houses of worship.

I: The smiling San Zeno was probably a better conspirator in his time than you are now.

Mara calls me names at every opportunity.

She calls me schizoid, indecisive, vacillating, timid, awkward, touchy, insecure.

In her eyes I am a swaying reed.

Today it said in the *Express:* Numerous wanted posters of the fugitive Mara Schneidereit were smeared over and thus made illegible with tar and paint some time during Monday night. According to a police spokesman, the identities of three persons participating in this action have been ascertained.

Mara at my home.
    Having welcomed us effusively, my mother served us a rich meal. Mara ate a lot, silently. My mother gave me a quizzical look. To divert her from Mara's dirty fingernails, I started talking about the upcoming election. Promptly Mara spoke up with her mouth full, those you're expected to elect are, of course, all con men, and the pinkos are the worst. My mother replied defiantly, when you people wave your black flags in the streets, you don't change anything either! Thereupon Mara, we've long since discarded the silly idea of running through the streets with some slogans and letting our heads be bashed in! That put a definite end to our conversation, and Mara resumed slicing the potatoes with her knife and tearing off large chunks from the cutlet she was holding in her hand. I left the room, and my mother followed me. Gently she took my arm, trying hard to look into my eyes, and said, you know I have nothing against the girl, but why doesn't she at least go to the beauty parlor once in a while? I said, when her hair has just been shampooed, she's very beautiful, and then you would again have said, pretty but dumb. Do me a favor, my mother said, go away before father comes home. Mara was standing in the door and said in a loud voice, don't worry, we haven't got much time anyhow.
    I'll never take her home again.

Always killing time.
    I have managed to lure her into a museum. Mara says, Madonnas everywhere, how disgusting! I say, their faces are often those of very plain women. Mara says, as long as they don't do anything but have babies, I don't give a hoot for those plain women. I say, you have children yourself, haven't you? She says, true, but they're different types from the ones we see in the pictures here. Don't forget that they toddle along with us from one hideout to the next and can't even attend a public school. I say, now here you see something different for a change: the descent from the cross. Mara says, they won't catch me!
    Always killing time.

Gladiator bouts, manhunts, tragedies. . . .

The arena, first century

... and now we return to the subject of Euripides, who allowed himself to be bribed with the sum of five talents by the Corinthians into having his Medea kill her children, while in fact the murder was to be blamed on the city fathers. Nonetheless, he had his heroine say something like this—of all the creatures that have been endowed by Nature with reason and feeling, we women are most unfortunate. With excessive efforts we get ourselves a man who immediately makes himself the proprietor of our body. If you get a divorce, people bully you with nasty words. The men say that we live in comfort and perfect security, while they have to run to the place where they work and occasionally have to plunge into the turmoil of warfare. How wrong! I'd rather wield weapons three times than be a servant and play the part of a birth machine once.

And what does this have to do with Mara?

If women stop submitting to patriarchy, they will necessarily shake the foundations of the state, too. And in this process, they will generate a thousand times more energy than the men. Due to their past history, women are rebellious, regardless of how badly they are mistreated. Mara, too, will be thrown into prison, but she will never change. . . .

The arena, twentieth century.

... tragedies, manhunts, gladiator bouts.

Heaps of plucked birds as small as eggs.

Mara apparently likes to roam around at the market. In the midst of the scolding, rummaging women doing their shopping, she looks carefree and very attractive. First she gobbles up half a chicken, then an apple strudel—made from an Austrian recipe. Then she heads for the wieners. I seize her by both her wrists and pull her close to me. She eyes me ironically and says, if you think you can play Romeo and Juliet with me, you're fooling yourself. I let go of her and console myself with two fritters, also of Austrian origin. Mara unhurriedly strolls from one stand to another.

I myself am a plucked bird.

those construction workers on strike how they shuffle and sing the masons' shoes leave chalk marks right and left white as snow as if apple blossoms were thawing in autumn no I wouldn't tear off one of my legs at demonstrations

at the movie theater the mouths are stuffed full and smell of
something fried from the last rows whispered and hummed confessions pour forth but in front there are beds of light white vests and
teeth bleached with hydrochloric acid no I wouldn't tear up my
mouth crying for changes

yet from what sky does the snow fall on the peaks from what
partisan sky below which the caves are as black as the hole in my
heart yes something black digs into pierces me grows exuberantly
stabs its tension is so terrific that it tears me apart

Should alms for the one who gives them be labeled as medicine?

We began to drift with the crowds. There you have your Ma-
donna, Mara said in a harsh tone. She pointed to a young woman
worn by drudgery, who was sitting on the pavement of the street.
Her legs were spread apart, and between them there lay a whimpering baby wrapped in motley clothes. The beggar woman, an Arab
or a Gypsy, had her lowered eyes fixed on her outstretched hand
and gave off a quaintly hissing sound. Hey, doesn't she have a truly
plain face, Mara asked sarcastically. I stepped forward and put a
coin in the woman's open palm. Mara emitted a short laugh, bent
down, and took the coin away from the beggar woman. I felt my
face turn red as a turkey cock and I pulled violently at Mara's
shoulder. I expected the flow of the pedestrian traffic to grind to a
halt. Mara looked at me pitilessly and put the money into the
pocket of her overcoat. How absurd, how humiliating, I said, this
time you've gone too far; I won't play along any more. Pugna-
ciously Mara answered, even though you don't understand what
I'm driving at, you won't revolt; you're too lazy for that.

Are alms actually just a sop for the bad conscience of the one
who gives them?

Lucie has shown up. She surprised us in front of the Palazzo
Canossa.

What are you looking for here? says Mara, startled.

They've rubbed us out, Lucie says hastily, and I couldn't call you
up on the phone. Incidentally, the price on your head has gone
up again.

That doesn't interest me, says Mara, what happened?

They caught Karola, says Lucie

And the others, and Johann and the children? Mara asks.

They've absconded to the Taunus, but that isn't all, says Lucie.
Well, what else? Go ahead, tell me! says Mara.
Your husband keeps seeing Littauer, supposedly an old friend of
his father, says Lucie. Her voice grows louder and louder.
Johann paying visits to a police commissioner? Don't make me
laugh! says Mara.
Come along, we'll sit down together some place, Lucie suggests.
And Christoph? asks Mara.
What I have to tell you is none of his business, says Lucie
unmoved.
We had planned, I cautiously object, to visit this building. I mean
the Palazzo Canossa.
Go inside, nobody's stopping you, you're always on your way
to Canossa anyway, says Lucie to my face and takes Mara's arm.
Lucie's nickname is Iron Lucie. Why not Lucifer?!

Mara looks slovenly.
Mara walks crookedly.
Mara doesn't wash herself.
Mara doesn't sew on any buttons.
Mara looks fatigued

She can't quite bring herself to believe that Johann is associating
with a police commissioner. And even if she and Lucie should slip
away three times, I know Johann Schneidereit. His gun is just as
fast and loose as his slick smile. The dashing glances he metes out
come right from the ramp of fashion shows. All spruced up in his
smartly fitting leather suit, he gives the impression of having grown
up on parquet floors, watched over by two nurses. From head to
toe the man is as smooth as silk. Am I jealous? No, I wouldn't
want to change places with him. What I am afraid of is this: egged
on by his vanity, he might drag all of us down with him. His wife
and children will be the first to get caught on account of him. I
don't worry the least bit about myself personally.

There is yet another member of our gang—I mean theirs. Gregor
Tomalin, Mara's brother. Whenever I saw him, I noticed a certain
animosity between him and Johann Schneidereit. I have never
heard the two men exchange a single word.

After having spent two and a half years also without an address, in other words, in the sewers of any political order, he picked out the most plausible of his forged passports and settled down somewhere. It doesn't matter where, for his mailbox is anything but inactive; still, it can't be far from here.

I don't know whether Mara wants to meet with him.

Mara begins to bloom, she disguises herself, that is, she dresses correctly.

Yes, I spy on her, naturally from a proper distance. With flying hair, the auburn wig becomes her damned well, she stops in front of the house in which young Montecchi is said to have lived. Is she perhaps about to enter the decaying building forcefully. No, lifting her head high, she looks with curiosity at the crumbled brick façade. How beautiful is Mara when she concentrates, showing her profile. For a moment, she disappears behind someone who's taking a walk. The man has moved on, and now Mara is carrying a small parcel under her arm. I scurry into a restaurant, and from a window I watch her stomp by. Once again her face has assumed the most indifferent expression conceivable.

Judging from the shape of the parcel, it might be a book they have slipped into her hand.

I can't stand the sight of blood.

On a Sunday morning, in the middle of Garibaldi Street, if that doesn't prove a sense of tradition, there's a dull rumbling, then a splintering crash. The blast presses our backs against a show window. Mara smiles. The window to which we are glued trembles. And so do our backs, mine does, at any rate. What game is being played here? Why don't I take the next train? The sun radiates not a single degree of warmth. It hovers low on the horizon and blinds us. I'm curious, that's why I don't budge, why I stay at Mara's side. How long have I been here? Or rather: how long will I remain? Parts of a vehicle shoot through the shining coldness of this autumnal sun. Now it is only a display piece, not really the sun any more. Pieces of glass and metal hit the ground. Having unfolded slowly and neatly, shreds of fabric tumble down in the light coming from the opposite side. At first deadly silence, then people, yelling madly, pour out of the houses in the neighborhood. The vehicle is ablaze. I grip Mara's arm and hear her say quite matter-of-factly. The prefect. Beads of sweat gather on my forehead. Was it for the purpose of this spectacle that she dragged me along to Verona? No, no, she couldn't possibly have anticipated it. On the other hand: The prefect! What put that idea into her head? The fire is swiftly extinguished, the puddles have a reddish color. Something is leaking from underneath the wreckage, thickened water, or rather, diluted blood. Mara takes me to a cafe and calmly orders a cup of chocolate.

On this earth there flows more blood than water.

how meticulously they have undermined everything sway back and forth a little bit here or there yes just where you're standing don't you feel that you're trembling that's how far we've come already the earth is moving.

everywhere there's the danger of falling into their traps if you happen to be in a curve or to cross a street at your leisure.

they've dared to advance into the paved streets into the big cities.

a network of passageways strongholds centers hiding places extends in all directions below the surface.

Mara doesn't make requests; she makes demands.

Would I run through Verona in alternately cold or foggy, that is to say, miserable weather, if she hadn't, one day, appeared at my door totally exhausted? The devil knows who had given her my name. Oh no, she didn't ask me for shelter. She demanded a bed and she lay down in it without ceremony. And at once she would issue commands: get me this and that, call up this person or another, introduce yourself with such and such a word! Since she was emaciated, I served her hot meals with a lot of meat four times a day.

At the end of a week she was in fine shape, she stuffed money into my pockets and said, leave everything as it is and come along with me. I need someone just like you, an orderly, reliable, and above all an unobtrusive fellow. Instead of giving her a box on the ear, I obeyed her.

May the devil take her!

The assassination on Garibaldi Street keeps disturbing me.

I say, doesn't it matter to you to see human beings die?

Mara says, it depends on what kinds of human beings they are. And after a while she asks me in her turn, did you ever lose your appetite at breakfast from reading those news reports about the great slaughters?

I say, yes! Yes! Yes! I did lose my appetite because of those things!

Mara says, you're lying, otherwise you wouldn't strut about, fat as a Christmas goose and with puffed-up plumage!

Her vulgar meanness makes me speechless; and how does she know that it was the prefect?

* * *

A forged passport is better than none at all.

I rummage through her belongings, I want to find out what's in that small parcel: It isn't a book. It's passports, a stack of authentic passports. Two of them have each a neat, complete hole; another one is covered with dried blood. It would be stupid of me to broach that subject with her. Do you know what you're talking about, she would answer, you're talking about a mixture of leukocytes, platelets, and red corpuscles, disklike and colored by ferro hemoglobin. That's all. I wrap the passports up again and put them back into the place where they were concealed.

An authentic passport is certainly better than a forged one.

I try hard to remain neutral.

Lucie had found ever-new opportunities to needle me. She has declared war on the entire male sex and is angry with me because I don't fall into line. She vanished from the scene of Verona in the same manner in which she had appeared on it.

Lucie calls me a neuter.

On Sunday the weather cleared up once more. Sunshine, no clouds, but an icy wind. We had climbed the Petersburg, on the far side of the River Adige, and the scent of snow was in the air. Mara stood still, and I was baffled by her tortured face when she suddenly began to talk about her brother.

How cold it is, she said, now that I think of Gregor . . . he is sitting in his little house where it's warm.

Why don't we pay him a visit? I inquired.

That's out of the question, she said, I simply don't know what's eating me; today I hate myself.

She smoked and stamped the ground. Her wide-open eyes looked like stagnant ponds and were aimed at something or other on the horizon.

Damn it, she said, I might even begin to bawl! I said, you're free, aren't you, to settle down in some out-of-the-way place, too. Given your imagination, you'll have more life stories to tell than there'll be neighbors to ask you about your background.

All of a sudden she became angry, trampled on her cigarette, and hissed at me.

Ah, you pig, how you do annoy me! As soon as you suspect some weakness, you start exploiting it. There's no private life, don't you forget that! Just as there's no such thing as an individual, contrary to your stubborn conviction. Yes, for a moment I was dog tired. But do you think I could settle down in a house? Ha, ha! I wouldn't find peace until every piss pot stinking of hierarchy has gone up in smoke, including your Verona!

It was you, after all, who wanted, or had, to go to Verona, I said in an attempt to defend myself.

Mara had already set out on the return trip.

consider the transitoriness of the stone in one's fist in one's pocket
which nobody sees
the transitoriness of the police radio
the gaping wound
the wanted poster is washed off by the rain

I played the part of the faithful dog, the retriever. Mara departed. And I don't know where to.

Translated by Peter Spycher

Lutz Rathenow

Struggle

He was trying to drown the moth. The moth was trying to get away from him.

The whole time he was sitting on the pot, he was trying to drown the moth.

He was sitting next to the washbowl, without getting up—without being able to get up, because he was sitting on the pot.

With his left hand he turned on the water faucet, held his hand under the steadily growing stream, held his opened hand under it to increase the radius of the area sprayed by the running water.

The moth was to be sprinkled, was to be hit, was to drown. That same moth that had accidentally strayed onto the smooth white bottom of the washbowl was scrambling upward on the bright, slippery surface. Toward the rim.

He wanted to finish the moth off and was trying to squirt the moth. It was to be rendered incapable of flying. It was to be crushed. To be squashed, stomped—that's what ought to happen to these moths. They were everywhere, crouching in the cupboard, sitting in the kitchen, in the lamp. In the bread. When he started to brush his teeth in the morning and opened his mouth, a moth flew out.

He had to destroy them once and for all.

He wanted to drown the moth that had climbed into the washbowl to frighten him. He had to keep going, destroy the moth—

keep going, this one stood for them all, even if it didn't work right away.

He tried to get closer to the washbowl without having to get up—he tried to edge closer to the bowl because in that way he could aim better.

He had to aim better because he hadn't hit the moth; he had to aim better because he wasn't hitting the moth. It evaded him, it trembled, clambered, crawled, evaded him, trembled—it made it to the top. Was gone.

He couldn't see the moth anymore, raised up, wiped himself, and pulled the chain.

He couldn't see it anymore.

As he inspected below and next to and behind and everywhere else around the bowl's rim, it became clear to him that the moth wasn't there anymore.

He could have flooded the bathroom, but the moth would fly up to the ceiling, and the water wouldn't come up to the ceiling because the doors weren't watertight. If the doors were watertight, he would flood this room.

He wanted to drown the moth and had not drowned it.

Were the doors watertight, that would have been the way out. As it was, they were coming, ought really to come any minute, right away or almost right away they would come, the one will incite the others, stir them up; and then they will all come together, will fly at him, jump on him, eat up his things, eat up the furniture, eat up everything he has—the apartment, which has been in their hands for a long time now already, and with the mothballs from the cupboard, long since useless, to which they have long since been addicted, with that they will come, shower him with the stuff, they'll impregnate him, turn him into a moth if he doesn't capitulate, assuming he hasn't already been one for a long time.

He had wanted to drown the moth. He could have drowned the moth.

He could burn down the house, or the block, or the whole city, as long as the house went. If the windows were sealed beforehand, there would be no chance for the moth to get out. If everything is properly doused with gasoline, the moth wouldn't be able to escape. Only he'd have to stay inside, so that nothing gets out the door, stay inside, so that nobody can come into the house to put out the fire. If he were to stay in the house, nobody would be able to break in a window or the door, he'd make sure of that. The house would burn right down to the ground, the moth wouldn't escape. But he didn't know where the matches were. Didn't know if he had any matches, had any gasoline. If he were to go and get matches, the moth could escape through the door when he opened the door to leave the house. He couldn't go get matches if he wanted to kill the moth.

He listened for sounds, listened carefully all around him and heard nothing except for the silence of the moth.

Because of the stench he pulled the chain a second time and waited until enough water had flowed back into the tank to pull the chain a third time.

He pulled the chain the third time and would pull it again if necessary.

Perhaps moths will soon become extinct, he hoped, perhaps they will quickly and totally die out.

He began to tremble. He began to sweat. He was beginning to catch a cold.

Surely it was waiting in ambush, lurking with the others, they were all waiting, that one with the others, waiting for him to keel over, cave in. The others, which he didn't see, which he felt, which were upon him, clinging to his back, covering his eyes.

He felt deaf.

He wanted to kill it.

He was waiting until enough water had flowed into the tank and he could flush again. He still wanted to finish off the moth, this or another one, he still wanted to catch at least one, any one at all.

With great show he climbed into the bowl on which he had recently been sitting and drew attention to himself. He waved his arms, sang a children's song, and hoped that the moth that was tormenting him would follow him.

He wanted to drown one, at least one.

And he was in the bowl and pulled the chain and he flushed himself away. He had taken off his shoes beforehand so as not to get stuck.

The moth that was trying to attack him. That had attacked him.

And he undressed completely in the bowl so he wouldn't get stuck on account of the buttons, so that nothing would jam, so that his things wouldn't clog up the pipe.

Undressed completely and pulled the chain again.
Nothing happened. Nothing happened.
He climbed out of the bowl. He lay down and cried.

Translated by George F. Peters

Josef Reding

Disturbances All the Way to Baton Rouge

No, Wash, thanks. I don't want a sandwich now.

A good sandwich, Oldtimer. Mama fixed it. Liverwurst with horseradish. A really good sandwich, Oldtimer. Take it.

I'm not hungry, Wash.

If you get just one bite down, the rest will follow one by one. That's what Mama always said when I was too finicky at meals when I was a kid. Later that wasn't necessary anymore. Then I had such an appetite that I gulped down anything edible like a slot machine swallows coins. It's best for me if I get something to eat every hour. You need something, too, Oldtimer, otherwise you won't last to Baton Rouge. So have some liverwurst and horseradish.

I couldn't get it down right now, Wash.

Go ahead and try, Oldtimer.

No.

Liverwurst with horseradish keeps your stomach clear and puts you in a good mood, Oldtimer.

May be, I said.

Not just may be, Wash said. It's true, Oldtimer, it's true. If you're ever real down, take liverwurst with horseradish. It'll make you bright and bushy tailed.

I'll try it. Sometime, I said.

Now's the time, Wash said.

For what?

For liverwurst with horseradish.

I don't know whether I had cast my eyes heavenward or what. At any rate, Cora felt sorry for me. Cora was marching on my right side. Cora said: Why don't you just leave him alone now, Wash? Don't you see that you're getting on his nerves? His, and ours too. Always the same thing!

Cora imitated Wash's voice: Liverwurst with horseradish. It's making my head split.

I just wanted to give him something, Wash said, as offended as a butler whose masters have dismissed him without warning and without reason. Didn't want to rub anyone the wrong way, Cora, not you and not the Oldtimer either. Did I rub you the wrong way, Oldtimer?

It's all right, I said.

Why do you always call him Oldtimer? Cora asked. After all, he's no grandpop.

Anyone who's ten years older than I am, Wash said, is an Oldtimer. When were you born, Oldtimer?

1929.

Well, then, and I was born in 1939.

Cora turned around to me: If he says Oldtimer to you, then call him Greenhorn, Oldtimer.

That's not fair, Cora, Wash said. Oldtimer is a statement of fact. But Greenhorn is calling names.

Go on and eat your sandwich, Cora said. Then you'll have something to do. How come you're called Wash, anyway?

It's short for my first name: Washington. Want a bite of sandwich, Cora? Liverwurst with horseradish on it.

Good God! Why doesn't lightning strike you in the mouth? cried Cora.

Wash chewed. And swallowed. And said: The weather report doesn't predict it. Isolated disturbances. Cloudburst, maybe. But no chance of lightning. . . . Nice that we're having such good weather.

Wash was right! The weather was good. But that was all that was good about this march to Baton Rouge. If I had known that I was risking my neck for people like Wash, I would have stayed in my room in Snakeshore. Would've composed something new, instead. A protest song. Or fiddled around with my symphony, "Continent 82." Here I march, the only paleface among the Negroes, to Baton Rouge. And why? So that people like Wash can vote. Like Wash, of all people. He'll wind up voting for one of those sly Southern governors who'll take his right to vote away from him again an hour after the election. Good that others joined in the march, too. Cora, for example.

Cora said: Surprises me that you're marching with us.

It's fun, I said.

I don't believe you.

You're right.

Well, so why are you marching? You as—a white man?

Why are you marching, I asked, you, as—a black woman?

I don't want to be taken for a factory-second any longer. You know: velvet dress, but faded and with a flaw in the weave. Half price.

That's the reason I'm gong along to Baton Rouge, I said.

You don't need to, Cora, said. You're the genuine article.

I want all of you—so, you too—nobody to be exploited because of the color of his skin anymore.

And what does that get you? Cora asked.

A weakness for minorities, perhaps, Cora. Or a need for justice. Take your choice, Cora, I said.

By the way, Cora, it was neat what you said about the flaw in the weave, Wash said.

I didn't make that up. Whites taught me that. Shouted it at me. They come up with something like that—something neat, the whites do.

I don't know: There were half a thousand of us on the road to Baton Rouge. But sometimes it seemed to me as if I were trudging along alone there.

Listen, Wash said. Up ahead they're beginning to hum.

We had agreed on humming together as a signal for impending attacks on the march. Humming is better than singing. You can hum even while clenching your teeth. You can hum even when somebody's slugging you in the face. You can keep on humming until you have to scream.

Now all of us were humming. Some melody or other. I think we were humming: "It's That Old-Time Religion."

Suddenly, several cars were swarming around the march. A violet Studebaker pushed so close to our section of the march that we could touch the car with our elbows.

The occupants of the car—three boys and a girl—looked fresh and sporty. you could tell by looking they were having fun.

One of the boys raised a revolver and shot. A few in our group threw themselves to the ground.

Don't panic! Wash called. They're blanks. I know them from Alabama.

The fresh young people in the car called in a chorus:

> *Eenie meenie*
> *minee moe!*
> *Tell the niggers*
> *where to go!*

Then they laughed. Broadly. Beaming. The girl in the car threw the march a kiss.

We'll be right back, called the boy at the wheel. So y'all will have a little variety.

The cars about the column closed in together. The motley crew gradually disappeared.

The humming stopped.

Do they ever like us, Cora said.

Think about something else, Cora, Wash said.

Fine, Cora said. I'll tell you about Hacklethorp.

What was that? Wash asked.

I was involved in an auto accident at Hacklethorp, as a witness. Two white girls were badly injured. Very badly. Only a quick blood transfusion could have saved them. A doctor was there. But no blood plasma. None of the bystanders had the blood type of the one girl. Only me. I was willing to give the blood. But the girl, who was almost gone, stared at me and cried out: No nigger blood, as long as I'm alive! She lived another quarter of an hour. Then they put a worn-out blanket from the car over her white face. For the first time in my life I saw a really white fade, then in Hacklethorp.

Wash changed steps a few times. As if finding out whether his feet were still all right.

Are there actually any differences? Wash asked. I mean, if my blood type is O, and a white man is blood type O, too, is that the same O? Can they tell that one is black blood and the other is blood from a white man?

I asked that, too, Cora said. Later. I asked a bunch of doctors and technicians from the blood bank. No difference, they all said. In a few hours we can tell what's in a blood sample, malaria and leprosy, or just if somebody's had too much to drink. But their race? No way. Maybe the white lady in Hacklethorp could have used that information—in advance.

Don't let it bother you, Cora, Wash said.

But I do let it bother me!

I'll give y'all something else to think about, Wash said. Can I read y'all some poems?

Poems by whom, I asked.

By me, by Wash, in person.

You write poems? Cora asked.

Now and then. At the building site. Sometimes I write one during the break, making a sandwich. And sometimes I write one when I'm. . . .

Wash laughed.

Well, where else do you write? I asked.

Sometimes I write one on the can, at the site. You're all by yourself, there in the can. You can sit there meditating and get paid for it, even.

Go on, read, I said. But don't be surprised if we have to grin as we listen. Now that we know you write poems in the. . . .

Don't matter, Wash said. It makes me grin sometimes, too, when I'm making the poems. Well, this one's called:

Found, a Dead Backhoe

The open muzzle
stuck slanting into the gravel,
its neck out of joint:
steel-flesh too grows slack.
Without beating the chambers and
valves of
the heart of
screws and
pistons and
grease.
Quittin' time! the man
had said, had
casually spoken

the death sentence,
executed the backhoe
and gone for a snooze.
Now the cadaver
brown and rotting
lies before my shattered sleep.

Can you let me have your poem about the bulldozer sometime?
I might think of a tune for it, I said.
Now you're pulling my leg, Oldtimer, Wash said.
No, I said.
Here, take it, Wash said. But I'm warning you, Oldtimer.
Of what?
There's some bits left on the sandwich paper: liverwurst with horseradish.
We laughed. A few of our fellow marchers nearby laughed too. They had not understood what Wash had said. But they laughed too, because we were such good laughers.
Why do you write something so far out, Wash? Cora asked.
What do you mean, far out?
Well, who's ever had anything to do with condemned-to-death backhoes?
Lots of people, Cora. A whole lot. But many of them just don't know it. Sometimes the backhoe drivers don't even know it.
It would be better for you to write something about us here. A poem about our march to Baton Rouge.
Couldn't do it, Cora, Wash said. I'm too close to it. That stirs me up, makes me jittery. And when I'm jittery I can't write. Not until later, when I'm not jittery anymore, can I write about the times when I was jittery. Do you understand that, Cora?
I'll try to, Cora said.
And you, Oldtimer? Wash asked.
Yes, you've got something there, Wash, I thought. You've got a whole lot there. When I hear a few scraps of music somewhere, hurdy-gurdy and car horns and the pizzicato that gusts of wind pluck from the slack harps between the telegraph poles, I can't transform that immediately into notes of music. In his own way, Wash grasped this.
Once I tried to make a poem out of it right away, while I was jittery, Wash said. I was sixteen then. Some cops had come and

taken Pops away. For un-American activities, that's what it said on the arrest warrant. When the masons on the site asked me the next day: Did they bust your old man? then I said: That can't be. Pops is in Montgomery setting up a site. I was ashamed. And I wanted to write a poem right away about Pops's arrest and about my cowardice on the site and about un-Americanism. I couldn't. It didn't work.

You think what we're doing is un-American? Cora asked.

To those car-cowboys a while ago, sure, Wash said.

Oldtimer has it easy, there. He's not an American, so he doesn't need to have American or un-American.

Not an American? Wash asked. What is Oldtimer, then?

A German, said Cora.

Well, what are you doing over here? Wash asked.

I want to take some time off from my countrymen, I said.

Are your countrymen a strain? Cora asked.

Some of them, sometimes, I said. And many of them, always.

Just like over here, Wash said. Do blacks demonstrate over there, too?

Over there they call the clergy blacks. And they don't demonstrate.

Do y'all have any Negroes? Wash asked.

A few thousand, I said.

And how do they get along with your countrymen? Wash asked.

Sometimes my countrymen rent rooms to Negroes. And charge more than to white students.

Did you go out onto the streets for the Negroes in Germany, too? Cora asked.

Not exactly for black Negroes, I said. But for yellow Negroes, for Vietnamese. And for white Negroes, for white workers.

How long have you been this way? Cora asked.

How long? I thought. Perhaps since then. At the time I had just turned sixteen. I was wearing field gray and carrying a short Italian carbine with as three-edged bayonet on my back.

Tell us, Cora said.

I repeated what I had been thinking . . . three-edged bayonet on my back. We had to blow up a few bridges. Little bridges over little rivers: Amper, Paar. And sometimes we had to dig in and fire our bazookas at Sherman tanks. And back again. Forwards, comrades, we have to turn back. And somewhere or other between

Aichach and Dachau, an emaciated man in striped rags was running across the road. A few guards after him. When they had caught him, they led him past me. Then this man spoke to me—why me, out of hundreds. Quickly, pleading. In a language I didn't understand. I looked at his emaciated face.

And then you helped this man, Cora said.

I looked at the others, I said. The ones standing around. I saw what they were thinking. Then with one sentence I cut through the connection that the prisoner had established with me. I said—and it was supposed to sound brusque: Shut your trap!—Nothing else: Shut your trap! And the prisoner stopped speaking immediately and turned away. And everything was as it had been before. And nothing was as it had been before.

Watch it, Wash said.

What's up? Cora asked. Are the whites coming back?

No, rest stop! Wash said.

Cora and Wash were glad that they did not have to follow up on what I had said. That they did not have to console me: You were only sixteen at the time. I would have acted the same way.

Crackling of dry blades of grass. Wash groaned contentedly.

Does one of y'all have anything to drink? asked Cora.

Only to eat, Wash said. Sandwich with liverwurst and. . . .

Forget it, Cora said.

I saw a gas station. I'll go over there, I said. They're bound to have soda water or cola in the cooler.

Why don't we all have a blue or a gray skin color? Wash asked.

You moron, Cora said.

Why do you say that? Wash asked. Look up there! The sky isn't white or black, either. It's blue or gray. Or mixed.

Cora pulled a tiny transistor radio from the pocket of her windbreaker. She fiddled with the buttons. Scraps of Glenn Miller music.

A unified color wouldn't be bad, I said. But then come the professional hairsplitters: long hair and short hair. Big noses and little noses. Occidentals and Asians. God-fearing and godless.

Dumb and smart, Wash said. You didn't like me until I told you that I write poems and don't just haul stones around, Oldtimer. You're a professional hairsplitter, too.

I'm going to go get us something to drink now, I said.

A refreshment stand was stuck to the gas station: an icebox, with a few sheets of plastic around it as a housing. And ads on sheet metal: "Fresh up with Seven-Up" or "Lucky Tastes Better! Cooler! Fresher! Smoother!"

The four bottles of colored water injected with carbon dioxide cost eighty-five cents. I put down a dollar and said: That's OK.

I did not hear the car until it stopped between me and the line of marchers, cutting my way off.

One of the occupants in the car was called Sharpy by the others.

Sharpy jumped over the door of the sports car. Sharpy sauntered up to me, with his hands in the back pockets of his jeans.

How very nice, Sharpy said. Here we meet our white blood-brother all alone, in the middle of nowhere. So we've got time for a man-to-man talk, one you won't forget for a long time.

Get out of the way, I said.

The others were standing behind Sharpy.

Now wait, Sharpy said. They don't always have to be blanks, blood-brother.

Sharpy had a snub-nosed revolver in his hand.

We stood facing one another on the sand like two gunslingers in front of a saloon in a Western.

Why are you stirring up the niggers, blood-brother? Sharpy asked. If they're starting their mass attack on the whites, then at least step aside instead of running over to them right away! To the enemy!

My enemies are somewhere else, I said.

Spoken like a hero, blood-brother, Sharpy said. But cool down and think about it. Today you're still running with them, and to-morrow they'll throw you out of your job and take it for themselves. What do you do?

I'm a composer, I said.

There, you see! So tomorrow some eager niggers will be there, like Armstrong or Gershwin, and you'll be polishing shoes.

The one wasn't a composer, and the other wasn't a Negro, I said. What do you do anyway? I asked.

Why am I wasting my breath! Sharpy said. Come on, put him in the car. We're taking him for a looong, looong ride.

Hands off! said Wash.

Wash was holding the tip of a knife between his fingers so he could throw it at any time.

Our blood-brother's getting reinforcements, Sharpy said. Drop that thing, shoeshine boy!

Wash raised his hand a little. Sharp fired. A few men were running towards us from the gas station.

Make tracks, said Sharpy. He did not shout. He said it calmly. His voice was casual as a shrug of the shoulders. The quartet loped to the car.

Wash groaned. He was sitting in the sand, holding his upper arm with one hand.

Cora was there. Someone or other brought up a first-aid kit. A black doctor in an old army jacket diagnosed: flesh wound.

I don't know how Wash managed to get permission to keep on marching. At any rate, he was with us again a half hour later.

There was not much more talking until Baton Rouge was in sight.

First, the jeering crowd advanced on us. We did everything that we had learned in our preparation sessions. We moved closer together, we linked arms with our neighbors, and pulled in our heads, expecting projectiles.

But no projectiles came. Water came. Hard, compact water that rammed into our stomachs and threw us to the pavement. The police had moved up water cannons.

It looks funny, a shower from water cannons. Funny, on a TV screen. Funny and harmless, like whipped-cream fights in silent movies.

But it's not funny. It's as if you were being flogged. All over the place.

But not only we were being punished by the heavy whips of water.

There—the police have turned . . . turned the cannons on . . . on . . . the whites . . . too. Wash yelled and gurgled. You . . . know, Oldtimer . . . you know what that means? We're being . . . treated equal . . . For the first time . . . equal! Finally equal! . . . It wasn't for nothing. . . . Equal!

Wash was laughing, he threw up again, kept on laughing.

Translated by Ralph R. Read III

Uwe Timm

The Dinner Party

I recognized her at once. I had gone to the departure terminal at Kennedy Airport ahead of time, into the smoking section. It was there where I saw her sitting, as delicate as she had always been. Of course, she was older now, but she'd scarcely changed. Even the color of her hair had retained its radiant chestnut brown. If I figured correctly, she was around forty-six at the time. Casually dressed, she wore jeans and a faded blue T-shirt over a long-sleeved white shirt. Next to her chair stood a sizable photo bag. Absorbed in an American paperback, the title of which I couldn't recognize, she occasionally raised her cigarette to her mouth. She smoked casually, leisurely, without glancing up and without the slightest haste, yet with distinct relish.

I had met her only once, at a dinner party some twenty years ago. Undoubtedly one of the most offbeat dinner parties I've ever experienced. She and her husband had invited us, Gisela and myself. The thing with Gisela was one of those short-term romantic ties, which—it being the freewheeling '70s—sparked up as quickly and unproblematically as it later came to an end. I had already heard a little about Renate, she was a friend of Gisela's, and was familiar with her nickname: Princy or Princess. Lionel, a friend of mine at the time, had studied art history, as had Renate. He described her to me as a definite knock-out, but hard to put up with. She always carried around a cushion inside a small fabric bag. She sat on the cushion on the benches at the University, as well as on chairs and stools, not particularly to avoid back pain, but in order to sit a little higher. When someone goes somewhere with her she always gives him this bag to hold for a minute, and then forgets to take it back, so that someone is always having to carry it along behind her. The princess and the pea.

"Perfect," Lionel had said, "outwardly flawless, a real knock-out and very delicate, but at the same time endowed with this fragile self-image. Just like the little bag she carries a motto around with her: ALL OF YOU EXIST TO FULFILL MY WISH. PRINCESS. Now she's even found her frog. Ramm is his name," he said, "he's got money, also has a bald spot, but otherwise he's got the hair of an orangutan."

"Have you all ever been swimming together?"

"No, but his shirts are always too small, so that his belly bulges out red-brown between the buttons. He's got the skin of a yeti." Lionel had already had quite a bit to drink when he told me all of this, and his excitement about Ramm and Renate confirmed the suspicion that he had a definite thing going for her.

"No," said Gisela, who knew Renate best. "She's really quite different, very resolute, but also very helpless. It's almost like she fell from another world."

Needless to say, I was rather intrigued with the both of them. I was just as curious about Ramm as I was about Renate. They had been married for only three months and had just moved into an older apartment with six rooms in Eppendorf, vastly oversized for two people. The apartment had been totally renovated. The old stucco had been carefully scraped off, and it still smelled like paint. Rooms of a quiescent white void, a black table with black chairs; the couch was a chrome-reinforced black ottoman from Corbusier. On the wall hung something abstract: red and blue ladled over a linen canvas.

Renate, if I recall correctly, had just turned twenty-four but still looked as though she were seventeen or eighteen. Everything about her had a delicately balanced perfection. Her legs, her fingers, hands, ears, ear lobes, throat, nose, and everything was perfect, totally flawless. You searched for a disturbing detail, if she'd at least had a crooked tooth, but even her teeth were perfectly straight. Only her voice threw you off. It was incredibly deep, and it just didn't fit into that delicate body. Nor did her laughter, a deep and peculiarly husky laughter. I liked it because it always drew my attention. When we all laughed, I heard only her, and when I watched her, it was as though one of those mannequins—

those perfectly formed plastic models that populate the display windows of all the shopping malls—were laughing warmly and full of animation. I went out of my way that evening in the attempt to make Renate laugh.

Ramm was a good twenty years older than she. At forty-five he was for us, we being in our mid-twenties back then, ancient. His silk shirt stretched over his belly, and where a button had actually come undone a few dark hairs hung out. Ramm had a thin head of hair but by no means a bald spot, as Lionel had claimed.

"Of all people why him?" Lionel had asked again and again, "that yeti-frog."

"It's actually quite simple," Gisela had said.

"Well then, why?"

"She doesn't get bored with him. Ramm is funny, and he's full of surprises. Apart from that, he's an outstanding cook, and he lays everything, including himself, at her feet."

Ramm was, in fact, friendly and self-confident. He had a good sense of humor, and a knack for appreciating the more ironical side of life. He'd been around in the world, worked for an internationally based company that handled management consulting. We talked about professors, papers, and lecture halls, while he was fresh out of New York. One taxi trip through Manhattan aroused far more intrigue than an entire month at the University of Hamburg. Back then, it being the mid-70s, things at the universities had settled down again. There were no more strikes or sit-ins, no more water bombardments in front of the tower of the College of Humanities. In the concrete gray cubical buildings people had gone back to their studies, if they weren't thinking of suicide.

Gisela had said that he'd asked Renate during an otherwise monotonous Sunday walk in the park if she would marry him. And when she answered, "Are you crazy?" he'd said: "Yes," had stripped down to the skin—it was winter, a winter with an extraordinarily heavy snowfall in the city—and proceeded to waltz naked in the snow down the path in front of her. "Marry me?" he'd called again and again: "Will you marry me?" At first she'd only laughed, but then had quickly said "Yes," when a group of people began heading in their direction: a family with three kids and a dog.

Besides—the underlying drive of concrete wishes shouldn't be underestimated—she'd always wanted to move into a renovated apartment complex. As a child she'd roller-skated down the long corridor of her family's old apartment. Her father had died while she was still young, and her mother had been forced to move into a smaller and more recently built apartment complex. "Would you open the wine, please?" Ramm asks, carefully handing me a bottle from the wooden shelves. "Diamond Greek 1967, a Cabernet Sauvignon from California. And you Renate-Honey, if you'd go ahead and set out the red wine glasses."

Renate-Hon stretches, poises on tiptoe, and the pointed heels of her pumps rise as her miniskirt inches a little farther up her delicate thigh. She reaches out her copper-tanned arm, and the deeply cut sleeve of her blouse offers a glimpse of her small, vulnerable white breast; her hand extends, but her fingers still don't reach the wine glasses. She could have pulled a chair over and stood on it, but she glanced around helplessly.

"Hang on," says Gisela, who measured a good six feet and had been awarded several prizes in the student rowing club on the bank of the Alster as the stroke of a scull without a coxswain: "Hang on, let me do it." Gisela reaches into the cabinet and gets the glasses out.

After an extra-dry port, Ramm had directed us into the kitchen, a kitchen with ample elbow room and furnished according to the latest technical trend: everything gleamed, shone.

"Only sometimes," Renate says, "when Ramm cooks," she only called Ramm by his last name, "it smells like burnt horn."

"No," says Ramm, "that isn't horn. It's varnish, but a natural varnish. I insisted on that particularly. It'll lose its smell once we've cooked a few times."

"Maybe it has something to do with the stove. Maybe you really should've had a microwave put in," says Renate.

"No," he answers, that he refused to do as a matter of principle. "Everything is becoming accelerated, on the streets, in the air, in the office, in relationships. You've got to take your time at least with cooking. Unfortunately, there's no gas stove here. To cook precisely, it's really got to be done over flame." He shows us a brand-new technological contraption. We stare at an electric stove with a glass stove-top, under which the heat rings glow red. "A product," Ramm explains, "that resulted from the billions invested in landing a man on the moon." Ramm put on some music by Eric Clapton and was tapping to the beat with a wooden spoon on the black granite counter. "First, the burner has got to get hot, really hot," he explains. "Only then do you set the pan on it, then you've also got to let that warm up. Hot! Hot!" Ramm pulls the potato au gratin out of the oven with two Mickey Mouse potholders and sets it on the table.

"Hey!" says Renate, who never cooked, can't cook at all, but who nonetheless claimed to have a good nose: "There it is again! That stench. It reeks like burnt horn." On the stove something sizzled and evaporated.

Ramm goes back to the stove, looks around: "No, nothing here. Maybe it's a piece of cheese from the au gratin."

"That's odd," says Renate. "Just like yesterday and the day before. Every time we cook there's this sizzling, and then this revolting smell of burnt horn."

We all sit and drink the Diamond Greek, and while Renate munches on the au gratin I tell about an uncle of mine. An uncle who could distinguish particular types of potato dishes by their flavor, and whom I mention every time potatoes are served. Everyone savors the flavor of the potato and tries to describe how it tastes. How does the Clarissa taste? Language simply doesn't cut it there.

Ramm sits contemplatively, tastes and tastes, and then says: "At any rate there's garlic in there, so of course that'll cover up the natural flavor." He taps again to the beat of Clapton with his index finger on the kitchen table, and again another poof is audible on the stove, followed by the odor of burnt horn.

"Weird," says Renate, munching on the au gratin. "It smells like horn again." She chews, says: "Disgusting." And again comes another poof, and another.

"There! Look over there," says Gisela, "there's something crawling!" Everyone jumps up as the next one is already emerging through the galvanized ventilation shaft directly above the stove. A large plump cockroach falls onto the stove top and marches steadfastly straight for the burner. It hesitates and then scampers as though drawn to the incandescent coil, where it starts straggling, as though wading through a swamp into which it actually appears to sink. And, in the lapse of a moment, the chitin shell bulges up and makes this small poof as a faint cloud of smoke wafts upward. The stench of burnt horn. Renate looks at us. With deep-blue childlike eyes she glances pleadingly at me and then at Ramm, clasps her hand in front of her mouth, and bolts off down the hall.

One after the other we run after her, yelling: "Renate! Wait!" She retches. She spews a blurred streak left and right on the snow-white walls along the entire corridor that she so loved because it reminded her of roller-skating, dashes into the bathroom, and locks herself in.

Ramm knocks carefully on the door: "Renate-Hon? Come out," he says. "Come on now, it's not so bad. In Africa there are a few tribes that eat cockroaches. A good source of protein."

From the other side of the door he is answered with the distinct sound of heaving, followed by a poignant gasp.

Ramm taps gently on the bathroom door with his knuckles: "Renate-Hon, please open up. I want you to come out." For a moment everything is still and Ramm says: "You know, there's an Indian tribe in California that herds grasshoppers onto a slab over glowing coals in order to roast them. It's considered a delicacy."

Again, sounds of heaving.

"Come on," Ramm says, "she's a little sensitive about these things." We sit down in the kitchen again. "I've seen cockroaches in a New York luxury hotel as big as mice," says Ramm. "Next to them, the ones here are cute little critters."

"Hungry?" He hoists a steak up on a fork. I nod gallantly. Gisela, with a rower's resolve, says: "No."

"I understand" He lays two steaks into the skillet. It sizzles. "Never salt the meat beforehand; that draws the juice out. The surface has to seal up first, which is why the pan's got to be so hot."

I stare at the ventilation shaft. Oddly enough, no more cockroaches come out, despite the fact that the smell of frying meat is now wafting upward.

"Cockroaches are incredibly versatile creatures," says Ramm. "They can fly, run, swim. I figure they only come when there's knocking. They actually wait for this tapping, wait to be called.

"They're trained. You know why?"

"Not a clue," I say as Gisela continues to stare transfixed at the ventilation shaft. She could've just gotten up and gone out onto the balcony, could've said: "I'm gonna go get some fresh air."

"During the eighty years that this house has been standing, they've developed their own specialized genetic code that responds to the preparatory pounding of tough German beef. The beef is prepped and there's this pounding, then they know: now there's some grub out there. First, it was the kitchen maids, later the housewives who tenderized the schnitzel, all those years they never went hungry. They'd pitter-patter around, march on out, and plop straight down. Down there is where the trash cans used to be kept." Ramm takes the steaks out of the skillet, lays one on my plate, and slices into it. The meat is still red, still bloody. "Look right?"

"Yeah," I say valiantly.

He puts the pan into the sink and goes to the counter, taps a couple of bars along to the beat of Clapton with the wooden cooking spoon, and a cockroach actually appears. It comes promptly, as though called, and plops down onto the stove where it scampers around and then goes up in smoke.

Gisela stands up, not quite as frantically as Renate but with definite resolve, and walks, no, runs out of the kitchen.

Ramm savors his steak and nods his head with approval while chewing. The knife slides effortlessly into the meat, through the dark brown, then gray, finally red, from which a little blood still oozes. I force myself not to glance in the direction of the stove.

"Of course, they sit in the ventilation shafts. You can paint as much as you want. You can plaster everything over with steel and chrome. They'll hole up back there in the bowels of the house just pleased as punch. What they don't reckon with is this treacherous little stove. They plop right down just like the good old days, only they don't land in all that lovely trash, but end up on that toasty little spot. They scoot and slide around like they're on black ice, and suddenly it gets hotter and hotter, and then their little feet start sticking. They scamper around all the more and their feet melt. They want to use their wings to fly off, but by then it's a lost cause. Everything's blistered together and then—then, there's just that poof.

"Don't you want any of the au gratin?"

"No, thanks."

From the front door Gisela shouts: "I'm gonna get some fresh air." She slams the door behind her.

"You all should come with me to Lagos sometime," says Ramm, and spreads his fingers demonstrating the size of the cockroaches there. "They grow in proportion to the amount they eat." Gisela, however, was already outside by then.

"Too bad."

I also say, "Yeah, too bad," and hear the crying, no, the whimpering coming from the bathroom.

I call out: "Bye, Renate!" but the only response is a muffled sound of renewed heaving.

On the way downstairs I take a deep breath. Gisela stands there and waits. Outside, the street is filled with the fragrance of flowering linden trees. A week later Gisela told me that Renate had moved out of the apartment. Shortly thereafter I moved to Munich, and Gisela went on to Berlin. We haven't seen each other since.

The signal light for boarding came on, and then the announcement that the plane to Frankfurt was ready to board. I watched Renate put her book away and stand up. She took her heavy camera equipment and shouldered it confidently. I walked over to her, strictly speaking just to hear her voice, that extraordinarily deep voice.

"Renate," I said.

"Yes?" she answered, still in that husky tone. She looked at me, peered at me in an attempt to figure out who I was, but at loss for recognition.

I said that we had met each other at a dinner party, back then in the new apartment that she'd moved into with her husband. "There was that bizarre incident with the cockroaches."

"Oh my God!" she said gruffly, and laughed low. "Then you experienced the end of my short marriage. Maybe we can sit together on the plane," she added. But I was sitting in economy class with my low-fare plane ticket, while she was flying business class. Two different gates separated us while we were boarding.

After the meal had been served and the film *IQ* had been shown, Renate came back into the economy class and sat down beside me. She asked me about what I was doing. I asked her about Gisela. "Are you not in touch with her anymore?" she asked.

"No, shortly after that dinner party I ended up moving to Munich."

"Gisela is a pediatrician in Berlin," although she'd been out of contact with her for quite awhile.

"And what are you doing now?"

"Photography," she said. "I'm a photographer now. I started studying photography after I got my master's, and went to a photography school in Paris."

When she told me her last name, her maiden name that she'd taken up again, I was surprised. I was familiar with the name and had even seen some of her work, only until then I'd not been able to connect the name with her, whom I'd gotten to know as Renate-Hon.

She travels around the world and photographs artists, musicians, and politicians for *Time* magazine, *Life, Vogue, Du,* and *Geo.* She journeys through cities, jungles, and deserts. Unthinkable, had you known her back then, this strikingly helpless demeanor in the face of it all. The way Gisela had described her to me, not at all maliciously, rather with an affectionate pity: in the process of filling out one form for a bank transaction she could occupy the undivided attention of three different accountants. She'd stand in front of her bicycle, pump in hand, and in a state of such utter perplexity that a throng of men would accumulate and scramble to be the one to pump up her tire. Lionel claimed that she was lazy, a premeditated awkwardness that she used as a coy façade for her laziness.

Gisela said, "No. It's not laziness, that's just the way she is, really just terribly delicate and simply helpless. Lionel hadn't ever been able to get anywhere with her, but then again, that just goes to show how she is: very resolute.

"That incident," she said, "back then with the cockroaches. It was actually pretty significant. I couldn't bring myself to eat potato au gratin for years after that. Eventually I got over it. Since then I've managed to see how locusts are roasted and eaten, even made a great photo of it all. But then, I never got quite so far as to eat one myself.

"At the time it was my escape out of an Egyptian bondage. Until then, Ramm did everything, really anything and everything, that I wanted from him. When I said: I want to sleep alone tonight, then he didn't go and lie down in the guest room. He asked me if he could sit in the bedroom closet so he could at least hear my breathing. Fine. He sits in the closet. He crouches the entire night long in the closet. Well, he did want to hear me breathing. Of course, he didn't sleep, but, as I'd noticed, he'd made me not sleep either. I was worried that I might snore, although, as far as I know, I don't. The idea of him crouching in the closet and listening to me snore just didn't let me fall asleep, so that I'd always end up asking myself, shouldn't I just say: Come to bed? But I didn't want that either. In the morning he went to his office unrested, run down, but he went there anyway and stayed until evening where he oversaw the company's productivity. I'm not sure what it all involved, it also never interested me. Always had something to do with economizing, whether it was with people, time, or just plain cash. On the days when he'd spent the night before sitting in the closet, he'd come home and bring lingerie—crimson-red, olive-green, Prussian-blue, and light-gray silk panties, teddies, and chemise. I could've opened an exotic boutique back then. He'd say: 'Here, try this on,' and then he'd go back into the kitchen and ask: 'Renate-Hon, what do you feel like tonight?'

"To put it bluntly, he wanted me to punish him. He wanted that misery, that torment, because he knew I lay awake at night. He heard it through the closet door: the unevenness of my breathing, my suppressed coughs. I'd always thought that a belly like his and self-flagellation couldn't have possibly gone together, but I was wrong. When he ate, when he tasted his food, he looked like a spoiled child. I could have beaten him. Literally. I never would've thought such a thing of myself, but I think I actually could've beaten him, could've dressed up in leather and whipped him. There was something very vexing about his self-indulgence. At the same time, he kept thinking of me as *Renate-Hon*. But then there was that incident with the cockroaches."

She said that she had come out of the bathroom, eyes puffy and red, and Ramm had kissed her. He'd kissed her under the pretense of comforting her, but not on the cheek, he'd shoved his tongue down her throat, almost torn her blouse. He'd dragged her into bed, her, who'd felt so weak, to whom everything seemed so wretched, where he had forced himself on her, had pressured, pushed, prodded, and pawed her. And she had—her worst mistake—given into him, simply out of exhaustion, because she'd thought she would be able to distract herself that way. But then she'd had the impression that his hair smelled like burnt horn, and suddenly she'd had to vomit. She threw up over his shoulder, which, however, hadn't held him off, it had only made him wilder.

"Yeah," she said, "he did. He smelled like burnt horn.

"I can laugh about it now," she said, and laughed gruffly but shook her head. "The next morning Ramm was already at the office when I got up. I took a thorough shower, and packed my things—only one suitcase, then gathered up all of the lace panties. Took all of the crimson-red, Prussian-blue, lime-green, and light-gray bras and corsets, went into the kitchen, and dumped them all on the table. I got the jar of Dijon and the jar of weißwurst mustard, seeing as how Ramm was so passionate about his weißwurst, and emptied them both out on top of the lingerie. I went over to the stove and cranked it up to high, then took the mayonnaise tube and went to the black granite counter, where in a flamboyant mayonnaise cursive I wrote: "Happy landing!"

"I grabbed the wooden cooking spoon and tapped on the kitchen counter, ran outside, slammed the door behind me, and stood outside.

"Afterward, I moved into my mother's place in Osnabrück for a couple of months and divorced Ramm. The whole thing went without a single hitch. Then again, I also never requested alimony."

The overhead lights in the plane came on, and the smell of coffee began wafting through the passenger compartment. Breakfast would soon be served. I raised the shade, and for a moment we just sat there, neither of us speaking, just looking out the window. Off to the east a soft-hued streak was already visible, before which the curvature of the horizon emerged distinctly. There the earth was turning slowly towards the sun. Delicate wisps of clouds far off in the distance were already beginning to take on an orange luminescence.

"So," she said and stood up. "Till later. See you in Frankfurt."

She had already disappeared back into business class when I noticed the cushion she had forgotten on the seat. A quaint little cushion onto which two cloth handles had been sewn. I hadn't noticed that she'd brought it with her. I also couldn't recall having seen it in the departure terminal, but it lay there and waited to be taken along. I picked up the cushion. It was as light as a feather.

Translated by Rebecca Penn

Wolfgang Weyrauch

Something's Happening

[St]

I'm a bootblack

at No. 1, the main train station, there are only two types of pedestrians, those who arrive at one minute after seven, Mondays, Tuesdays, Wednesdays, and those who depart at two minutes after seven, Thursdays, Fridays, Saturdays, the first group leaves the city at three minutes after five, Thursdays, Fridays, Saturdays, the other returns at four minutes after five, Mondays, Tuesdays, Wednesdays, and all others, meaning those from the hotels named after the four seasons (as if spring, summer, fall, and winter had something to do with camelhair overcoats and alligator suitcases), ride the trains whenever they have a notion to and not when they need to, and that's only when one of them gets born, marries, dies, or has a big business deal and the train at five after seven has to be taken, since birth, marriage, and death are merely means to the end of transacting business, I go on polishing the shoes of anybody and everybody

but one day, today, tomorrow, or a year from now, when the big blast blows, the earth will crack, but the stone giant Atlas remains, on the roof of the main train station, a globe out of stone on his shoulders

I'm a taxi driver

I'm a washroom attendant

I'm a bootblack

at No. 3, a department store, I have no choice, I shine shoes, I look at everything from down below, I know what dirt is, I know how to scrape it off, and put polish on them, and spit on them, and the cloth takes care of what's left, I ask myself what's left, one thing or another, the shoes head where the escalator moves, I don't care if I damage the shoeshine kit around my waist or not, it would be best if they took off their shoes at the right moment and walked on in their bare feet, anyone standing in front of someone else looks at the feet and not the shoes, the face and not the hat, the beds you people can buy in the store are totally useless to you, the important thing is how well you make love in the beds, and when you get things topsy-turvy you think happiness is right around the corner, I once walked all through this store at No. 3 Main Street, everything was fabulous, the employees were selling and smiling, the customers were buying and smiling, then suddenly I heard a call, at first I didn't know who or what was calling out since the voice came from all directions, and although it spoke as though it were human, it was only a loud speaker, Miss, it said both far away and nearby, you're not smiling enough, I've been watching you all the time, that lady customer is entitled to your amiability whether or not she buys a thing, thus the smile hadn't really been a smile but a shoe the bootblack shines without first scraping the dirt off

but one day, when the big blast blows, or the breeze, or the storm, in any case the breath that knocks the breath out of everyone, the bolts of silk will no longer be cut into yard-long strips, instead they'll fly about and toss about and whiz about throughout the store, from upstairs to downstairs, from downstairs to upstairs, and there'll be no stop to it

I'm a news vendor

I'm a nightclub doorman

I'm a taxi driver

I'm a washroom attendant

I'm a bootblack

at No. 7, the information bureau, I, a bootblack and nothing else, one of a hundred and one, one who could be taken for any of his colleagues, and vice versa, I know more than the information bureau, yet I'm no smart shit, no, I'm merely around people more, I don't need to be a detective, I don't need to be assigned to find out what somebody is or what he isn't, I don't have to tail anyone, I don't have to dissemble so the person being tailed won't recognize me, I don't accept pay for doing that, and no matter how much money might be offered me, it's not my business to collect evidence, no, it all comes to me without any effort, I remember it all, but for what purpose I won't say and mustn't say, let's just say I report it somewhere, and it's evaluated there as part of the judgment of what mankind is like today and what he can be changed into in the future, I can't do clever things, no, I'm only a bootblack, and that means I see nothing but feet, how they move about, they wade, they slip, they plod, they run, they drag, they crawl, pedestrians are dragons, serpents, bears, humans, or creatures that don't exist, they are garbage collectors, stockbrokers, shanty dwellers, or sailors, call girls, stenographers or housewives, they look straight ahead, stop, walk on, turn around, return the way they came, back again, take a sharp turn to the left, to the right, turn circles around themselves, they form something like I once learned in school, I think the math teacher called them figures, straight lines, circles, acute angles, obtuse ones, triangles, rectangles, polygons, but all feet make either the one or the other, some make room when somebody approaches them, others walk straight ahead as if those approaching did not exist, they are not with the others, they are against them, they are proud or quarrelsome, but the others are peace loving or cowardly, it's one way or the other, sometimes I'm afraid it's not enough to be just a bootblack.

but when the big blast blows, and nobody knows where it comes from and why it happens, not even the monstrous eye and ear of the information bureau will survive it, they will each shrink until they are as tiny as the eyes and ears of ants

I'm a street cleaner

I'm a waitress

I'm a news vendor

I'm a nightclub doorman

I'm a taxi driver

I'm a washroom attendant

I'm a bootblack

at No. 9, a watch shop, it will soon be eleven-thirty, I've got to go on, it occurs to the bootblack that he has more to do than to shine shoes, it's the very same with the street cleaner, he sweeps the streets and he observes and informs, and receives and passes on information, it's the very same with the waitress, she's serving and she's listening, also the news vendor does both, sells papers and keeps a sharp lookout, the nightclub doorman calls, beautiful girls under eighteen, and then whispers that everything is going as planned, the washroom attendant makes sure there's enough paper on the rollers the same time she tears off the sheets with something written on them, I won't say a thing about the taxi driver, he's a taxi driver and he's not a taxi driver, some know something about him but nobody knows everything, neither do I, it's got to be that way, yet it no longer makes much difference because it won't be long until it is time, it's only a short half hour until midnight, the clocks in the shop here will announce it, but they won't be right if they think it depends on the second and the minute and the hour, only the exact moment is decisive, the moment of moments of which some people will say that's when things began to improve and when others who knew nothing about the taxi driver will find it out

but when the big blast blows, which will turn into dust, into dust full of gravel and rubble, the hands of the clocks will fall off, the numerals indicating hours and minutes will disappear and the dials will become blank, blanked out like everything on earth

the bootblack

at No. 13, some sort of office building, doesn't matter what sort, is closed, the night watchman isn't one of us, walk on, quickly on, another ten minutes, and the bootblack's feet are old, but my feet make me think of the roof of the office building, on the roof a TV antenna is right next to a siren, the antenna transmits pictures that move as if alive, the siren acts as though it were dead

but when the big blast blows, which we perhaps are generating even within ourselves, the siren will shriek as it has always shrieked, and we just haven't heard it because we had no ears, and the antenna will be silent as it's always been, silent and motionless, but we'd always taken the false life for the true life

the bootblack

and all the rest

who intend to make a one

out of a zero

at No. 15, the Federal Building, I really should bow to it, twice, the first time different from the second, the first time with my rear end to it, that's how the bootblack will show his contempt for an administrator who harasses the citizens, then with the proper

greeting, namely with respect and support for our future minister who is at present the taxi driver, and because there are only a few more minutes to go I can say without fear, but no, be careful, bootblack, get hold of yourself, I do not fear for my life but things can go awry, and I will not be the one who has betrayed everything, so instead of bowing I'll go into the Federal Building, to the officer on guard, and depending on whether he's one of our men or not, I'll say Lasso, if not I'll ask him for some adhesive tape and say I got a blister, bootblack will stick to his boot tree
but when the big blast blows and the first breath is as always, ordinary, gentle, or violent or sleepy, the Federal Building will collapse, its walls, constructed to last forever, will burst and crumble and slip into the slime that will spread over everything
the bootblack
the street cleaner
and all the rest
who intend to make a one
out of a zero
except that
at No. 17, the fountain, but that's my own name for No. 17, bootblacks are clever, they always land on their feet, actually No. 17 is the building where, where two persons sit facing each other, with one doing the asking and the other the answering, but the one answering must not ask, and the one asking doesn't need to answer, and when the one answering doesn't answer, either because he can't or doesn't want to, or if he doesn't answer as the one asking wants him to, then the one asking will threaten him, with what, once anyone holds his tongue or gives the wrong answer, he will give the wrong answer from then on, for example, my answer is wrong, my answer is wrong, my answer is wrong, and so on, or, I'm a zebra, I'm a zebra, I'm a zebra, and so on, or he should hold his tongue forever, I hold my tongue because I mustn't speak, I hold my tongue because I can no longer speak, but the fountain in front of No. 17 babbles, foolishly and harmlessly
but when the big blast blows and the second breath falters as though the breather had forgotten what breath is, the fountain will surge up and flood over and so completely demolish the building at No. 17 that the tables and chairs will float away with the ice floes
the bootblack
the news vendor

and all the rest
who intend to make a one
out of a zero
except that each of them must first
at No. 20, the telegraph office, I once called up the taxi driver,
something he allowed only in case of extreme emergency, and that
was exactly my case, because the one whom I was to inform, that,
wasn't there and no substitute appeared, but hardly had the connection been made and we were exchanging the first insignificant
sentences, which nonetheless were exactly predetermined and
which contained the crux, depending upon the initial letters, when
my line got crossed with another conversation, in which two married men, a gynecologist and a neurosurgeon, admitted they had
had enough of a third man's wife, their common girl friend, and
now, if it turned out to be fun enough, they intended to try it out
with their own wives, topsy-turvy, not normal
but when the big blast blows, and the third breath is stifled as if
the breather had never lived, the phone receivers will swing, back
and forth, and throughout eternity, the voices of the callers will
swing, forth and back, my wife will become your wife, your wife
will become my wife
the bootblack
the nightclub doorman
and all the rest
who intend to make a one
out of a zero
except that each of them must first
renounce his own zero
at No. 22, the wax museum, here the murderers and the murdered
are collected, Alexander the Great with his smallest soldier, Charle-
magne who, like Alexander, was smaller than the humblest peasant
he slew, Attila, who was no less monstrous than Sweden's Charles
the Twelfth or Napoleon the First, all three roved about where they
had no business being and killed off cobblers and carpenters and
market women, Bismarck wasn't any better, it only seems so because he was more fortunate than those before and after him, the
misfortune he brought upon the people was the same misfortune
as a hundred or a thousand years before, misfortune is misfortune,
Hitler was a monster, yet Truman dropped the first atom bomb,
Stalin did away with the people at home, but Nasser intends to

drown the Jews in the sea, I, the bootblack, walk into the wax
museum, I'm no murderer, yet I might be murdered unless we can
prevent our murderers from murdering, I pretend I'm a curious
and carefree visitor until I find a place I can slip into, as a wax
figure, I am made of wax, I wait for the one to whom I am to
transmit the message that everything is ready, I wait, no one comes
but now someone is coming, who is it, it's the taxi driver, he steps
up to me, he examines me to see if I'm made of wax, he nods, I
breathe out my information, he smiles, he leaves the place, I stay
put, motionless, according to instructions, I do not leave the murderers and murdered according to stipulations until I've counted
to a hundred, then I go to the future victims, that is, unless we first
make victims out of the others, yet we won't harm them a bit
provided they can be convinced we are lambs trying to change
wolves into lambs
but when the big blast blows, the wax will melt because fire comes
from the blast, or it will solidify because the blast turns into ice,
otherwise everyone will be so that it can't blow
the bootblack
the washroom attendant
the waitress
and all the rest
who intend to make a one
out of a zero
except that each of them must first
renounce his own zero
since the least will become the greatest

[Item 11]

I've been hearing about something called *laser,* they say laser can
do everything there is and everything there isn't, that's all I know
about it, I don't have any idea whether it's a capitalized word or
not, whether it's pronounced like an English word or like it's
spelled, if it's the man's name who discovered it, or if it's made up
from the first letter of five words and the five words the letters
stand for make up a sentence, or if they combine five concepts into
one, maybe the combination stands for *labor and society energy
resource* , or maybe the sentence says *laß alles, sei ein Roboter,* I
just don't know, and it probably doesn't make any difference what

laser means, but it does matter what all laser can do, I've heard it can rip out one of my eyes, or possibly even both eyes and insert them somewhere else so I'll seem blind even though I won't be, and I can see what I shouldn't see, laser can cripple my left leg or my right leg or even both legs, and it can cripple the legs of a thousand men, that is, paralyze them, for a few hours or days, and even forever, laser can decipher my thoughts, or shut them off, or confuse them, or make them into their opposite, it can therefore turn a friend into a foe and a foe into a friend, laser can make an apple as large as ten apples, laser can reduce an apple until it is only one-tenth of its proper size, laser can let an apple shrink so long that it is no longer there, laser can combine an apple and a pear into a third fruit that might be called a pearple, laser can make me grow a third arm or a third ear, laser can delay the delivery of a letter sent from Paris to Versailles, laser can cause a telegram from Paris to Versailles to be relayed by way of an outer-space probe, circling in space, laser can change water into wine or wine into water, laser can enable someone to walk barefoot on a lake without sinking and drowning, laser can make the bread of five thousand people turn moldy, yet they don't even notice that the bread has become moldy, but I don't doubt that laser cannot feed five thousand people with one loaf of bread that didn't already exist, and I do not err when I assert that laser cannot alter itself, therefore that it cannot renounce evil, that it cannot change evil into good, violence into nonviolence, exploitation into assistance, egomania into compassion, lies into truth, godlessness into piety, hate into love, I'm right when I say that laser can do just about everything, yet what it can do is basically nothing, and if there were no laser we'd be better off, I and everyone else, indeed, laser cannot perform even the most minuscule of tasks, namely, keep me from thinking of myself whenever I think: things ought to be better

Translated by Earl N. Lewis

Wolf Wondratschek

German Lesson

For example.

Whenever an Italian soccer team wins in a big, international game, the German sports writers find out right away whether one of the Italian players is of German descent. Besides, they point out again and again that various German soccer players in Italy play a very good game of soccer.

We are famous for knowing exactly what Paradise looks like. It's just possible that this is because we never learned how to eat breakfast right.

For example.

German men's choirs have their songs. Adolf Hitler owned a German shepherd. Even in times of peace we like to talk about the readiness of our soldiers.

As was announced in Bonn, Berlin lies on the Rhine.

We believe firmly that everything had to happen as it had to happen. And we're proud of that, for we still have no idea of our fears.

German innkeepers are pleased when their guests discuss the Second World War. That promotes business. After the third beer the foreigners are homesick for Heidelberg.

On a map we show the tourists where Heidelberg lies; even in rainy weather Heidelberg looks exactly the way the foreigners have pictured Heidelberg in the sun.

For example.

The German national anthem has three stanzas. Sometimes it begins with the first stanza anyway. We recognize the melody by the trumpets.

At the rest areas on the autobahns Germany is very beautiful.

Most German highways are planned so that even at top speed you can see the church in the village. Order is a must.

The dread of Communists is still a part of our education. In school the teachers tell about Russia. They say that many Russians understand our language.

Parents cause children great concern.

In Germany, it seems only the wrong people keep running into each other. We've had practice at that. Our laws see to it. We have never profited from our reason. We prefer black clothes.

The Christian Democratic Union. The lawn in front of the building is mowed. Prosperity for all. Whiter than white. That's the main thing.

We are forgetful. Only in our mistakes is there a parcel of truth. But nobody wants to admit that. We believe in proper relationships, but not in political ones.

Humor is a matter for experts. On TV they have to persuade us to be amused. But then we laugh till we cry, because we want to be taken seriously in any event.

That the whole thing can't be half that bad—this always figures. One of the funniest words in the German language is "revolution."

For example.

Anyone who wants to get to know this country ought also to strike up conversations with barbers. In a passionate way they are typical of this country. Their training includes a lot of fury.

The queen mother is fine. The queen is fine. The king is fine. And the children of the royal pair are fine. German newspapers report that normal conditions prevail once again in Greece.

Anyone who doesn't belong to a party or a sports club is considered a rabble-rouser hereabouts. In the Black Forest the strollers greet one another. The neighbors have a dog, too. Among other things we read a newspaper. In the confessional the priests are enlightened. A German woman is not a naked woman. Exceptions prove the moral.

In the front yards of one-family houses little garden dwarfs bloom. Our cabinet members look likable. It is said that we are living in a democracy. In the future Germany doesn't want to have any past. Since we have had too much past, and since we haven't come to terms with the past, we have gotten rid of the past altogether. Now we are getting along better.

For example.

We have enough federal presidents. The Mediterranean is again a German swimming pool. Nothing else is in the air.

We act as though everybody in Germany understood something about physics, but otherwise our indifference is almost a historical condition.

A single refugee is sufficient to justify our lack of political originality. The equation of Germany and German Federal Republic is more than simply an error in translation.

Because simple reflections are so difficult for us, we simplify the difficulties.

For example.

Misfortune remains the privilege of the misfortunate. Labor remains the privilege of laborers. Politics ought to remain the privilege of politicians, they say in Bonn. But this continuation has consequences. The pessimists criticize the optimists. And the optimists check on the pessimists. What we understand by political dialogue functions in this way here. But I hope that will be much clearer some day than it has been up to now.

Germans no longer look like they might be named *Maier* and *Müller* today. We have gotten that far meanwhile. And we call this illusion progress.

That is typical. A nice funeral is more important than convalescent leave in Switzerland. The little man in the street has not grown taller, of course, but fatter instead.

For example: Goethe, Adenauer, made in Germany.

We are all extraordinarily capable of being influenced optically. Anyone who speaks into more than six microphones here naturally has more to say than anyone else. Better arguments correspond to better clothes. We have learned these permutations. We are not politicking. We want to make an impression.

We never get tired of trying to prove to one another that we aren't actually at all the way we actually are.

In Germany shortcomings are getting rotund. We can't take a joke. The police help out their friends. Youth is a risk that the German populace doesn't intend to let itself in for anymore. That's why our government talked about natural catastrophe and passed the emergency laws.

We wear our destiny like a uniform. We applaud lies. Even the wrong track is made of German oak here. We recognize Jews at a glance.

Translated by A. Leslie Willson

Biographies

ALFRED ANDERSCH (1914–80), born in Munich, became an apprentice in the book trade, was unemployed in the early thirties and, after the Reichstags fire, was incarcerated twice in the concentration camp in Dachau in 1933 because of his Communist activities, after which he gave up his involvement in politics. He served in the German army, took part in the occupation of France but deserted in 1944 on the Italian front and spent several months as a prisoner of war in Louisiana and Rhode Island. With Hans Werner Richter he edited the literary magazine *Der Ruf* (The clarion), which began as a magazine for German prisoners of war. After the publication was shut down by American occupation authorites in Munich in 1947, Andersch was instrumental (with Richter) in founding the famed literary Group 47, after the successor to *Der Ruf*, *Der Skorpion*, was denied publication permission. He worked in radio, edited the literary magazine *Texte und Zeichen*, and moved to Berzona, Switzerland, in 1958. His work includes the novels *Die Kirschen der Freiheit* (The cherries of freedom), 1952, *Winterspelt*, 1972 (both of which have appeared in English translation), as well as radio plays and many stories.

STEFAN ANDRES (1906–70) was born near Trier. He tried to accommodate his father's wish that he become a priest, but eventually gave up that path and studied German literature and art history. In 1937 he was expelled from the writer's association after National Socialist censure of his work and moved to Positano in Italy in the same year. He returned to Germany in 1950 but moved to Rome in 1961, where he lived with his wife Dorothea until his death. His works include the short novels *El Greco malt den großen Inquisitor* (*El Greco Paints the Grand Inquisitor*), 1937, a thinly veiled story of the unmasking of the evils of dictatorship by an artist, which unleashed Nazi attacks on his work. The short novel *Wir sind*

Utopia (We are utopia), his best-known work, appeared in 1943. The anti-Nazi trilogy *Die Sintflut* (The flood), 1949–1959, treats the concept of inner emigration. *Die Versuchung des Synesios* (The temptation of Synesius), was published posthumously.

JÜRGEN BECKER (1932–) was born in Cologne and has worked for many years as a radio-play editor with German radio there. For a time he edited editions of plays for Suhrkamp in Frankfurt am Main. He is best known as an innovative author of radio plays (more than a dozen) and a productive poet. Only in recent years has he also turned his finely tuned and highly personal diction to prose.

ULLA BERKÉWICZ (1951–) was born in Giessen, attended the Frankfurt Actor's School from 1966 to 1969 and has acted in several German theaters. Her work includes the narratives *Josef stirbt* (1982, which appeared in English translation as *Josef Is Dying*), *Michel, sag ich* (1988), *Adam* (1989), *Maria Maria*, three stories (1988), the play *Nur wir* (Only us), 1991, *Mordad*, a novella (1995), and the novels *Engel sind schwarz und weiß* (1992, in English, *Angels Are Black and White*, 1997) and *Zim Zum* (1997).

ELISABETH BORCHERS (1926–), who was born in Homburg on the Rhine, is a poet and prose author who works as an editor with the Suhrkamp Verlag in Frankfurt am Main. The prose texts published here were broadcast first on German radio in Stuttgart and appeared later in book form.

GISELA ELSNER (1937–92) was born in Nuremberg and studied German literature and theater arts in Vienna. Her first novel *Die Riesenzwerge* (1964, translated in fourteen countries) aroused great interest for an author described by Hans Magnus Enzensberger as a "humorist of the monstrous that comes to view in ordinary life." An attractive woman, Elsner was unable to shake off an image that alienated some critics, from whom she took shelter in an ironic distance. The novel *Das Berührungsverbot* (Do not touch!), 1970, came to grips with the hypocrisy of the sexual revolution. Her novel *Abseits* (Living in the shadows), 1982, was uncannily prophetic, describing a woman's increasing isolation and persecution mania that end in her suicide. Elsner killed herself in Munich.

HUBERT FICHTE (1935–86) was born in Perleberg and spent his childhood and adolescence in Hamburg and Upper Bavaria. He was an actor in Hamburg, sheepherder in the Provence, and after establishing himself as an author conducted anthropological studies in Brazil, Haiti, and Trinidad. "I am my own best guinea pig," he wrote in his novel *Versuch über die Pubertät* (On puberty), 1974, a novel that features what Fichte called the mixed Afro-American religions of South America and the Caribbean. Much of his work has an autobiographical foundation, as in his first novel *Das Waisenhaus* (1965, appearing in English translation as *The Orphanage*), which recounts the conflagration in wartime Hamburg and the effect of the war on a young boy. His novel *Die Palette* (1968, the name of a Hamburg gay bar) was the first of several that focused on the gay scene in Germany and was followed by other works on that theme. Fichte died before he could finish his monumental nineteen-volume novel *Die Geschichte der Empfindsamkeit* (The history of sentimentality), which is being published by the Fischer Verlag.

GÜNTER BRUNO FUCHS (1928–77), born in Berlin, was evacuated as a child to Czechoslovakia where he got acquainted with political and social outcasts, persecuted Gypsies. After the war he studied art in Berlin and sold small cards with his own illustrated poems. He was himself an outsider and Bohemian all his life, critical of society. Active as a writer and graphic artist, he frequented bars and sympathized with the likes of children, alcoholics, policemen, and the elderly retired. Fantasy and childlike inventiveness tinged with irony and humor color all his work, which has been described as the "difficult work of a great clown."

MAX VON DER GRÜN (1939–), born in Bayreuth, wound up as a miner in the Ruhr area, where he became a mine train engineer before turning full time to writing. He was involved with the group of worker writers that met under the name of the Group 61. He was driven to become a writer by his wish to set his ideas and experiences down in stories. He is the author of novels, stories, and children's stories, especially *Vorstadtkrokodile* (Crocodiles in the Suburbs), 1976, an immensely popular book about a heroic handicapped child, written by von der Grün for his own stricken son.

PETER HANDKE (1942–) was born in a small community in the Altenmark in Austria. His father was a married German soldier and his mother wed another German before his birth. His upbringing contributed to his rebellious spirit and helped form his resistance to an oppressive system of prohibitions and wearisome habits. His defiant play *Publikumsbeschimpfung* (1966, translated both as *Offending the Public*, and as *Tongue-Lashing*) established his fame and the provocative attitude of his later work. His novels seek to come to terms with language, literary genres, and automated social ideas, all of which he challenges and dissects, and established a sub-genre position described as subjectivity. Most of his works have been widely translated.

HERBERT HECKMANN (1930–) was born in Frankfurt am Main, where he later studied literature and philosophy. For his novel *Benjamin und seine Väter* (Benjamin and his fathers) he received the Bremen Literary Prize in 1962. He has published novels and short stories, some for children. His work reflects a satirical and humorous attitude toward contemporary political and social mores in Germany.

HELMUT HEISSENBÜTTEL (1921–96) was born in Rüstringen and lost an arm in World War II. He studied architecture, German literature, and art history in Dresden, Leipzig, and Hamburg and worked in radio as an editor and producer. His works may be described as avant-garde in the sense that they depart from and challenge literary norms, but in an eclectic manner. "Actually, I have nothing to say," wrote Heißenbüttel, and then proceeded to eat his own words by saying a lot, by examining language and taking part in what could be said. He was foremost in presenting pieces that he called "Texts," which did not fit customary generic forms of literature and wrenched even ordinary sentence structure. His genius consisted of describing events, situations, and even language itself in new and unforeseen ways, such as in his *Textbuch 5. 3 × 13 mehr oder weniger Geschichten* (Textbook 5. 3 × 13 more or less stories), 1965.

MICHAEL KRÜGER (1943–), poet and novelist, is the director of the famed Hanser publishing house in Munich. His first works were volumes of poems, distinguished by a probing and lively personal retrospective of everyday observations. He is the author of three novels—*Das Ende des Romans* (1989, *The End of the Novel*), *Der Mann im Turm* (1991, *The Man in the Tower*), and *Himmelfarb* (1993)—all of which have appeared in English translation.

ULRIKE LÄNGLE (1953–) studied in Innsbruck and lives in Bregenz. Her first book, *Am Marterpfahl der Irokesen* (On the martyr's stake of the Iroquois), a collection of love stories, was published in 1992.

FRIEDERIKE MAYRÖCKER (1924–) was born in Vienna, where she still lives. She was an English teacher in Viennese secondary schools. Mayröcker published her first poems when she was fifteen. Often described as an experimental writer, she resists such categorization staunchly. She insists that she just does her own kind of work, work that reflects her personal engagement with the world about her, a relationship that has been called an ambivalence between dream and trauma. Her poems and short prose texts have always reflected an intensely private and personal confrontation with language. The text in this volume is a collage based on an exchange of letters between Mayröcker and her long-time friend Ernst Jandl, and the editor of this book. Her work in English translation includes *With Each Clouded Peak*, *An Offering for the Dead*, and *Selected Poetry and Prose*.

HANS ERICH NOSSACK (1901–77) interrupted his study of law and philosophy at the University of Jena after five semesters and worked in a glass factory and in banks. Because of his opposition to National Socialism he was prohibited from writing from 1933 until 1945, though he wrote in secret during those years. His conviction that what could not be dreamed had no reality was a basis for the visionary, mythical, and introspective in his work, which included poetry, novels, and plays. His novels include *Spätestens in November* (In November at the latest), 1955; *Spirale. Roman einer schlaflosen Nacht* (Spirals: novel of a sleepless night), 1956; *Unmögliche Beweisaufnahme* (Impossible proof), 1959; and *Der Fall d'Arthez* (The d'Arthez case), 1974.

HELGA NOVAK (1935–   ) was born in Berlin and studied journalism and philosophy at the University of Leipzig. After working as a lab assistant and bookseller she married an Icelander in 1961 and worked in Islandic factories. She returned to East Germany but lost her citizenship there in 1966, whereupon she returned to Iceland. She has traveled widely and has lived in Frankfurt am Main and Berlin. Wolf Bierman once remarked that Novak was not only unacknowledged in Germany as a poet and storyteller but that she was actually unnoticed, all unfairly. She has stubbornly refuted and criticized political and personal despotism and in her writing points out the violence that language can possess. Her work includes powerful poetic utterances, journalistic documentaries, and volumes of stories.

LUTZ RATHENOW (1952–   ) was born in Jena and studied German literature and history at the university there, though he was expelled in 1977 because of his outspoken criticism of the East German regime, accused by his persecuters of intellectualizing political problems. He was arrested in November 1980 after the publication of his first book in West Germany, *Mit dem schlimmsten wurde schon gerechnet* (We already expected the worst), but he was released a week later. The chief theme of his work is the contentious relationship between the individual's search for happiness and the norms of society that resist that search. He is the author of volumes of poetry, dramatic sketches, radio plays, and prose, such as the volume of stories *Jeder verschwindet so gut er kann* (Each one disappears as best he can), 1984.

JOSEF REDING (1929–   ) was born in Castrop-Rauxel. He was a concrete worker after high school for two years before he continued his education with the study of German and English literature, psychology, and art history. He was chosen for a Fulbright scholarship for the 1953–1954 academic year at the University of Illinois. During a guest professorship at Xavier University in New Orleans in 1959 he took part in civil rights marches in Louisiana and Alabama. In 1952 he received a Young Authors literature prize and in 1961 was awarded a fellowship at the Villa Massimo in Rome. His work reflects the social contradictions of his age and the attendant political perils. Numerous collections of short stories by Reding appeared between 1958 and 1981, including stories for children.

UWE TIMM (1940–) was born in Hamburg and studied German literature and philosophy in Munich and Paris. He co-edited *Literarische Hefte* and Autoren/Edition and lives in Munich. He is a poet, storyteller, and novelist. His first novel, *Heißer Sommer* (Hot summer), 1974, centers on student restlessness in the late sixties. It was followed by several others, including *Der Schlangenbaum* (*The Snake Tree*), 1986; *Kopfjäger* (*Headhunter*), 1991; *Die Entdeckung der Currywurst* (*The Invention of Curry Sausage*), 1993; and most recently, *Johannisnacht* (Midsummer night), 1996.

WOLFGANG WEYRAUCH (1907–80) was born in Königsberg, spent his childhood and school years in Frankfurt am Main, and died in Darmstadt. He was a trained actor and studied German literature, Romance languages, and history in Frankfurt am Main and Berlin. A Russian prisoner of war toward the end of World War II, he afterward became an early and influential member of the Group 47. He was principally a poet, who coined the phrase *Mein Gedicht ist mein Messer* (My poem is my knife), and was the author of short narrative prose, though his legend *Der Main* (The Main River) was hailed and his anthology of short prose of 1949 *Tausend Gramm* (A thousand grams) heralded a new generation of authors. With his concept of *Kahlschlag* (clear cutting) he struck a chord for the cleansing of a Nazi-tainted German language. Weyrauch was noteworthy for his constant, always youthfully exuberant readiness to strike in new directions. Echoing the famed annual Büchner Prize awarded by the Darmstadt Academy of Language and Literature, Weyrauch became the sole juror for an annual award for poetry, which he financed as well, called the Leonce and Lena Prize (from the title of a Büchner play), through which he identified a promising new poet each year.

WOLF WONDRATSCHEK (1943–) began his career with poems and short stories, distinguishing himself as an impudent best-selling poet with volumes such as *Chucks Zimmer* (Chuck's room), 1974, 1982. He was a typical rebel of the decade of the sixties, sharp-tongued and sarcastic, reckless and inventive, as his first collection of stories demonstrates, *Früher begann der Tag mit einer Schußwunde* (Earlier the day began with a gunshot wound), 1969. Wondratschek is also the author of radio plays and film scripts.

Acknowledgments

Every reasonable effort has been made to locate the owners of rights to previously published works and translations printed here. We gratefully acknowledge permission to reprint the following material:

From *Das Alfred Andersch Lesebuch*. Translated by A. Leslie Willson. Copyright © 1979 by Diogenes Verlag AG Zurich.

Stefan Andres, "El Greco malt den Großinquisitor" (from "El Greco malt den Großiniquisitor und andere Erzählungen, pages 65–93) © Piper Verlag GmbH, Munich 1992. Also by kind permission of Dorothee Andres. English translation © 1989, The Dimension Press.

Elisabeth Borchers, "Mord oder diese Geschichte ist kein Beweis": in: "Eine glückliche Familie" © 1970 Hermann Luchterhand Verlag, Neuwied, Berlin.

THE GOALIE'S ANXIETY AT THE PENALTY KICK by Peter Handke, translated by Michael Roloff. Copyright © 1972 by Farrar, Straus & Giroux, Inc. Reprinted by permission of Farrar, Straus & Giroux, Inc.

"Schematische Entwicklung der Tradition," "contrat social," "Endlösung, Katalog der Unbelehrbaren," "Shortstory": from *Textbuch 5* (1964/65), in: Helmut Heißenbüttel, *Textbücher 1–6*, Klett-Cotta © J. G. Cotta'sche Buchhandlung Nachfolger GmbH, Stuttgart, 1980. From TEXTS by Helmut Heißenbüttel, translated and selected by Michael Hamburger, Marion Boyars, Publishers.

Ulrike Längle - DER TEUFEL IST DER FREUND DES MENSCHEN from: DER UNTERGANG DER ROMANSHORN. © 1994 S. Fischer Verlag GmbH, Frankfurt am Main. English translation © 1998 *Dimension²*, reprinted by permission of Ingo R. Stoehr.

Friederike Mayröcker, "In einer zerfallenen Nachbarschaft © Friederike Mayröcker 1993. All rights reserved Suhrkanp Verlag, Frankfurt am Main. "From the Story of a Separation," by Jürgen Becker, by permission of Suhrkamp Verlag. "Hi, Wendy," by Ulla Berkéwicz, by permission of Suhrkamp Verlag. "The Pocketknife," by Hans Erich Nossack, by permission of Suhrkamp Verlag.

Wolfgang Weyrauch, "Something's Happening," in an English translation by Earl N. Lewis, by kind permission of Margot Weyrauch.

282 · Acknowledgments

Taken from Wolf Wondratschek, *Früher begann der Tag mit einer Schußwunde* © 1969 Carl Hanser Verlag, Munich, Vienna.

"The Pet" by Michael Krüger appeared in *Aus dem Leben eines Erfolgsschriftstellers.* © Sanssouci-Verlag, Zurich, 1998.

"Shorthand Text" by Max von der Grün and "UBUville—the City of the Grand Egg" by Herbert Heckmann © 1972 and 1973 by Verlag Eremiten-Presse.

"The Garden" by Hubert Fichte from *Der Aufbruch nach Turku. Erzählungen* © 1963 Hoffmann und Campe Verlag, Hamburg. All rights with S. Fischer Verlag GmbH, Frankfurt am Main.

"Disturbances All the Way to Baton Rouge" by Josef Reding from *Ein Schlafmacher kommt,* © 1967, Georg Bitter Verlag.

"The Dinner Party" by Uwe Timm, translated by Rebecca Penn, published by permission of the author and the translator.

"Confessions of an Elderly Cane Maker" by Günter Bruno Fuchs from *Gesammelte Fibelgeschichten und letzte Gedichte. Erinnerungen an Naumburg.* © 1978 Carl Hanser Verlag, Munich and Vienna.

The following texts appeared in *Dimension* [issue number indicated in brackets] and are reprinted with the kind permission of A. Leslie Willson:

Jürgen Becker, "From the Story of a Separation" [*Dimension, America 54*]

Ulla Berkéwicz, "Hi, Wendy!" [17/30]

Elisabeth Borchers, "Murder; or; This Story Is No Proof" [2/452]

Gisela Elsner, "The Engagement" [7/128]

Hans Erich Nossack, "The Pocketknife" [1/568]

Helga Novak, "Journey of a Woman Nihilist to Verona in Late Autumn" [6/490]

Lutz Rathenow, "The Struggle" [11/330]

Josef Reding, "Disturbances All the Way to Baton Rouge" [Special Issue on America, 1983]

Wolfgang Weyrauch, "Something's Happening" [2/1]

Wolf Wondratschek, "German Lesson" [2/60]

Max von der Grün, "Shorthand Text" [5/250]

Herbert Heckmann, "UBUville—The City of the Grand Egg" [6/186]

Frederike Mayröcker, "In a Rundown Neighborhood" [6/100].

Titles Available in
The German Library

*All titles available from The Continuum Publishing Company,
370 Lexington Avenue, New York, NY 10017*

Volume 1
GERMAN EPIC POETRY: THE
NIEBELUNGENLIED, THE OLDER
LAY OF HILDEBRAND, AND
OTHER WORKS

Volume 2
Wolfram von Eschenbach
PARZIVAL

Volume 3
Gottfried von Strassburg
TRISTAN AND ISOLDE

Volume 4
Hartmann von Aue, Konrad
von Würzburg, Gartenaere,
and Others
GERMAN MEDIEVAL TALES

Volume 5
Hildegard of Bingen, Meister
Eckhart, Jacob Boehme,
Heinrich Seuse, Johannes
Tauler, and Angelus Silesius
GERMAN MYSTICAL WRITINGS

Volume 6
Erasmus, Luther, Müntzer,
Johann von Tepl, Sebastian
Brant, Conrad Celtis, Sebastian
Lotzer, Rubianus/von Hutten
GERMAN HUMANISM AND
REFORMATION

Volume 7
Grimmelshausen, Leibnitz,
Opitz, Weise and Others
SEVENTEENTH CENTURY
GERMAN PROSE

Volume 8
Sachs, Gryphius, Schlegel, and
Others
GERMAN THEATER BEFORE
1750

Volume 9
Harmann von Aue, Wolfram
von Eschenbach, Luther,
Gryphius, and Others
GERMAN POETRY FROM THE
BEGINNINGS TO 1750

Volume 10
Heinse, La Roche, Wieland,
and Others
EIGHTEENTH CENTURY GERMAN
PROSE

Volume 11
Herder, Lenz, Lessing, and
Others
EIGHTEENTH CENTURY GERMAN
CRITICISM

Volume 12
Gotthold Ephraim Lessing
NATHAN THE WISE, MINNA VON
BARNHELM, AND OTHER PLAYS
AND WRITINGS

Volume 13
Immanuel Kant
PHILOSOPHICAL WRITINGS

Volume 14
Lenz, Heinrich Wagner,
Klinger, and Schiller
STURM UND DRANG

Volume 15
Friedrich Schiller
PLAYS: INTRIGUE AND LOVE,
AND DON CARLOS

Volume 16
Friedrich Schiller
WALLENSTEIN AND MARY
STUART

Volume 17
Friedrich Schiller
ESSAYS: LETTERS ON THE
AESTHETIC EDUCATION OF
MAN, ON NAIVE AND
SENTIMENTAL POETRY, AND
OTHERS

Volume 18
Johann Wolfgang von Goethe
FAUST PARTS ONE AND TWO

Volume 19
Johann Wolfgang von Goethe
THE SUFFERINGS OF YOUNG
WERTHER AND ELECTIVE
AFFINITIES

Volume 20
Johann Wolfgang von Goethe
PLAYS: EGMONT, IPHIGENIA IN
TAURIS, TORQUATO TASSO

Volume 21
Novalis, Schlegel,
Schleiermacher, and Others
GERMAN ROMANTIC CRITICISM

Volume 22
Friedrich Hölderlin
HYPERION AND SELECTED
POEMS

Volume 23
Fichte, Jacobi, and Schelling
PHILOSOPHY OF GERMAN
IDEALISM

Volume 24
Georg Wilhelm Friedrich Hegel
ENCYCLOPEDIA OF THE
PHILOSOPHICAL SCIENCES IN
OUTLINE AND CRITICAL
WRITINGS

Volume 25
Heinrich von Kleist
PLAYS: THE BROKEN PITCHER,
AMPHITRYON, AND OTHERS

Volume 26
E. T. A. Hoffmann
TALES

Volume 27
Arthur Schopenhauer
PHILOSOPHICAL WRITINGS

Volume 28
Georg Büchner
COMPLETE WORKS AND
LETTERS

Volume 29
J. and W. Grimm and Others
GERMAN FAIRY TALES

Volume 30
Goethe, Brentano, Kafka, and
Others
GERMAN LITERARY FAIRY TALES

Volume 31
Grillparzer, Hebbel, Nestroy
NINETEENTH CENTURY GERMAN
PLAYS

Volume 32
Heinrich Heine
POETRY AND PROSE
Volume 33
Heinrich Heine
THE ROMANTIC SCHOOL AND
OTHER ESSAYS
Volume 34
Heinrich von Kleist and
Jean Paul
ROMANTIC NOVELLAS
Volume 35
Eichendorff, Brentano,
Chamisso, and Others
GERMAN ROMANTIC STORIES
Volume 36
Ehrlich, Gauss, Siemens, and
Others
GERMAN ESSAYS ON SCIENCE IN
THE NINETEENTH CENTURY
Volume 37
Stifter, Droste-Hulshoff,
Gotthelf, Grillparzer, and
Mörike
GERMAN NOVELLAS OF REALISM
VOLUME I
Volume 38
Ebner-Eschenbach, Heyse,
Raabe, Storm, Meyer, and
Hauptmann
GERMAN NOVELLAS OF REALISM
VOLUME 2
Volume 39
Goethe, Hölderlin, Nietzsche,
and Others
GERMAN POETRY FROM 1750
TO 1900

Volume 40
Feuerbach, Marx, Engels
GERMAN SOCIALIST
PHILOSOPHY
Volume 41
Marx, Engels, Bebel, and
Others
GERMAN ESSAYS ON SOCIALISM
IN THE NINETEENTH CENTURY
Volume 42
Beethoven, Brahms, Mahler,
Schubert, and Others
GERMAN *lieder*
Volume 43
Adorno, Bloch, Mann, and
Others
GERMAN ESSAYS ON MUSIC
Volume 44
Gottfried Keller
STORIES: A VILLAGE ROMEO
AND JULIET, THE BANNER OF
THE UPRIGHT SEVEN, AND
OTHERS
Volume 45
Wilhelm Raabe
NOVELS: HORACKER AND TUBBY
SCHAUMANN
Volume 46
Theodor Fontane
SHORT NOVELS AND OTHER
WRITINGS
Volume 47
Theodor Fontane
DELUSIONS, CONFUSIONS AND
THE POGGENPUHL FAMILY
Volume 48
Friedrich Nietzsche
PHILOSOPHICAL WRITINGS

Volume 49
Hegel, Ranke, Spengler, and
Others
GERMAN ESSAYS ON HISTORY

Volume 50
Wilhelm Busch and Others
GERMAN SATIRICAL WRITINGS

Volume 51
Bach, Mozart, R. Wagner,
Brahms, Mahler, Richard
Strauss, Weill, and Others
WRITINGS OF GERMAN
COMPOSERS

Volume 52
Mozart, Beethoven,
R. Wagner, Richard Strauss,
and Schoenberg
GERMAN OPERA LIBRETTI

Volume 53
Luther, Heine, Brecht, and
Others
GERMAN SONGS

Volume 54
Barth, Buber, Rahner,
Schleiermacher, and Others
GERMAN ESSAYS ON RELIGION

Volume 55
Arthur Schnitzler
PLAYS AND STORIES

Volume 57
Gerhart Hauptmann
PLAYS: BEFORE DAYBREAK,
THe WEAVERS, THE BEAVER
COAT

Volume 58
Frank Wedekind, Ödön von
Horváth, amd Marieluise
Fleisser
EARLY TWENTIETH-CENTURY
GERMAN PLAYS

Volume 59
Sigmund Freud
PSYCHOLOGICAL WRITINGS AND
LETTERS

Volume 60
Max Weber
SOCIOLOGICAL WRITINGS

Volume 61
T. W. Adorno,
M. Horkheimer, G. Simmel,
M. Weber, and Others
GERMAN SOCIOLOGY

Volume 64
Heinrich Mann
THE LOYAL SUBJECT

Volume 65
Thomas Mann
TONIO KRÖGER, DEATH IN
VENICE AND OTHER STORIES

Volume 66
Benn, Toller, Sternheim,
Kaiser, and Others
GERMAN EXPRESSIONIST PLAYS

Volume 70
Rainer Maria Rilke
PROSE AND POETRY

Volume 71
Hermann Hesse
SIDDHARTHA, DEMIAN, AND
OTHER WRITINGS

Volume 72
Robert Musil
SELECTED WRITINGS: YOUNG
TÖRLESS, TONKA, AND OTHERS

Volume 78
T. W. Adorno, W. Benjamin,
M. Horkheimer, and Others
GERMAN TWENTIETH-CENTURY
PHILOSOPHY

Volume 79
Winckelmann, Burckhardt,
Panofsky, and Others
GERMAN ESSAYS ON ART
HISTORY

Volume 82
Einstein, Heisenberg, Planck
and Others
GERMAN ESSAYS ON SCIENCE IN
THE TWENTIETH CENTURY

Volume 83
Lessing, Brecht, Dürrenmatt,
and Others
ESSAYS ON GERMAN THEATER

Volume 87
Plenzdorf, Kunert, and Others
NEW SUFFERINGS OF YOUNG W.
AND OTHER STORIES FROM THE
GERMAN DEMOCRATIC
REPUBLIC

Volume 89
Friedrich Dürrenmatt
PLAYS AND ESSAYS

Volume 90
Max Frisch
NOVELS, PLAYS, ESSAYS

Volume 92
Peter Weiss
MARAT/SADE, THE
INVESTIGATION, THE SHADOW
OF THE BODY OF THE
COACHMAN

Volume 93
Günter Grass
CAT AND MOUSE AND OTHER
WRITINGS

Volume 94
Ingeborg Bachmann and
Christa Wolf
SELECTED PROSE AND DRAMA

Volume 98
Hans Magnus Enzensberger
CRITICAL ESSAYS

Volume 99
I. Aichinger, H. Bender,
G. Köpf, G. Kunert, and
Others
CONTEMPORARY GERMAN
FICTION

Volume 100
P. Handke, F. Mayröcker,
Uwe Timm, and Others
CONTEMPORARY GERMAN
STORIES

Printed in the United States
203173BV00001B/76/A